On the last census form Antony Hopkins listed eight
professions – six valid ones and two bogus ones – 'as a way
of bogging up the computer'. He is: composer, conductor,
author, pianist, lecture recitalist, broadcaster, sportscar
enthusiast and mad golfer, and his life has been full of
variety. *Beating Time* tells the story of that life in hilarious
detail. It presents a rather different image from the serious
broadcaster on music with thirty years of 'Talking About
Music' behind him, the composer of incidental music for a
huge number of films, radio features and plays, or the
recipient of numerous honours including the CBE, a
Doctorate at Stirling University, Fellowship of Robinson
College, a Medal of Honour from the City of Tokyo as well
as the highest awards the Royal College of Music and the
Royal Academy can bestow.

Antony Hopkins lives with his wife, various animals and
a turbo-charged Japanese car in his late adoptive father's
cottage on an estate near Berkhamsted.

Also by Antony Hopkins

Antony Hopkins

Beating Time

Futura
Macdonald & Co
London & Sydney

A Futura Book

First published in Great Britain in 1982
by Michael Joseph Ltd

This edition published in 1983
by Futura Publications, a Division of
Macdonald & Co (Publishers) Ltd
London & Sydney

ISBN 0 7088 2343 2

Reproduced, printed and bound in Great Britain by
Hazell Watson & Viney Ltd, Aylesbury, Bucks

Futura Publications
A Division of
Macdonald & Co (Publishers) Ltd
Maxwell House
74 Worship Street
London EC2A 2EN

To the memory of my father, of whom I have no memory, but who left me his talents that I might develop them in ways that fate denied him.

CONTENTS

BEATING TIME

PREFACE

I nevitably there are many gaps in this story since it is one I
never really planned to write. Not being a politician with an
eye to the future, I have kept no diary, except for a brief period
when, as a boy of fifteen, I was in hospital; nor do I have much
feeling for the chronology of my adult life. The years have been
full but have tended to bear a resemblance to each other. Indeed,
one of the few ways in which I can identify any particular year is
by association with the make and model of the car I had at the
time. I have a clear visual memory that such-and-such an event
happened in the year of the white XK 120 or of the green E-type,
but since I have been accustomed to change my car every year
since I first owned one I still find it virtually impossible to place
events with any accuracy. Nevertheless I have tried to set down a
tolerably accurate record of my life so far, although I have
changed a name here and there to save from embarrassment those
who, willy-nilly, have been dragged into these pages. Perhaps one
should not write an autobiography until one is ninety or more
and all the other participants in the story are dead or too far
gone to remember; but since I have no wish to live to so great an
age (and certainly have no guarantee that I shall do so) I have
taken the achievement of three score years as a suitable moment
to pause and look back.

1
Death before Life

I DIED when I was six months old — or so my mother fully believed. She had been out to the shops, having left the tiny sickly bundle that was me in my cot. When she returned I showed no sign of life; with sadness mixed with resignation she picked me up and started to walk to the doctor's house. It scarcely seemed worth hurrying, and when she found that the doctor was not at home she sat in the waiting-room holding what appeared to be my lifeless form. Her thoughts must have turned back to the time a little more than a year previously when she had had a major abdominal operation. Nobody at the hospital had told her that she was pregnant at the time, despite a six-week stay in the ward. It was at home, during her convalescence and while still bandaged, that her own doctor informed her that I was three months on the way. She had lost a considerable amount of blood, so much so that when I duly arrived I was all head and shoulders, a six-pound baby with the appearance of a famine victim, so wasted were my lower portions. Indeed, the nurse suspected that I was a hunchback, though she hesitated from telling my mother so. Something must have been wrong with my digestive system since I proved incapable of taking any nourishment. In the first six months of my life I had only gained eight ounces in weight. Having survived thus far against all the odds I must have been a cause for despair. With two other small children in the house aged four and two my mother had enough on her hands without the additional worry of a baby who maddeningly seemed unable to cope with food in any form.

My 'death' therefore was not unexpected and when the doctor returned my mother handed me over quite calmly, saying, 'I think the baby's dead.' The doctor, a kindly woman called Theodora

Johnstone who had been puzzling over my mysterious anorexic condition since my birth, took me in her arms and went over to a cupboard which contained a bottle of brandy. Using a small gold presentation spoon she trickled a few drops down my throat. There followed a splutter of protest, a choking cough and a gasp of incredulous delight from my mother at seeing me thus rescued from what she had believed to be a certain death. For the next nine days I clung on to life by the most tenuous of threads, watched night and day by my devoted parents; my sole diet was brandy and water which was fed to me from a teaspoon, an experience which has resulted in an intense and lasting dislike of alcohol and a pathological hatred of small spoons. Many is the time in adulthood that I have excused myself from eating grape-fruit, boiled eggs or a prawn cocktail because I have found it too complicated to explain that if I were to put a small spoon in my mouth I would be in danger of throwing up!

Two or three months after I had survived this traumatic period, Dr Johnstone arrived with a sample of Sister Laura's Baby Food, a new product which she hoped I might be persuaded to eat. 'I haven't given it to a baby yet,' she said, 'but I tried it on a sick puppy and it seemed to do some good.' Small spoon or not I took to Sister Laura's recipe with the avidity of a gourmet confronted with a dish of caviare. After my appallingly hesitant start I began to grow apace, although I didn't walk until I was two and, perhaps more disturbingly, spoke not a word until I was three. Curiously enough my mother was not unduly worried by this, despite suggestions that my brain might have been damaged through a persistent lack of nourishment. She remained quietly confident that in due course I would be able to speak, a confidence that was shown to be justified when, in a beach-hut at Whitstable, the assembled family became aware of a large and aggressive insect. Following its erratic flight with my eyes I suddenly enunciated the single word 'bumble-bee' with perfect clarity. This spectacular verbal début elicited some enthusiastic applause which presumably must have gone to my head since I have hardly stopped talking since. By the time I was four I had become positively garrulous, making friends with the ease of the totally unselfconscious. In particular I loved to go along the beach to chat to the fishermen, cultivating the undesirable habit of returning home with my pockets full of shrimps, delicious to eat but causing my clothes to stink abominably. I must have more than made up for lost time at meals since by the age of four I was a sturdy child showing no visible traces of the early crises.

The one thing that stilled my incessant chatter was the sound of music. My father, a writer by profession, was an excellent amateur pianist. He loved to play, and it seems that the minute he began I would drop whatever I was doing and go to the piano, standing silently beside the keyboard watching his hands as if spellbound. My elder brother Peter and my sister Pamela would happily bang away on the piano as most children will do, given the chance. I refused to touch it, preferring just to listen and to try to observe how it was done. With considerable perception my father used to maintain that I would be the musician of the family since music held me in such thrall. Sadly he did not live long enough to see his prophecy come true.

His name was Hugh Reynolds. His father was an engineer who went to New Zealand to work, leaving his wife and three children behind. While there he discovered a goldmine at a place called Wanganui, founded a mining company and became very prosperous for some years. Even the death of his wife (from cancer) failed to bring him back to England; the children had been placed at boarding schools and were cared for by relatives during the holidays. In due course the elder son went to join his father at the mine while Hugh went to Exeter College, Oxford. Quite unexpectedly disaster struck when a hot spring flooded the mine beyond repair. The supply of money, previously more than adequate, suddenly dried up and my father was forced to leave the university and find employment as a teacher at a preparatory school. This was in 1914, and with the onset of war his life changed course. As a boy at Berkhamsted School he had suffered a severe bout of rheumatic fever, which had badly affected his heart. Unable to pass his medical examination for military service he was directed into government work in London. It was there that he met my mother, Marjorie; they were married in 1915 and moved to Wisbech early in the following year.

Despite the war it appears to have been an idyllic time. For some reason he was allowed to return to schoolmastering, a life that he found quite congenial. The young couple set up home in a small but pleasant furnished house. Walks along the river were a source of delight with three-masted sailing ships nosing their way right into the town bringing loads of timber from Scandinavia. Even in winter my mother found the surrounding countryside lovely to explore, relishing the sight of the great shire horses stamping their massive hooves into the rich black soil. Came the spring and the ugly news from France could almost be forgotten as the fruit-trees burst into opulent flower and huge fields of tulips and narcissi stretched their colourful length to the far horizon. Sixty-five years later my mother was still able to recall vividly the wonderful scent of an entire field of Parma violets.

Had Fate dealt more kindly with them my parents might well have stayed in Wisbech indefinitely but an epidemic of typhoid broke out and they had to leave. All the schools were closed; the local hospitals, already full of wounded men from the front, were unable to cope with a sudden influx of fever-racked patients. The few doctors in the district were worked so hard that they could scarcely stand at a bedside, nor did an acute shortage of food help to sustain their strength. In three days there were ninety deaths and many a family must have been doubly hurt by news of casualties abroad and this unforeseen plague at home.

The shortage of men was such that my father had no difficulty in finding a job in the accountant's office of the Enfield Small Arms Factory. Peter, the first child, had been born in October 1916 and the little family of three settled into an unfurnished house in a district called Bush Hill Park. Though it was less picturesque than Wisbech the address, 13 Gardenia Road, at least served as a reminder of those flowery fields. It was there that my sister Pamela was born followed in fairly regular succession by me and my younger brother David; it was there also that I died my premature 'death' and taxed the patience of my parents so sorely with my inability to eat. (My birthday, March 21 1921, was later to become a source of pride when I discovered that I shared it with the great Johann Sebastian Bach — same day, different year . . . .)

In 1923 we moved to Whitstable, all six of us. Hugh had been very ill, his chronically poor health exacerbated by twelve-hour working days during the war. He was advised to get out of London, preferably to the sea; it was a decision he welcomed as he longed to sail again as he had done when a boy. During the last year of the war he had begun to write adventure stories for boys' magazines and, with the help of a good literary agent, had achieved enough success to feel he could safely make a career as a freelance author. It meant that he could be at home with his children, with whom he willingly spent hours, teaching them through play; any Reynolds child was expected to be able to read tolerably well and to do mental arithmetic by the age of four. Sailing was a great joy for him and he regularly raced in a yacht called 'The Belle' which was owned by a stockbroker with more money than maritime skill. In 1924 Hugh even won a handsome shield for the best overall record in the yacht club.

Although he was clearly determined to be as active as possible his health continued to be a worry, and the following year he decided to take us all to Italy where a kindlier climate might be advantageous. He could write as easily there as at Whitstable and he had always wanted to travel. My own first memory is of seeing the channel steamer on which we embarked at the start of our journey. I was amazed at its sheer size as we walked up the gangplank; I knew we were going to sea but, with Whitstable experiences in mind, I assumed it would be in a rowing-boat or at the most a fishing smack. My mother tells me that I shouted 'It's a liner!' in high excitement.

We duly arrived at a small coastal town called Bogliasco, near Nervi in the Gulf of Genoa. There we settled at the Villa Viacava; it was my father's intention to stay for at least a year but the hoped-for improvement in his health did not materialise. My own memories for the period are scanty, isolated incidents such as a second brush with death when I slipped on some seaweed-garnished rocks and fell into the water. My poor mother had to rush in fully clothed and drag me screaming from the waves.

By November 1925 my father had become gravely ill and the doctor insisted that he should go to hospital in Genoa. In those days the ambulance service in Italy was voluntary; one Sunday morning four uniformed sailors came to fetch him and carried him down the long garden path. It was a sad little procession and he may well have realised that it was to be his last day at the villa. My mother couldn't go with him as we four children were too young to be left alone, but the following day we were entrusted to a friendly neighbour, Countess Abriani, who despite her Italian name was English. She was wonderfully helpful during those final weeks of my father's life and enabled my mother to go almost daily to the hospital. Hugh was in a small private room with a large window overlooking a pleasant garden. There my mother would sit with him by the hour, undisturbed by a sympathetic staff who knew that he was beyond help. He was able to talk, but only with long rests to gather his rapidly waning strength. Nowadays he could have been saved by heart surgery, but an operation to replace a main valve was unthought of in those times. On December 12 1925 he died, aged thirty-four, and a day or two later he was buried in Genoa cemetery. Exactly a week after his death my mother brought us back to England to face what must have been the saddest Christmas of her life.

The prospects for a young widow without any sort of pension were not good; to earn enough to support and bring up four children seemed an almost insuperable problem. David and I, the two youngest, were parked for a time at a nursery school where I remember feeling that it was a terrible indignity to be made to sleep after lunch with our hands folded on the dining-room table. The smell of well-scrubbed wood so close to my face comes back to me now, and I would peep furtively through my fingers to detect any movement from the other children. With the help of a relative Peter was admitted to Christ's Hospital in Horsham, while Pamela began her formal education at a school near Sloane Square. She was a very bright child and at the age of ten won a scholarship to Christ's Hospital Girls' School, a feat sufficiently unusual to justify a half-holiday for the whole school at Greycoat. Meanwhile, and before this notable event, my mother had written to Dr Fry, Dean of Lincoln, who had been the headmaster at Berkhamsted in my father's day. She was seeking help of any kind to get her through an appallingly difficult period. One Sunday, on Dr Fry's recommendation, she went down to Berkhamsted to discuss her plight with the new head, Mr Charles Greene (father of Graham, the author). There at School House she was introduced to one of the housemasters, a Major Hopkins, quiet and shy to a degree that made him seem almost unapproachable, but the kindest of men as I was to discover. My mother had perforce taken Pam with her and 'Major' (as I was subsequently to call him) took them both back to Incents, a vast boarding-house with sleeping accommodation for nearly forty boys.

Now I have long nourished the fantasy that my mother took at least three of us down on that momentous day and that I was chosen because I got on best with the dogs. Major Hopkins's wife was devoted to animals and habitually kept a *ménage* of horses, dogs and canaries. Cats were only accepted years later and even then she never really took to them. They must have heard on some feline grapevine that good lodgings were to be had for the asking and they would appear mysteriously in the garden. If they were brave enough not to be deterred by terriers, beagles and a St Bernard they were allowed to stay. Anyway, I still have this vision that rather in the spirit of a dowager duchess breezing through the pet department of Harrods, she said, 'I'll take that one!' pointing at me, simply because I was lying on the lawn covered with fox-terriers and showing no fear. My justification for this quite misleading tale is a photograph taken on the day of my arrival showing me, diminutive and scruffy, with a string of assorted dogs beside me.

The truth of the matter, if less bizarre, is an even more striking tribute to the kindness of Major and Mrs Hopkins towards a complete stranger. On the afternoon of that very Sunday Mrs Hopkins took my mother for a walk and, after a further discussion of the problem, turned and said, 'I'd like to take the five-year-old for a time if you'd let me have him.' (It seems that there had been some talk of a temporary adoption of Pam, but it was felt that a boys' boarding-house was not the ideal environment for the up-bringing of a young girl.) While regretting the necessity for such a course my mother realised that there could hardly be a better solution. The wonder of it was that the Hopkinses had not even seen me at the time and yet agreed to take me on. A properly legal document establishing a joint guardianship was drawn up; there was to be no attempt to separate me from my family, it being fully understood that if the arrangement failed to work some alternative would be sought. I have sometimes said jokingly that I was 'on approval' for seven years since an official adoption with its consequent change of name did not occur until I was twelve; yet to use such a phrase with its implications of doubt would be less than just, for there was never a hint of reluctance on the Hopkins's part. Whether for physiological reasons or, as I used seriously to suspect, from excessive reticence on Major's part, their marriage had proved barren; it appears that they had always wanted a boy. Suddenly, quite out of the blue, they were offered one by Providence, and it was my good fortune that they decided so unhesitatingly to seize the opportunity of acquiring a son. For my mother it was a welcome solution to an awful dilemma; for me it was the beginning of a new chapter.

2
Home Is Where The Pianola Is

The house I arrived at one spring day in 1926 seemed immense. Perched high on a bank, to the left of Chesham Road as one went up the hill towards the school playing-fields, it was surrounded by a fortress-like wall. To reach the front door one had to climb a steep flight of stone steps; the house towered above, three stories high. On the other side of the road was about an acre of land with a tennis court, a garden, and a small paddock beyond a dense shrubbery. Lurking far in the back of my mind is a vague memory of my arrival, though I have no recollection of the journey nor of attaching any significance to the day. I am told that Mrs Hopkins was delighted when I announced quite firmly that I would call her 'Signora', a habit I had acquired in Italy. I am sure that at the time I didn't think of them as parents, and Major and Signora seemed perfectly suitable titles; indeed I continued to call them by those names until their dying day. They were both older than my natural parents would have been and, as I look back, seem to have been curiously opposed in temperament since he was one of the most silent men I have known and she one of the most talkative of women. His reluctance to speak caused him to have a little mannerism of clearing his throat every few words. He had been at Berkhamsted School as a boy, graduated at Oxford and then returned to the school as a junior master, housemaster and, ultimately, bursar. His identification with the school was a mainstay of his life; in time he virtually became a 'Mr Chips'. His subjects were classics and history but he was widely read in English and was delighted when I proved to be a voracious reader. He was also a keen sportsman, deriving great enjoyment from tennis, golf, hockey and riding. Indeed the only severe criticism I could make of him would concern his driving which, in later years, I found quite terrifying. Not that he drove fast; far from it. His most alarming habit was to coast clutchless from side-roads into main streets, a procedure which would have me shrinking below the dashboard, sick with fear.

Signora on the other hand was not in the least intellectual. Brought up on a large and prosperous farm in Essex she had a great affection for animals, regarding them as superior to people in many respects. Although she was kindness itself she found it extremely difficult to see any viewpoint but her own. Before her marriage she had been assistant matron at another of the school houses so she was well accustomed to a crowd of boys. There were half a dozen or so servants to cope with everyday domestic tasks and a full-time groom to look after the horses. The social order seems hardly to have been questioned, perhaps because behind the traditional green baize door, butler and cook wielded as much authority as any master or mistress.

After Signora had died (in her late eighties) I found a few diaries that she had kept in a rather sporadic way. Surprisingly I can find no mention of my first appearance on the scene even though I have the volume dated 1926. It's confusing to read owing to her characteristically thrifty habit of making entries for '26, '27 and '28 on the same page, quite often on the wrong date.

It seems that I was for the most part a bright and cheerful child, precocious in my use of language and rather given to nauseatingly arch remarks that were better fitted to the Dickensian period than to the brittle and sophisticated 'twenties. At that time Major was accustomed to go to the Norfolk town of Hunstanton each January for a golfing holiday. He would spend the day on the links while Signora would hire a horse from Mr Callaby's stables and go for exhilarating rides along the seemingly endless beach. She was accompanied everywhere by a beloved fox-terrier called Tan, her favourite from the Incents pack. Her diary for 1 January 1927 offers her first surviving record of my existence as part of the family:

At Hunstan [sic] once again. Another year gone. Tan not a day older nor are we I think. Tony added unto us: he is most attractive, good and very interesting. Everybody noticing him, but he is shy just now and will not talk to people at first. Utterly devoted to Tom and always after him.

The 'Tom' referred to was of course her husband. The next day —

> ... Tony and I walked along coast beside the links, he playing at 'Mowgli' with great spirit and intelligence. His intellect and *common sense* amaze me. As Mr Burns remarked, 'the mind of a boy of 14 in a child of 5'. ... Tom has him on his knee now reading *Winnie the Poo* [sic]. I keep hearing 'Come on Major' when Tom stops. ... [Tony] has a perfect passion for books .... The sky tonight perfectly wonderful, red and lovely. Tony and I spoke of God's wonderful works; he said, 'Don't forget Jesus helped Him, Signora.'

Later in the week we visited a rectory nearby where I distinguished myself by asking the canon's sister, 'Why do you have such a statue as that?' — referring to a crucifix on the wall — 'It's so sad it makes me want to sob.' I do not remember being a particularly devout child, but Signora clearly relished these Fauntleroy moments. From a very early age I did in fact read aloud a chapter from the Bible on Sunday evenings and I vividly recall the humiliation of being unable to cope with NEBUCHAD-NEZZAR at first sight. I was shaken at the sight of two Zs.

We came back from Hunstanton ten days later, Signora having bought a large bay mare called Duchess to add to the *ménage*. That spring an epidemic of mumps swept through the house filling the sick-room to overflowing. I must have been kept strictly segregated from the boarders as I avoided infection. In April, though, I was taken ill with agonising earache. Major and Signora were away at the time and it was the house nurse who rushed me to the Ear, Nose and Throat Hospital in Golden Square on the urgent instructions of the doctor. Mastoid, tonsils and adenoids were all removed in a single operation, a surgeon's benefit which I doubt if I appreciated at the time.

> Apr. 29. To London to see Tony. Found him lying mute and looking dreadful all bandaged up. I could hardly bear it.

Neither could I. I was a sore and bewildered child, and I can still remember the relief I felt when familiar faces came through the ward door. Apparently I refused to fraternise with the other children; indeed I was mildly shocked by the East End kid in the next bed who used to lick his plate both sides to ensure that not a speck of food was missed. I was too ignorant of poverty to understand that he had certainly never been fed so well.

When I returned from hospital I was put in the charge of the first of a number of nannies. It was understandable, especially while I was recovering from the operation, that I needed looking after. They didn't all inspire an equal affection. One I recall clearly dressed habitually in black, wearing an all-enveloping dress modelled on Queen Victoria in mourning. She had a number of quite separate but lengthy black hairs sprouting from her chin and neck, a feature which I found gruesomely fascinating. Her skirt was so long that she appeared to glide rather than walk, taking a permanent shadow with her as though she was covered by a huge cloche of black glass. I dreaded her approach and found the intimacies of the bedroom rather embarrassing in her presence. I much preferred one who came later, though, to my regret, only for a short time. She had a wooden hand, perpetually gloved, which aroused intense interest on my part. How was it fixed on? Did she take it off at night? I would badger her with such questions, no doubt to her considerable annoyance. She used to read to me from a long, romantic and I suspect rather poor novel in which a castle bell tolled with some dreadful significance which I have forgotten. I used positively to hear its hollow tone clanging in my mind's ear and never tired of the melancholy tale.

My favourite nanny was a gorgeous buxom girl called Rose, a perfect Renoir with creamy skin, shiny black hair and mischievous eyes. I suppose I must have been seven or eight during her brief stay, old enough to have become aware that certain parts of the body were regarded as naughty. Bath-nights with Rose were fun, taking on something of the character of mild Victorian pornography. One night she left me alone in the bath for a moment or two, presumably to fetch a clean towel. I prepared myself for her return by propping my bare bottom over the rim of the bath so that it would be the first thing she saw when she came back. I was rewarded for this exhibition with a gale of rustic laughter and a playful slap. She proceeded to wash me with a touch of salacity to which I instinctively responded by beseeching her to show me her bottom. This request, at first refused, was repeated night after night until at last, to my delight, she turned round and flicked up her skirt like a cancan dancer. It was a famous victory but I may have been indiscreet enough to arouse suspicions about our orgiastic behaviour for, to my sorrow, she was shortly asked to leave.

Although sex and sexuality were absolutely taboo subjects I was seemingly preparing myself to write a definitive treatise on female anatomy with the willing co-operation of a small girlfriend known as Tinker. (Her curious nickname arose from a visit to Peter Pan; she had identified herself with Tinkerbell.) Our acquaintance had ripened to familiarity from the time we were about seven. At one end of the tennis lawn was a somewhat ramshackle pavilion to which our steps would regularly lead us. Its pale paint peeled and flaked in the summer sun; old cricket bats garlanded with dishevelled string stood in the corner; croquet balls lay like huge coloured eggs in broken boxes. Within its shadowy interior we felt safe from observation. Off would come knickers, down would fall trousers and the endlessly fascinating exploration of inexplicable differences would begin. For years we hardly ever met without pursuing this mutual interest. It was truly done in the cause of pure knowledge since we neither of us experienced any sexual satisfaction. Of course the secrecy, the knowledge that we were doing something strictly forbidden, gave us a thrill. The ultimate peak of the exhibition was for each to observe the other spending a penny in the shrubbery. The different ways in which this astonishing bodily function was performed never failed to elicit murmurs of wonder.

Our intimate knowledge of each other's bodies created a marvellous bond between us and we were more than bosom friends. One day, when we must have been all of eleven, she struck me a cruel blow by refusing to disrobe. I was incredulous at this betrayal of our bond and asked her why. 'Because I've joined the Guides and taken an oath that I wouldn't,' she replied. In vain did I protest that no oath could have been that specific; did they actually make her swear that she wouldn't lower her knickers for Antony Reynolds (as I still was)? Well, not exactly, she admitted, but that was the gist of it. I felt horribly let down even if my trousers weren't, and our friendship was never quite the same again.

That same shrubbery was the scene of a much more positive sexual experience which I recount merely to give assurance that it did me no harm although, had it been discovered, it would have brought expulsion at the least on the perpetrator. The forty or so boys at Incents ranged from fourteen to eighteen in age. I was given a great deal of freedom and mingled with them happily, quite possibly being something of a nuisance. During the first three years that I was there I became a sort of mascot; the senior boys in particular treated me with great kindness partly no doubt because, even with all his reticence, Major inspired great devotion. One summer evening I had been playing on the lawn among a small group of boys. A ball was lost in the quite dense bushes nearby. Being the smallest I wriggled my way through the outer fringe of branches to look for it. Another boy, about sixteen, joined me in the search. There was a small clearing a few feet across in the centre of the shrubbery, a spot I knew well from adventurous sorties with Tinker. Suddenly the boy lifted me and laid me down. I imagined it to be a friendly wrestling game but to my surprise he lay on me and started to jog himself around in a distinctly weird manner. 'What can he be doing?' I thought to myself as his breathing started to quicken. There was a sort of convulsion and then he got up, flicking the dry dirt off his knees in some agitation. It had been an intriguing and not unpleasant experience, but chatterbox though I was I felt it was best to keep quiet about it.

I suppose I must have been about six when I first went to a little private school in Berkhamsted. It was called Rothsay and was run in her own red-brick semi-detached by a delightful woman called 'Wicky', or, more formally, Miss Whittaker. (It still exists, albeit in a different building.) Largely owing to the very adult way in which Major treated me I was streets ahead of the other children. While they wrestled with 'The Cat sat on the Mat' I would be put on my own in a corner to read National Geographical Society magazines or Arthur Mee's *Children's Encyclopaedia*. I can see the classroom now, with light pouring in from the big window behind us and a mottled yellow upright piano, its woodwork curiously veined. On the wall hung a large picture of a farmyard in the country, painted on oilcloth. It was used for French lessons which I hugely enjoyed. 'Le coq,' Wicky would say, picking out a gaily caparisoned cockerel with her long wooden pointer. 'LE COQ' we would all chant back with the fervour of a devout congregation. 'La poule' — 'LA POULE', 'La forêt' — 'LA FORÊT', — 'L'arbre' — 'L'ARBRE', and so on until we had named every part of the picture, with special stress always being given to the mysterious matter of gender.

Normally I would walk the mile or so to and from the school, but on High Days and State Occasions I would ride there, much to the excitement of the other children. Tooley, the groom, would ride Duchess, Signora's big bay mare, while I would be perched on a sizeable grey called Kelpie. Of course I was on a leading rein, but it is an indication of how little traffic there was in the High Street that such a mode of transport could even be contemplated. In time I was given my own pony, first a little black Shetland called Nib and then a self-willed Dartmoor whom I proudly named Pegasus. I adored riding and seem to have had not the slightest fear of horses. On one occasion I was seen to be having trouble with Pegasus, who resolutely refused to jump a very small fence in the paddock. Exasperated by her obstinacy I dismounted and jumped the fence myself. 'There, silly,' I said in piping tones, 'you see how it's done?'

In the house there was one piece of furniture which had a compelling appeal for me. It was a pianola, a form of mechanical piano operated by foot-pedals rather similar to those on a harmonium. One opened two sliding doors at the front and inserted a perforated paper roll which was then fixed to a roller beneath. Along the leading edge of the keyboard were several chromium-plated levers with mystical symbols attached, *ff, f, p, pp*, and even *cresc.* and *dim.* I didn't at first fully comprehend what they meant but I would manipulate them eagerly, pedalling away the while. The paper roll would glide upon its way and, wonder of wonders, the piano would play. It seemed miraculous, and I would watch in fascination as the notes went down, seemingly played by invisible fingers. There was a whole cabinet full of rolls, mostly ballads or Gilbert and Sullivan but including a few light classics such as the *Faust* ballet music or Suppé's 'Light Cavalry Overture'. The one really solid piece was the finale of Tchaikovsky's Fourth Symphony, a veritable torrent of notes which had my heart thumping with excitement. (On reflection it could have been from the effort of pedalling, the density of the transcription apparently causing the instrument to require more air. I developed grotesquely large calf-muscles from an early age and sometimes claim with pride that I was not a marathon runner but a long-distance pianola player!)

Being a naturally curious child — perhaps in more senses than one — I would place tentative fingers on to the keys that I had just seen depressed, and in this way I acquired quite a repertoire of Last Chords, teaching myself the basis of harmony. One day the matron of the house heard the piano being played. She came in to investigate and found me on my own. 'Were you playing the piano?' she asked. At first I denied it, but she reassured me that she wouldn't be cross so I admitted that I had been. 'Show me,' she said, and I sat down and played an adequately harmonised tune of my own devising. In a non-musical household this was regarded as a phenomenon of a prodigious kind and I soon found myself having piano lessons from a kindly lady called Miss Hedges. She used to write down my earliest compositions as a reward for Good Work, and for years I treasured a blue cloth-bound manuscript book containing the first musical fruits of my childish mind. When I was at home not a day would pass without recourse to either the pianola or the gramophone; the records consisted almost entirely of complete Gilbert and Sullivan operettas or vigorous and manly ditties sung by Peter Dawson. (Many years later I discovered that during recitals he used to slip out his false teeth and place them inside the capacious belly of the grand piano — 'to give the voice better resonance'. During the applause he would perform a veritable conjuror's bow, simultaneously popping them back into his mouth so that he could give the audience a flashing smile.) The Sullivan I loved; indeed I knew *Trial by Jury* literally by heart by the time I was twelve. One voice in particular bewitched me, a soprano called Helen Lawson; she was a regular member of the D'Oyly Carte Company which at the time enjoyed considerable prestige. One day, greatly daring, I looked up her name in the London telephone directory and wrote in the margin, 'Helen Lawson has the most beautiful voice in the world.'

At the end of August 1927 we went to East Wittering in Sussex for a holiday, travelling in Major's favourite make of car, a Trojan. It was a rugged bone-shaker of a vehicle with solid tyres and a crash gear-box. The soft-top folded back, to the accompaniment of sharp exclamations of pain as fingers were pinched in the collapsible frame. Signora sat in front with the ubiquitous Tan on her knee while lovely Rose sat with me in the back. We stayed in a rented bungalow called 'The Do-Do', close to the shore. The only blot on the day was the pre-breakfast bathe. Major was a great believer in the therapeutic powers of cold water, taking a cold bath every morning of the year, and welcoming the bonus of the even colder sea. He would stride into the waves like a Commando while I stood pathetically at the brink, toes curled in agony. I have never been much of a swimmer and even now tend to sink to the bottom like a stone if I commit myself to the waters. Far happier were the hours spent on the sands building not the traditional pat-a-cake sandcastles but relief-maps of Europe or the British Isles. Major gave me a better education during the holidays than I ever had at school, continually fostering an interest in the history of the cathedrals and castles we frequently visited. Almost the only childish books I read were those of A.A. Milne; otherwise my taste ranged over Kipling, who was my favourite, Henty, and W. Harrison Ainsworth (now virtually forgotten but the writer of splendid historical novels), not to mention innumerable versions of the tales of King Arthur or Robin Hood. As evidence of this literary bent I quote again from Signora's diary, this time concerning a holiday at Dymchurch in the summer of '28:

> ... After tea we three went for a walk over the marshes to nearby Lym [sic = Lympne]. Tony was pretending to take photos with Tom's field-glasses, perfectly serious, and so of course were we. He said once, 'Next time we will play Pilgrim's Progress and we will bring a Bible with us and read it and I expect it will really help us should we get tired.' He felt the walk was a great adventure as we had to climb stiles and cross bridges. He said, 'This is almost as adventurous as Captain Scott, isn't it?'
>
> An extremely interesting and entertaining child — full of moods, but the whining or cross ones last a very short while. His is a very happy disposition.

Signora clearly felt the greatest affection for me but, as a counterpoint to her litanies of praise, I would quote what could have been a disastrous incident that took place in June '28. Opening a dining-room window that had slightly jammed I pushed my hand right through the glass. A nasty gash like a segment of a tangerine erupted blood. It was very nearly fatal, a millimetre from a main artery; equally at risk was the tendon controlling the movements of my hand. Even so, the relevant entry in her diary shows a good deal more concern over a dog than over me.

> ... Tony put his hand thro' the dining-room window and cut his wrist rather badly. Poor darling — dreadful crying. Tan sick and came out rushing about and I saw something drastically wrong. Got Mr Dixon [the vet], he gave her chloroform — [*I could have done with some!* —] — and found there was a pup! He prepared to stay but before long one was born. We felt happy about her then and left her. I came down at 4 am and found 4! During morning another born. All black with little white fronts and paws.

Since Tan was a white terrier with a tan-coloured splash on one shoulder she must have been mixing in dubious company to give birth to such progeny. The following day —

> Tony had stitches in his hand. I didn't stay. Poor little fellow. Sister said he bore it v. well though he was as white as a sheet. Tan alright. Several boys with sore throats and temps.

The winter of 1929 was particularly severe with deep snow that lasted for six weeks or more. I remember going for walks past the school playing-fields with walls of packed snow towering so high above me that there was no view. Naturally I fantasised that I was Captain Scott in the Antarctic, muttering 'Stick-it — Stick-it' to myself through gritted teeth as, accompanied by some heroic nanny, I trudged through the icy wastes where no man had been before.

Major and Signora's generosity towards my family almost surpasses belief. Every holiday one or all would come down to stay and when the time came, Major arranged for David to come to Berkhamsted School and helped with his education. Christmas was always a great occasion, and we Reynoldses would put on some improvised theatrical entertainment before the assembled staff. The pianola would be in danger of overheating, so vigorously was it put to use, and I was soon capable of playing a number of traditional tunes, always providing that the communal singing covered up deficiencies in the harmony. There could scarcely have been a better house for children's games; there were huge long corridors with innumerable doors opening off them, several staircases and, most intriguing, little attic rooms, some of them empty, in which I imagined ghosts. A skylight with an emergency fire escape opened on to the roof and sometimes I would climb out into the daylight and use the vast gullied slopes as a very private playground. There was a tremendous drop over the edge that added the spice of fear to my exhilaration, an emotion I have continued to enjoy throughout my life. By the time I was nine I was too old for nannies and too much of a handful for Signora to cope with. It was decided that I should go to Berkhamsted Preparatory School as a boarder. The idyll looked as if it was destined to end.

3
No Cane On Sundays

Since I was going to 'live in' at Hall Park, the prep. school, I cannot quite fathom why it was that for my first visit there I was expected to find my own way. Presumably it must have been for some sort of interview with the headmaster, a Mr Davis. Of course I was wholly familiar with the main buildings of Berkhamsted School and it was with perfect confidence that I walked down to the central quadrangle. However, once I arrived there I wandered round increasingly bemused until by chance the head boy, a giant of some eighteen years, came towards me. 'Can you tell me which part is the prep. school?' I asked, not a whit awed by his seniority since I felt protected by Major's status. 'It's miles away at the other end of the town,' he replied, at which my defences crumbled and I burst into tears. Not only would I certainly be late, but I would have let Major down — a recurring childhood dread that never wholly left me. His standards of conduct were so high that I felt constantly unworthy; to this day I have never met anyone with greater integrity. Shame-faced and tear-stained I crept back to Incents to explain what had happened. Major was not available but Signora rose to the occasion by asking Tooley to harness Kelpie to the smart 'trap' which was the alternative transport to the Trojan; soon we were bowling along towards Boxmoor, all sorrows forgotten as the brisk clatter of Kelpie's hooves resounded along the street. It was a glorious compensation for the bad start to the day.

Hall Park had originally been a splendid private mansion. It had about eight acres of grounds attached to it with magnificent cedars giving a special character to the garden. There must have been about sixty boys, most of them boarders. The atmosphere in those less permissive days was surprisingly relaxed. Corporal punishment was reserved for only the most heinous offences, though I did once receive a measured slap on the face from Mr Davis. The correction is remembered even though the sin is forgotten. During my first term I gave proof of my musicality in a rather strange way. It was while we were singing a hymn at morning prayers. The tune so stirred me that I found myself quite spontaneously improvising a descant, soaring high above my earthbound colleagues. There could be few better examples of the differences in educational attitudes then and now. Any child of today heard improvising a descant — moreover one that actually fitted! — would instantly be rushed off to a County Music Adviser, and his parents would set about applying for a grant so that he could be directed to a special school for the musically gifted. In my case the headmaster stopped the hymn, glared, and said, 'Who did that?' Up went my hand, somewhat hesitantly, and red of countenance I said, 'I did, Sir.' He pondered for a moment, wondering whether it was a punishable offence under the General Malefactor's Act, Para. 31, Subsection iv. Finding it impossible to think of a suitable sentence, whether judicial or grammatical, he gruffly said, 'Well don't do it again — it's *showing off* . . . .' His voice rose slightly as he identified my crime and heads were turned in my direction to offer general support to the reprimand. The awful truth is that I did do it again even though I hadn't intended to. I was literally exalted by the music and the sound of sixty treble voices singing with a fervour that the puny forces of Rothsay were incapable of matching.

Life at Hall Park was extraordinarily happy for the most part once the first pangs of separation were over. I was inevitably regarded as something of a swot, for Major's intellectual guidance had given me a head-start over all the other children. I once found a copy of the Schoolboy's Diary dating back to those days; hoping to find it full of descriptions of 'unforgettable' moments that had somehow slipped from memory I eagerly turned the pages. Nothing. It was a complete blank until, in the final section, there was a printed column labelled Position in Form. Beneath, in pencil, I found as succinct a summary of a term's work as one could wish to discover:

WEEK	PLACING
Week 1	1
" 2	1
" 3	1
" 4	1
" 5	1
" 6	1
" 7	1
" 8	1
" 9	3
" 10	1
" 11	1
" 12	1

What mental aberration, what dread malady caused Week 9's fall from grace I do not recall, but it wrecked my average for the term.

On 28 June 1930 I gave my first public performance, singing a novelty song called 'The Tin Gee'. The school magazine also records that I played Giuseppe the Puppet-master in a sketch called The Puppets. It was at the school speech-day and we performed out of doors on a glorious summer afternoon. Mr Davis filmed the occasion with his cine-camera and subsequently showed us the film a number of times to our universal delight. Having seen the film so often I have no hesitation in saying that I *also* sang 'Riding down from Bangor', wearing a beautiful flowery dress and a picture hat that would have been a joy to behold even at Ascot. I must have been an understudy called in at the last moment, for the programme gives credit to someone else. However I am determined to put the record straight after a gap of fifty years; since I can still sing the tune I'm sure I am not mistaken.

Two impressions in particular remain with me from Hall Park, the first of which concerns the innate cruelty of small boys when the pack instinct is aroused. Our frequent games of Cops and Robbers were for the most part enormous fun and played in an excellent spirit, but one day it was decided to 'bait' a boy called Stebbings, for what reason I have not the slightest idea. I can see him now, tall for his age, with long thin legs and very pale gold hair cropped rather short. I had heard a lot of shouting at the highest point of the grounds; naturally I ran up the slope to investigate. What I saw remains a vivid image still. They had blindfolded him and tied his hands. Spinning him round and butting him from side to side of a yelling ring they were flicking at his legs with supple twigs. One bright spark folded a handkerchief and seized a switch of stinging nettles by the root. To howls of excitement from the mob he began to flay the victim's calves. Up until then Stebbings had been brave enough but this new torment brought tears. 'A frog, a frog!' screamed a voice, and a boy came dancing out of some bushes holding a frog by its foot, waving it like a battle-won trophy. 'Stuff it down his shirt!' came the cry, and eager hands held the unfortunate boy still while the live frog was dropped down his shirt at the back. He let out a scream of terror and revulsion and I turned away sickened. As far as I recollect nobody was punished for this nasty episode, though I may be wrong. Schoolboy's 'honour' would have prevented Stebbings from reporting it; he would have known that the long-term ostracism that 'sneaking' would have earned would ultimately have been even harder to bear.

The second impression stems from the dormitory where about a dozen of us used to sleep. My studies in Comparative Anatomy here took a new turn, for everyone was expected to become involved in a nightly strip-show. No need to tell where the focus of interest invariably was, although I must say that after the mysterious attributes that Tinker had displayed I found the male organs rather boring. Again I would stress that there was nothing very sexual about this although I'm sure our behaviour would have earned the strictest censure from adults. There was only one truly vicious boy, head of the school at the time; he liked to exercise his power by getting into bed with the smallest boys and sticking a compass-point into their thighs. It was a visit to be dreaded though we were too unversed in psychology to appreciate its undoubted symbolism. No one sneaked.

One Saturday night virtually the whole dormitory was parading in the nude when the door crashed open and Matron stood there, her face a swiftly changing picture of horror, disbelief and gathering anger. There was a wild scuffle of bare feet across the lino and a muffled clang of iron bedsteads thudding against the wall as we dived for cover. 'You will all report to Mr Davis first thing after breakfast,' she said in icy tones, 'and if I hear so much as a peep from any one of you I'll . . .' I forget what dreadful threat she uttered but it was enough to ensure a very silent breakfast.

There was some quiet speculation as to 'how many' we were each likely to get before we filed sheepishly into the head's study. To our infinite relief he told us that it was against his principles to use the cane on Sundays and gave us whacking impositions instead. It was the first time that I felt that religion had a really *practical* value.

(How different from a school I visited in Adelaide in the '60s. When the headmaster, a clergyman, arrived in his very elegant rooms for lunch his wife remarked how tired he looked. 'I know, dear,' he replied with a heavy sigh, 'I've been flogging an entire form.' At first I thought he was joking but no, he was painfully serious.)

The two episodes I have just elaborated may well create the false impression that the prep. was a terrible place, quite unfit for young children. Of all my school years, those spent at Hall Park were the happiest. Looking back now I realise that this was almost certainly because of its beautiful grounds, vast banked lawns extending away into the distance. There were no tarmac paths, no roads to cross; restrictions on our freedom were remarkably few. On Saturday nights there would be a film show (without sound of course), or sometimes an entertainment from a staff-member or visitor. We were far easier to please than the modern child and major excitements like a trip to the Zoo in Mr Davis's posh Riley were anticipated so keenly that the day was bound to be a success. (*Going up the Watford by-pass, craning over his shoulder to see the speedo. 'Go faster, Sir!, Go on Sir, go faster!' 'Coo . . . we're doing SIX-TY!'*)

In 1931 I won the Reading prize, the Music prize and the Latin prize, the last being particularly gratifying to Major since he had laid a secure foundation. I still have a letter he wrote to me in Latin neatly inscribed in capital letters on a sheet of cardboard. He took it for granted that I, a ten-year-old, would read it with pleasure. Meanwhile I was allowed home two afternoons a week to ride, as an alternative to playing organised games. I include the following extract from Signora's diary for that year not only for the little drama but also to show the conversational level I sustained at the time:

Feb. 11, 1931. A trying day. Started riding at 12.10 with Tony. He had been discussing the battle of Blenheim and Marlborough's tactics all the way and galloping and waving this sword. We were galloping up the narrow path on the common on our homeward journey. Duchess and I had only just begun to gallop; as we went *down* the slope I suddenly saw Pegasus fall right down and her rider of course. To my horror he lay moaning . . . dreadfully knocked out.

I can vaguely remember being hoisted aboard Pegasus like the traditional sack of potatoes. Signora walked to Coldharbour Farm leading horse and pony. Our arrival was inauspicious since the two dogs with us promptly attacked the flock of chickens in the yard and killed a plump hen. There was no telephone at the farm so one of the workers rode Pegasus back to Incents and organised a rescue party.

. . . Tony very indignant I found at Matron having put him on his bed with curtains drawn! He came down to tea and Tom showed him a book about the Civil War — Cavaliers and Roundheads. Tony full of interest and excitement about it and quite his normal self . . . . He returned to the Hall at 6 in taxi. What an *intensely* eager spirit is his . . .

'Intensely eager' I may have been but I was also a very strange mixture of prematurely adult (with Major) and distinctly babyish with her. I constantly spoke of myself in the third person, usually saying 'Tiny' instead of Tony. I think a psychologist would say that I was trying to experience an infancy that circumstance had in a way denied me. Much of the time I was treated as a grown-up and subconsciously I may have tried to counter this by acting the infant as much as the precocious scholar.

Although Signora was not really at all musical she encouraged my piano-playing. Alas it *was* play rather than work and throughout my professional life I have paid a heavy price for not having built a proper technical foundation when I was young.

Sept. '31. Tony improvises so nicely before going to bed, looking away and it just comes . . . . This evening I made up tales of Pooh while he was playing and he composed a march to attract lots of Poohs and then he played to them pretending the room was full of them. He played on and on — surely very wonderful!

Well, not really; certainly not by comparison with true child prodigies.

One day in April 1932 my ear started to play up again. I remember being carried down the main stairway at Hall Park wrapped in a blanket, my face screwed up in pain. I was taken to a nursing home in Nottingham Place and for a second time endured the nightmare of a mastoid operation. The subsequent dressings were a form of indescribable torture, nearly a yard of narrow blood-soaked gauze pulled from the side of my head each morning. I was determined not to cry out and used to hold a bristly hairbrush in my hands, squeezing it tightly to transfer some of the pain away from my ear. After a week the stout bristles were completely flattened but I hadn't given in.

I was away from school for a time and lost ground, so much so that at speech-day Major pointed out that I had won no prizes. 'But I got one for being Captain of the Hall,' I said, showing him the shiny new volume in my hand. 'That doesn't count,' he replied, 'it's automatic.'

4
A Year with a Dancing Girl

I returned from the operation to a new home. During the previous year Major had bought a pair of almost derelict cottages buried in the heart of the wood about four miles from Berkhamsted. Two acres of land came with them, infested shoulder-high with nettles, cow-parsley and bindweed. Many an hour was spent hacking through this jungle with sickle and scythe. On one side of the cottages were extensive beech woods, on the other the common, liberally decked with gorse, bracken and silver birches. Most of the nearby land was owned by the National Trust, for which worthy cause Major had been a tireless worker. (There is a Hopkins Pavilion near the Bridgewater Monument to commemorate him.) For months we had been making regular treks across the common to see how the conversion of two cottages into a single home was progressing. A dank musty wash-house complete with giant copper (a large wash-tub) was to be transformed into a pleasant living-room with windows on three sides. Two bathrooms were installed and a new 'front' door was placed at the side of the house facing a small courtyard hollowed out as a patio. A huge bank that pressed right against the south wall was dug out and re-shaped into terraces. There were no machines to do such work, just a delightful little Irishman called Billy Mahon. He was a boon companion to me and probably welcomed the chance to down tools and entertain me with his animal imitations.

In so remote a situation we had neither electricity nor water from the mains. A small petrol engine in an outhouse thumped away during the dark hours to provide us with light, and all the gutters from the fairly extensive roof area funnelled their water into a large underground cistern. Perhaps the most intriguing feature of the garden was a deep excavation, larger than the average public swimming-pool. The story of how it comes to be there is worth re-telling. Ashridge House, the vast pseudo-Gothic castle which dominates the adjacent park, was built in early Victorian times by the seventh Earl of Bridgewater. He was a typical autocrat and resented the market traffic that trundled to and fro less than a mile from his stately home. The road, which was of great local importance, ran from the village of Aldbury below the escarpment of the Chilterns to the much larger town of Hemel Hempstead. It may even have dated from Roman times since it traced an almost straight line across the woodland. Without the slightest legal right to do so the Earl decided to close the road; his method was effective to say the least — put a fence *across* it, build a house *over* it and dig a pond *in* it. Just in case this wasn't enough to serve his purpose he also made a wood yard for the foresters, built 'our' two cottages on the site and ordered that a vast hole should be dug in the road itself, too deep ever to be filled in by indignant libertarians. I like to imagine someone nowadays digging a great pit across an arterial road to stop the traffic; things are not what they were in 1822.

In addition to a new home in truly idyllic surroundings I found one new face to greet me on my return. Pegasus had gone and in her place was a one-time polo pony with whom I fell instantly in love. Her name was Dancing Time but I re-christened her Dancing Girl, perhaps instinctively sensing that she was not merely beautiful but distinctly fast *and* temperamental. We got on splendidly and she won me the prize for Best Boy Rider at Tring Show when it was the biggest one-day show in Southern England. I say that *she* won it because after we had been circulating the ring rather boringly a military band struck up a brisk march. True to her name Dancing Girl rose on to her hind legs and two-stepped round the ring while I tried to preserve my dignity and look as solemn as the occasion demanded. I think the judges must have felt that as I was still on board at the end of this circus turn I really knew how to ride.

With her polo-playing past, 'Dancy' was a wonderful gymkhana pony, so quick on her feet that I became unpopular with the locals and had to be handicapped in bending races. Perhaps our greatest moment of glory was when at the age of fourteen we won a junior point-to-point for under-nineteens. The hot favourite to win was a girl called Ann Blackwell, of the Crosse and Blackwell family. Rumour had it that the race was rigged in her favour since she and her sister Mary had been practising over the jumps for some time. I'd never jumped real hedges before and when the field of about twenty ponies thundered towards the first one I decided to hang well back. Dancy was no show jumper and often refused in the ring if her attention was diverted. I didn't fancy a refusal in the midst of this cavalry charge, still less the possibility of being tipped over the hedge to soften the landing for the backmarkers. Once over the first fence I relaxed and began to move up through the field. Familiar voices shouted to me as I galloped alongside friends; the cavalcade streamed across fields leaving a wake of barking dogs and screaming mums. After half a dozen fences I found myself in a little group of three led by the redoubtable Ann, of whose neatly-shaped posterior I now had a fair view. We rose to the final fence together and she glanced across at me, indignant at the challenge. The final run-in was a long sweeping curve to the left. She had the inside and we galloped knee to knee, the drumming rhythm of hooves quickening the blood. I was urging Dancy on almost lying on her neck and as we came to the post she found a few longer strides and edged in front. We won by a neck, and I do not remember being asked to the Blackwell home again.

Most of the Pony Club events took place at a house called Beaney in Little Gaddesden. The Gibbs family who lived there were all keen riders, especially the eldest daughter — radiant, dark-haired Mary, the village beauty. There we would meet for team games on horseback and have tuition in the application of aids in riding. One day an examiner came down from London head-quarters to test us in all-round horsemanship. 'Now boy,' he said to me in the clipped tones of an ex-cavalry officer, 'I want you to demonstrate the use of a wisp in grooming.' Dancy was standing in the yard, a dark sweat-mark where her saddle had been. I took a handful of straw, roughly plaited it and tied it in a loose knot. I started to rub the sweat away, her moist coat shining brightly in the sun. 'Put some guts in it, boy,' came the angry voice behind me. 'No, not like that; here, give it t'me.' He took the wisp from my grasp and gave Dancy a mighty thump. Quick as a top she spun round and barged him in the back, knocking him flying. 'You see, Sir, she doesn't like it,' I said, trying not to laugh.

Some good came out of the ear operation because, in order to make a proper recovery, I was allowed to stay away from school for a year. I was formally adopted by Major and Signora and had my name changed to Hopkins, which confused some of the older masters horribly when I returned. During this period of blissful leave I had a tutor, a rather dry and proper individual called Mr Smith who clearly felt (with some justification) that I was neglecting my studies. In such surroundings I could hardly be blamed for wanting to spend every available moment out of doors. Dogs and horses were my constant companions. I had a gorgeous St Bernard called Cornelia and we would wrestle together for an hour at a time on the lawn, her great furry paws slapping at me. Every day I would ride, and poor Mr Smith, who was not at all horsy, would stand gaping as I tried some foolhardy stunt in the paddock, jumping bareback with only a halter to check my beloved Dancy. How I loved to feel the warm barrel of her body against my bare legs as I cantered her up to the big field at Coldharbour where we grazed the horses in summer. At harvest time I went and led the big cart-horse up and down the cornfield while the men loaded the sheaves on to the creaking wagon. I swatted the horse-flies on its twitching belly, leaving little smears of red blood and counting the kills.

It is hardly surprising that music was relegated to second place. A friend of the family, Patrick Cory, a born pianist with a fine technique, was very disappointed in me on one of his infrequent visits. He confided to Signora that I had enough talent to become a first-class musician if only I worked, but that riding horses over the common was no way to go about it. He was right of course. I was squandering precious years, the vital time when I should have been training my fingers and building the foundation of a repertoire. One day, exasperated by my ineffectual playing, he stuck a Schubert piece in front of me and said to me, 'Go on, learn that. I'm going to lock you in and I won't let you out till I can hear you playing it properly through the door.' With a heavy heart I sat down and started to read my way through. It was an arrangement of the beguiling B flat tune from the 'Rosamunde' suite. I stumbled badly over the central G minor section, finding the three-against-two an almost insoluble problem — this at an age when any gifted child today can rattle through a dozen sonatas. In my defence I will say that I was given no indication of my potential. In the Junior School I had been taught piano (and violin) by a truly lovable woman called Muriel Rogers. She had the greatest enthusiasm for music and gave me my first 'classical' records — the overture to *Hansel and Gretel*, and Kreisler playing 'Tambourin Chinois' and 'On Wings of Song'. However, one twenty-minute lesson a week was scarcely adequate preparation for a career as a professional musician. Although I loved playing I was bone lazy about working. I never took an Associated Board grading examination in my life with the inevitable consequence that my scales never developed any real fluency. To this day semi-quavers in the left hand set me all a-tremble. What talent I had as a child was truly spontaneous:

> ... He puts verses (once Shakespeare) to music — sort of recited to music. Awfully good and moving. He sings so charmingly.... He played in my RSPCA concert v. well. His own composition was encored. Mrs D. remarked as he started the concert, 'He is an amazing boy.' She has often said he is quite out of the ordinary and so he is. A great talker, and very keen now on drama and pictures — good ones.

Unfortunately this flattering assessment from Signora's diary is completely misleading musically since she had no standard to judge me by and was herself virtually tone-deaf. She was not unlike that lady in one of my favourite stories who, seated in a deck-chair listening to a military band playing a lugubrious air, whispered to her neighbour, 'Can you tell me if this is Handel's 'Largo' because I do so love it if it is.' I think I *was* precocious in my literary taste and in my conversation, but pianistically I was disastrously slow in developing. The music may have been there but the technique certainly wasn't.

Returning to school after a year of liberty was a depressing anti-climax, although I was allowed to become a day-boy. With the move to Woodyard, Major had retired from house-mastering but since he had been appointed bursar he still went down every day, thus providing me with transport.

It was the most boring period of my school life, only relieved by music lessons with Miss Rogers and singing in the Glee Club. There was another musical boy in the school much more gifted than I; his name was Peter Lubbock. His father was PT instructor and bandmaster and Peter had an uncanny knack of being able to play any wind or brass instrument he laid his hands on. He and I were the two leading trebles and would nudge each other delightedly when, during Glee Club rehearsals of some large choral work, Forbes Milne (the music master) would say to the thirty or so boys around us, 'Now do it without Hopkins and Lubbock.' The pathetic mewing that ensued as the pack wandered leaderless was highly gratifying to our egos. Years later when I was a student at the Royal College of Music I met Peter and he showed me some orchestral scores he'd done which were far more accomplished than anything I had produced. He didn't take up music as a career but became a test pilot for the Fleet Air Arm. Tragically he was blown to pieces when an experimental aircraft he was flying exploded in mid-air.

In a school that had the usual obsession with games I was not cut out for success, though I did win the under-14 100 yards in the quite creditable time of 12.6 seconds. (The school athletics were dominated by a magnificent sprinter called Alan Pennington who went on to represent Britain in the famous Berlin Olympics. He was my boyhood hero and had set some incredible records, winning the 220 yards *under 16* in 23.2 seconds on a grass track.) In due course I moved up to the senior school and was made a boarder again since Major was very dissatisfied with my work. I settled into communal living with a reasonably philosophic attitude though I hated sleeping in a narrow wooden cubicle in comparison to which Dancing Girl's box was palatial in size. A new and even more compelling distraction suddenly and unexpectedly dominated my life; I fell deeply, romantically, consumingly in love.

As though the four thousand acres of National Trust land surrounding Woodyard were not enough I also had the run of the splendidly picturesque gardens of Ashridge House. During the period I have just described my main companions — apart from Tinker who gradually became less available as well as less willing — were the two daughters of Lady Davidson, the local MP. Margaret and Jean were happy extroverts, keen riders, fond of music and great fun to be with. The Davidson family lived in the end wing of Ashridge House beneath a handsome archway leading to the stables. Ashridge was then known as the Bonar Law Memorial College and was the headquarters of the Conservative party. The grounds were a children's paradise with a huge avenue of rhododendrons extending into the distance. There was a grotto made from massive pudding-stones, a secret tunnel that took some courage to walk through in inky blackness, a fascinating tomb for a horse with a beautifully crafted ceiling made from hundreds of flints; there were two quite sizeable houses made from trees skilfully trained over a frame of metal rods and my favourite spot — a tree 'chapel' made of tall incense cedars planted close together in a ring. A little stone lectern with a carved book on it stood in the centre, and as one looked up towards the sky, the treetops formed a coronet of stunning beauty. It was said that fairies danced there in the light of the moon and local children would sneak in at midnight, hoping to catch a glimpse of them.

In the spring of 1936 Air Vice-Marshall MacEwen took over as the principal of the college. He had a daughter called Brownie who was the most beautiful living creature I had ever seen. She was a mere ten years old with an exquisitely formed little face, hair so dark brown that it looked black in certain lights and fragile bones of such delicacy that even the supplest Oriental would have looked clumsy beside her. I was ripe for the picking and as soon as I saw her I fell. Needless to say the relationship was totally innocent and, for that reason, all the more romantic. She could not have had a safer nor more gallant lover for my ideals were based on Sir Galahad, Bayard and Chaucer's 'very gentil parfit knight'. Each morning before breakfast I would walk the half-mile to Ashridge and stand beneath her window calling to her softly. (I feared to ride lest the sound of hooves should arouse her parents and bring them out to shoo me away.) My little Mélisande would appear, framed by the grey stone of the turret where her room was situated. Brushing her hair, she would smile bewitchingly at me and we would carry on a hushed but urgent conversation making plans for the day. Although I had always loved animals, the human relationships in my life had up until then consistently lacked real warmth. My fondness for Major was tinged with awe, my affection for Signora strangely babyish, subconsciously playing up to her need for a small child of her own. Other adults I treated as equals and was sometimes disliked for it. Here though was a tiny enchantress who brought out in me a vein of tenderness that had never previously been revealed. My whole day revolved around her whim; I was her protector, her groom, her slave, and I loved to do her any service. She had a beautiful little black pony about twelve hands high and we would ride together for hours at a time. There were often other children with us but I had eyes only for her.

One day we were riding at the far side of Northchurch Common some three miles from home. It had rained heavily the previous day and the grassy rides were bisected by broad puddles of water which were the greatest fun to jump. After one such leap she suddenly pulled up her pony sharply. I reined in Dancing Girl and turned back swiftly to see what was doing. 'He's gone terribly lame,' she said, looking up at me with a worried expression that stabbed my heart. I dismounted and ran what I confidently felt were expert hands down the pony's slender legs. I could feel nothing, no lumps, no inflammation. 'His legs are sound,' I said, eternally optimistic. I took the reins and walked him on a little, the squelching mud tugging at my boots. He staggered and it was clear something was desperately wrong. 'You ride Dancy,' I said, 'and I'll lead him home.' I lifted her, feather-light, into the saddle, sweet momentary thrill, and together, unusually silent, we started the long trek home. That night I phoned to find the outcome and learned that he had ruptured a gut and had to be destroyed. Soon after, the MacEwens left — I used to think because they feared for their daughter's safety with so intense a lover in the neighbourhood. I only saw her once more after their departure. It was at a dance a couple of years later and there she was, hair flowing loosely down her back, swaying deliciously in another's arms. I hated dancing and had no aptitude for it; even so I asked her if I might... she tossed her head almost contemptuously and glided off in the stiff embrace of some gilded youth. I felt like a gelded youth; it was an early lesson in the perfidy of women, for my devotion had been purity itself.

I think Major was worried by my unconcealed adoration for Brownie. One afternoon he said that he felt he ought to have a talk with me about 'a few things'. He suggested that we should go for a walk to avoid being overheard. His expression was rather grave as we set off up the hill through the woods. For three miles or so we walked in a great circle, returning home in time for tea. Not a word had been spoken. He could not persuade the word 'sex' to pass his lips and for once I was tactful enough not to press him.

A chance encounter was a little more enlightening. On one

occasion when my sister was staying with us she and I had set out to walk the four miles to Berkhamsted. After a mile and a half the road goes up quite steeply through Frithsden Copse. Coming down the hill towards us was a man wheeling a bike with a small fox-terrier seated in a basket on the handlebars. 'Can you tell me the way to Mrs Low's kennels?' he called to us. I started to give him directions, my gaze meanwhile drawn inexorably towards a large sausage-like object protruding from the front of his trousers. 'Oh, sorry about that,' he said, looking down not a whit self-consciously and giving its plummy head a friendly pat. 'Felt a bit hot so I took it out to cool it.' Pam and I exchanged glances looking for an indication of the polite thing to do. 'Taking my bitch to Mrs Low's to be mated I am,' the man went on to say. 'D'you know how they do it — you know, make puppies?' We shook our heads. 'Well, the dog gets on top of my bitch here and sticks this bit' (pointing to his own comparable member) 'inside her.' His hand began flicking up and down the sausage which seemed to inflate alarmingly. 'Then he squirts his stuff inside her and that's how puppies are made.' It scarcely appeared to be a logical consequence but we were prepared to take his word. A little pool of white fluid rather resembling condensed milk formed on the road. 'Like that, see ...' the man said. We nodded silently. 'First right you said and then along the valley?' 'Yes,' I replied, 'you can't mistake it; it's a big yard on the left before you get to the pub.' 'Righty-ho, I'll be off then.' We resumed our upward trudge intrigued by the unusual interlude. 'Suppose we'd better not say anything,' I said to Pam. 'Suppose not,' she said. We walked on in silence, pondering this interesting exposure of hidden truths. Maybe it was something to add to one's store of knowledge but it clearly could have no application to humans.

5
Public School, Private Thoughts

L ife at School House revolved around the original hall, built
in 1544. Three long lines of narrow reading desks stretched
from end to end, giving seating for some sixty boys. On the
opposite side were three considerably more substantial desks for
prefects to sit at, each raised on a dais so as to give a commanding
supervisory view. Small lockers, one for each boy, were provided
on one end wall while the seniors and house prefects shared an
additional line of lockers placed above the back row of benches.
Further desks, their tops slightly angled in two directions, were
placed between the prefects' vantage points. There we would
congregate in little groups reading the *Daily Mirror* or model-
makers' magazines. The cultured background which I had truly
enjoyed since I was five was abruptly removed and I found myself
in a strictly organised society in which to read anything other
than the Saint or Bulldog Drummond was regarded as an
eccentricity. Signora made me wear a brown mac — 'No gentleman would wear navy' — and this sartorial distinction made me
acutely self-conscious since I was the only boarder to do so. I was
inevitably teased about my riding and quickly acquired the nickname of Horace, after the Disney character Horace Horsecollar.
During my first year I was a fag, though the system was not as
unjustly abused as it was in some schools notorious for petty
tyranny. I found the total absence of privacy a cause for misery
and longed for the immeasurably more sympathetic company of
animals. The termination of my brief but intense love for little
Brownie left a huge gap in my life. The experience of loving, of
giving myself had given me a deep satisfaction that I had not
known before; the emotional void within me demanded to be
filled.

It is unfortunate that the word homosexual has even today a somewhat grubby connotation. The '-sexual' half of the word has a very positive force suggestive of genital contact. I doubt though if I would have survived if it had not been for a 'love-affair' in which sex played no part. Inevitably sixty or more young males cooped up together and denied any contact with girls generated an unnaturally repressive atmosphere. Sex was certainly on our minds although I was probably the most innocent boy in the house. (Thanks to Tinker I knew what 'little girls were made of' though neither of us had ever had an inkling of how things worked, except for watering the garden.) One boy with a murky countenance tried to corrupt me by boasting of his holiday conquests. He described the amusement he and his pals had derived from hanging over the Embankment wall watching the French letters float by. I was amazed by this, wondering how he could tell they were French; surely the water would make the ink run? Anyway, who could read them at that distance? I voiced my disbelief giving my reasons. It was his turn to look incredulous.

'Don't you know *anything*?'

'Well . . . not about that sort of thing — at least I don't think so . . .'

'Do you know any bad words?'

'Not really; I can swear in Latin . . . oh, and in Greek . . . a little . . .'

'Cor, you are daft. Shall I teach you some bad words?'

'Oh do. Please do.'

'Well, I'll have to write them down because if anyone hears me I'll get reported.'

He searched in his pockets for a diary, pressed it open on his knee and took out a rather messy fountain-pen with the sort of nib that tore holes in the page as you wrote.

'I'll start with the very worst one of all and then if we have to pack it in at least you'll know that.'

I felt my cheeks flush with excitement; I sensed that I was on the brink of some tremendous initiation into a world of unspeakable evil. Like some legendary figure, Faust perhaps, or did I mean Dante, I was being drawn into an abyss With great deliberation he wrote the magic word. PHUK. I wondered if he'd finished. When I realised that he had, I waited for a bolt from heaven to strike us down, but no divine retribution came and I was content to know this black incantation without having the slightest idea what it meant.

My innocence of sexual terminology remained exceptional. When I was sixteen the headmaster had a heart-to-heart talk with me in his study one Sunday evening. 'Are you circumcised?' he asked — I can't imagine why. 'I don't know, Sir.' 'Oh come on boy, you must know.' 'Really I don't, Sir. It's something to do with religion isn't it, Sir?'

Sandy had fair hair, blue eyes and a rather wide face with high cheekbones and a faintly negroid nose; he had the most winning smile and a good scientific brain with quite different aptitudes from mine. We arrived at School House on the same day and got on famously from the start. Gradually his company became completely indispensable. I haven't the slightest doubt that the intensity of my feelings towards him was due to our absolute segregation from the opposite sex, a deprivation the day-boys did not have to endure. By chance rather than design almost all my childhood companions had been female, apart from my younger brother David who had frequently stayed at Woodyard. Nearly all the friendships established at prep. school had been severed in the intervening years; my year's absence had seen to that. Wildly romantic by nature, my head filled with tales of ancient gallantry, I needed a 'fair maiden' to whom I could dedicate myself. Fair maidens were quite unattainable in our monastic society so I made Sandy the object of my devotion. It is very hard to describe how deeply I felt for him for some four years. He was flattered, touched, enjoyed my company but did not reciprocate my love.

One night, aching with loneliness, I felt I had to be near him or die. Barefoot I stole silently up the cold stone stair to the upper dormitory where he slept. Any traffic between the two dormitories was strictly forbidden and I knew my entire school career was at risk. If I was caught I would certainly be expelled; the disgrace I would bring upon Major would be unendurable but I was mad enough to take any risk. Scarcely moving the curtain to his cubicle in case the rings made that unmistakable metallic slither I edged my way in. As silently as I could I lowered myself to the floor by his bed. A slight movement of the bedclothes. The quietest possible whisper, slowly enunciated, in curiosity not annoyance — 'What . . . are . . . you . . . doing . . . here?' 'Nothing.

Just here.' Silence, and in a strange way contentment despite the blood hammering in my ears. I sat there for about ten minutes, my pyjama-clad back pressed against the chilly stone wall. Suddenly I heard footsteps coming up the stairs, authoritative footsteps that filled me with stark fear. Not only would I be expelled but Sandy too, and for nothing. We would both surely be beaten, for no one would ever believe my protestations. His dressing-gown was on the bed (we were always cold at nights); I grabbed it and jammed myself full-length against the heavily varnished wood of the partition, face to the floor. Awkwardly I pulled the dressing-gown around me, hoping its dark grey wool would obliterate the striped pattern of my pyjamas. *Oh God, it's not long enough; my feet will show. The mat; there's a mat on the floor. Reach down for it; scrabble it over my frozen feet. Terror now, absolute terror as the footsteps stopped just outside. He must be able to hear my heart. The tiny rattle of curtain-rings as he opened a hand's breadth. Hold my breath; don't move an eyelash.* I was a hunted animal, a hare lying flat in its form, the hounds sniffing the grass inches away. I sensed eyes peering into the dark cabin. At last, unbelievably, the reassuring sound of the curtain re-drawn. Slowly the footsteps measured the length of the dormitory, returned, stopped again as though he smelt the scent of fear and then, blest relief, scuffled down the stairs. I suppose I must have waited for twenty minutes or so before I heard the bathwater running in the first-floor bathroom, heard the lock click into place. Palms pressed against the wall I crept downstairs. It was as risky a journey as the ascent had been. I could not have devised any excuse that would explain my presence on the staircase. The boy in the cubicle next to mine must have heard me and guessed where I had been. 'You filthy little sodomite,' he said to me some time later in tones of utter disgust. He didn't sneak though; that would have been against the code.

With a little over sixty boys packed into one building it was hardly surprising that we suffered the occasional epidemic. 'Suffered' is not the right word though; we welcomed them. A bout of measles, mumps or chicken-pox would put the house in quarantine, a happy state since the school timetable would be reversed. Whilst the rest of the school worked we would play games, and vice versa. Someone devised an immensely enjoyable game that was a crazy variant of soccer. It was played on a rugger pitch with about thirty players on each side. So far as possible everything was done in multiples of three; there were three balls, three goalkeepers to each team, nine forwards and so on. Play stopped and restarted each time a goal was actually scored, but it was quite common to have three goalkeepers under attack simultaneously. If it was raining we would play a very rough alternative called gym rugger in which there were no organised scrums but no end of scrimmages. During one such game I had clasped the ball tenaciously to my chest when someone tried to throw me, judo-fashion, from behind. Seizing me by the shoulders he exerted powerful leverage against my left leg; unfortunately there was a prostrate body lying on the floor between my ankles and my leg could not give way. There was a painful snapping sensation in my knee and I gave a yelp of pain, inaudible in the general hubbub. The rest of the term I limped around the school suffering from a badly displaced cartilage which the school doctor refused to diagnose, accusing me of faking to get off games. In the Christmas holidays I was taken to see a specialist who said that there was nothing for it but to have the cartilage out. I was booked in to King's College Hospital for the operation, a depressing prospect since I was also due to have yet another operation (the fourth!) on my wretched right ear. The small pit behind the ear had been surgically closed; it was then found necessary to do a sort of rebore. Small wonder that I had my fill of being brave; for many years afterwards I used to faint if a doctor even looked into my ear. It was nature's way of avoiding more torture and however much I would say, 'It isn't going to hurt,' I would simply keel over.

It was during the period of the knee operation that I kept the only diary I have ever written. It is a very revealing document; I had plenty of time to write in the ward and I poured out my heart for page after page. The entries begin on 18 December 1936. I was fifteen. With my dispatch to boarding-school Dancing Girl had been passed on to a friend but we still had horses, a noble old racehorse called Captain and a skittish mare of a rather stubborn disposition named June. Although my brothers and sister were all due to stay for Christmas the diary starts in a mood of depression from having seen Sandy off at the station. However, a logging expedition into the woods, chopping up fallen timber, seems to have cheered me up a little.

... It's so utterly glorious being back at home free and comfortable, out in the lovely wild country. If only Sandy were here I would be completely happy. My dread is that when he comes to stay (after the operation) I won't be able to ride and walk with him as much as I'd like to.

In the afternoon, for a ride with Pam. Old Captain delightful ... We see a lot of deer, one being snow-white, another a huge stag, white with fawn markings. I had always wondered at, 'And herds of strange deer, silver-white came gleaming through the forest green.' Now I know what he meant. They looked very romantic and rather strange ...

A quiet evening playing Beethoven and Mozart. Bro (one of the dogs) had hysteria just before dinner; poor little beggar, he has an awful time when he is taken — just like I feel before being operated on, only I don't howl.

Sat. Dec. 19. Gorgeous day, blue sky, not a cloud in sight, bright sun and a keen nip in the air. Much carolling in the bath and down to breakfast in time. Letter from the vet about Cornelia who has an objectionable skin disease — all the symptoms of sarcoptic mange but no parasites externally ... After breakfast a hard smash at Clementi, Pathétique, Haydn D major and Mozart G. Then a jazz medley. To the garden-room where Pam and I dressed Corney's sores.

The entry for this day alone runs to some thirteen hundred words. We had a stocky little pony called Sabrina trained to go in harness and when we went logging we used to rig up chains so that she could pull in the timber. We never lacked firewood.

Dec. 19. cont. . . . Changed into complete rugger kit including boots and went down to the stable, where we collected rope and axes and marched off with Sabrina in halter with chest-strap traces. Collected loads all the afternoon. Sabrina great fun with the loads tearing up the ground behind her as she cantered along. There was a lot of fun near the end of the afternoon when she reared ... and cleverly turned round and backed out of her tackle! We laughed so much that she could have got away easily if she had chosen to. A lot of people about and hounds kicking up the devil of a row up on the ridge towards the brick kilns. It was rather funny — Miss C. and Anne H. were returning from the run looking terribly proud and aristo-cratic just as we came haring round the corner with a couple of logs making a terrific noise, kicking up the mud and looking terribly savage and primitive. Miss C.'s horse, being a true blue-blooded nobleman, at once threw a fit at the sight of us and endeavoured to dash up the road, thus completely upsetting their dignity as members of the band of English 'Sportsmen and women'. Anne looked absolutely disgusted at me, as I was dirty and doing lowly manual labour in primitive clothing; she more or less passed by on the other side. . . . We also saw Peter Gibbs returning from the hunt, and Cornelia booed so loudly that his pony fled up the hill like rather tired lightning. . . .

It was a lovely evening with great banks of cloud piled up in the West flushed a dull red by the setting sun. Behind them was a soft blue sky, which grew an ominous black to the North and East. There was no wind at first, and the delicate skeletons of the tree-tops showed up gauntly against the sky. However, when I turned back homewards a keen wind sprang up against me, and it felt marvellous swinging along through the mud with the breeze in my face and the weird night-feeling of expectancy all around me. I thought much of Sandy and in my mind was blended a curious mixture of sadness and joyousness, sadness at his absence, joy at the very thought of him . . .

And so it continues through the remainder of December with long and lyrical descriptions of an extremely healthy life outdoors alternating with maudlin passages about my quite obsessional longing for Sandy's company. Almost every day I would go and sit for a time in the straw in Captain's stable and talk to him as my only confidant. The beauty of telling one's secrets to animals is that they don't spread them around.

On Christmas Eve my elder brother Peter arrived to stay. He was very keen on music though nothing exceptional as a pianist. He played a cruel trick on me which I have never forgotten.

. . . Peter showed me a colossal MS. written by him which he then played — extraordinarily good and better than any of my improvisations. Well built-up but inclined to be over dramatic while seeking for effect in some places; very hard to play . . .

rather a mixture of Chopin and Grieg with regard to melodic and harmonic treatment but really very good — some weird harmonies and some really lovely melodies with rippling accompaniment. With polishing it would be good enough to publish. Perhaps a trifle too long for the theme.

As musical criticism this at least has the benefit of being honest, although the sequel was humiliating enough to make me realise that I should never be a critic.

> ... I shall never forgive P. for fooling me .... His so-called composition was a MS copy which he'd made of the Chopin B flat minor Scherzo. I nearly spotted it about five times but never had the courage to say I definitely disbelieved him. He apparently heard the piece, liked it, and decided to copy it out to get to know it better — and took me in very badly. The cad!

Christmas passed happily apart from acute pain in my knee during Morning Service. Every day there was a ride, every day communal music-making round the piano; regrettably, serious practice seems to have been non-existent. On the 29th Signora escorted me to London to go to the hospital. I felt that my sojourn there would give me a good opportunity for some serious reading. I took an impressive number of books with me, meticulously listed in the diary: —

Beethoven's Symphonies	— piano version
" "	— Grove
Complete Works	— Shakespeare
English Journey	— Priestly (sic)
Plays	— Galsworthy
Canterbury Tales	— Chaucer
Tales of Imagination	— Poe
The Opium-Eater	— De Quincey
Tale of Two Cities	— Dickens
Golden Treasury	— Palgrave
The Progress of Music	— Dyson
Studies of Great Composers	— Parry
The Hunchback of Notre Dame	— V. Hugo

I took considerable care over the choice of this extraordinarily pretentious selection even though the weight was arm-breaking. I did not realise what life in a public ward was going to be like. Apart from the two Beethoven items I read not a word from this miniature library. Other patients foully seduced me with Edgar Wallace and Leslie Charteris. I was a lost soul.

During my stay I chronicled every event in the ward, savouring the misfortunes of others with glee only occasionally tempered with sympathy.

... Inhuman yells coming from the chap who's just been operated on. He is just coming out of his chloroform and is coughing, being sick, groaning and moaning and occasionally giving the most awful shrieks and crying out, 'Oh dear! Oh dear!' Nurse is sitting beside him and telling him he's alright and it's all over. More shrieks — I should imagine he's just getting conscious. Terrific hoarse screams and nurse telling him it's naughty of him to shout. Poor devil — I pity him intensely and hope to goodness I shall control myself .... People are quite happily reading and writing with all this din going on. He has now stopped, and just gives an occasional cough getting the muck out of his lungs.

The operation took place on 31 December and I must have gone on with the diary very soon after I came round as the handwriting appears very wobbly. After the agony of the ear surgery it seemed almost pleasant; a knee feels so much further away! I became the ward clown and was nicknamed 'the Imbecile' by the nurses.

Jan. 7. ... Given a horrible-looking dose of cascara by the night-staff. Took about quarter of an hour to summon the courage to drink it and nearly spilt it I was laughing so much at myself The nurse nearly had hysteria from laughing too. As soon as I had drunk it I ate a whole tangerine in as quick a time as I could. Then to sleep.

Jan. 8. ... had one of the nearest shaves of my life. Nurse arrived, drew the curtains and told me she was going to give me an enema. I nearly fainted with horror and she went off to get the B.P. and paraphernalia; arrived with the B.P. and in pathetic tones I implored her to allow me to try and use it ordinarily first. She did while she went to get the stuff and by the grace of heaven I succeeded. What a stroke of luck! . . . to recover from the shock lay back listening to records 'over the air'. Heard the most divine song by Schumann called 'The Almond Tree'.

I still remember the effect Elizabeth Schumann's voice had on me, even through the crackling headphones. The diary ends the moment I returned home but before putting it away I will quote one more extract, an extravagant literary send-up brought about by an absorbed reading of Gilbert Murray's translation of the *Medea* of Euripides — from an era before I had encountered Leslie Charteris.

A MASTERPIECE — BY ME — Written in bed — probably under the influence of a drug.

Deep and dark, e'er the first low notes of Atheris
Had died, soft-shrouded in its sultry pall
Came Night, and closed his lids 'neath sleep,
While the laving waters of the limpid lake
Lapped lovingly upon the shore.
Whispering through the trees
Came a breeze,
And the little cloudlets tossed lamb-like
In the archèd heavens. Luna, the
Queenly Goddess of the Night rose haltingly
Into her azure courts, and the flocking
Hosts of stars, deep flushed in gold array
Bowed humbly to her gorgeous state.
Moted beams swam feather-light through space
And nightingales cuddled the cool night air
In breathless song. Windily wafted
Came sweet notes of long-drawn music
Spun thread-like o'er the craggy hills
To flood his ears in liquid harmonies.
Then rose he passionate and smote him on the breast.
Closed his visor and took his mighty sword.

Temnithora was its name and its steely shard
Was stained in good men's blood.
Strode he forth into the dark Unknown,
For ever to be lost in Scythian solitude.

It is gibberish of course but sounds quite impressive if declaimed in the grand manner.

If I seem to have spent overlong on an episode that lasted a mere three weeks it is because it is the only period of my entire life that is documented in detail. At least it is my authentic voice and gives evidence that I had inherited some gift for words from my father. As to the Sandy affair, whose intensity I have not exaggerated, I would point out that there have been societies in the past where it would have been regarded as perfectly normal. I do not know if the Greeks had a word for it but they would certainly have understood it. It is a sad commentary on the outlook of our moral guardians that the two purest emotional involvements of my life should be the two that would be most condemned.

6
Music in the Mountains

The summer of 1937 was one of the most significant periods of my life. A girl called Margaret Young came to stay with the Davidson family at nearby Ashridge. We were almost exactly the same age but she was a truly gifted violinist, far more advanced than I was in musical proficiency. She was already tackling the big solo repertoire, the concertos of Beethoven, Brahms, Mendelssohn or Max Bruch, sonatas such as the 'Kreutzer' or the César Franck, the unaccompanied works of Bach, not to mention innumerable show-pieces by Kreisler, Sarasate or a host of eighteenth-century composers whose names all seemed to end with the letter I. Virtually every day she would come down to Woodyard and together we would plough through these great (and for me uncharted) works with rather differing degrees of success. One sometimes reads in concert reports that 'the accompanist followed the soloist perfectly'. I often followed a couple of bars behind, unable to keep up with her flashing bow and flying fingers. It is hard nowadays to imagine that a potentially musical boy of sixteen could *not* have heard the standard works of the violin repertory, yet there I would sit gazing apprehensively at the opening pages of the Beethoven concerto wondering if I dared reveal my ignorance by asking how fast it went. A wily alternative wording came into my mind. 'How fast do you like it?' I queried, as though I'd played it with a dozen or more violinists already. Using her bow as a commanding baton she flailed the air and I began, my confidence draining in sick unease when the first D sharps appeared. Could it really be correct I thought, in all innocence reacting precisely as Beethoven intended us to do.

Despite my dreadful inadequacy I greatly enjoyed these daily sessions and the challenge of Margaret's excellence proved to be a spur to my complacency. I actually began to practise instead of just fooling around at the keyboard. In conversation Margaret frequently referred to her elder half-sister Jane, a cellist of the very highest quality. She had been a pupil of Feuermann and was a born teacher, her superb musicianship being radiated to all and sundry on infectious waves of enthusiasm. I think Major was becoming seriously worried by my lack of application; in place of the precociously intellectual child he now had an insouciant teenager who spent more time in the stable than in the study. He wrote to Jane asking if she would hear me and give an honest assessment. Was I capable enough to take up music as a career?

I cannot say honestly that I had given much thought to my future; I was coasting along very nicely and had no wish to change my course. When I had first entered the senior school I had toyed with the idea of becoming a doctor, though Lord knows I had suffered so much at their hands that it was a strange choice. I would like to feel that my motivation was idealistic and humanitarian but the sad truth is that since Tinker's defection to the Guides my treatise on female anatomy had made no further progress. In those less permissive days I despaired of ever finding any practical answers to the questions that frequently plagued my adolescent mind. It seemed that only through the legitimate channels of the medical profession would I be able to satisfy my natural curiosity. I had decided therefore to become a doctor with a secret bias towards gynaecology. (I didn't know the word but, as the saying goes, 'It's the thought that counts.') The prospects of studying such forbidding subjects as physics, chemistry and biology to the required levels was a daunting one since I had no aptitude for the sciences. Fortunately I was further dissuaded by a schoolfriend whose elder brother actually was a doctor. 'That's daft,' he said when I revealed my base motive, 'it's seven years before you get to the interesting bit . . .'

Late one afternoon in midsummer I arrived at a large house in Addison Crescent to display my meagre talents to Jane. I had heard so much about her that I felt we were almost acquaintances. Whether I was early or she was late I cannot remember but I shall never forgot my first impression of her as she let herself in through the front door. She wore a black beret set at a jaunty angle on her jet-black hair while her long leather coat confirmed a distinctly un-English appearance. Her expression was more vital than any

I'd ever seen, dominated by eyes that seemed to taunt me, amused, teasing or provocative by turns. In due course I sat down and played my one adequately prepared piece, the Allegretto from Beethoven's Op. 10, No. 2. My sole reason for choosing this was that Major had kindly given me Schnabel's recording of the sonata as a birthday present; the first and last movements were quite beyond my feeble grasp but I could just about manage the middle movement, especially as it begins with the two hands in unison. I had played the Schnabel record until the needle had almost worn its way through to the other side, copying his slightest nuance in my own performance. Even if Jane didn't actually clap her hand to her forehead exclaiming, 'My God, he plays just like Schnabel!' she was apparently sufficiently impressed to write back to Major that I was at least worth further observation. She suggested that I should go to Austria for a few weeks, there to join a small group of largely professional musicians who gathered in a little colony to make music for the sheer delight of it. By watching my reactions she would be able to judge my musical receptivity, a fairer test than a brief hour in London could provide. To my great excitement, it was agreed that I should go. I hadn't been abroad since the ill-fated expedition to Italy which I scarcely remembered. All alone, with the princely sum of fifteen pounds in my pocket, I duly set off for Schwaz on the Innthal.

The journey through Nazi Germany opened my eyes to a situation of which we were naively unaware at school. Twice we had played host to parties of German youths in the cause of Anglo-German friendship, hoping no doubt through the civilising influence of cricket to dissuade them from any warlike inclinations. We mostly thought of Hitler as a rather absurd little man, an easy butt for the cartoonists. Our history studies scarcely brought us into the twentieth century and I remember being taught hardly a thing about current affairs. Suddenly I found myself travelling through a country in which uniforms seemed to far outnumber civilian clothes. At every station halt I would watch with rather amused disbelief as arms were raised in stiff salute, heels clicked, and the monotonous parrot-cry 'Heil Hitler' rang out. The jerky movement of the puppet-like figures seemed faintly risible but the smile was wiped off my face when a bulky policeman came into my carriage and started to search my bag. He came across a sheath-knife, a relic of a brief period in the

Scouts. He grunted as he held it up accusingly, his eyes suggesting that he had by chance discovered a plot to assassinate the Führer. 'Vy you haf zis?' he growled at me. My command of German was absolutely minimal and I felt quite incapable of explaining that any English schoolboy going on a holiday in the country would automatically take a knife. As a virility symbol it seemed a lot more harmless than the guns that joggled on nearly every male hip in Germany. My blushes and my halting attempts to explain must have convinced him that if I were to be involved in an assassination attempt I would make a complete botch of it. I can joke about it now but the atmosphere at the time was genuinely nasty. To be surrounded by armed thugs is never a pleasant experience, especially when they are masquerading as policemen. It was with a feeling of relief that I emerged into free, happy Austria. Jane and Margaret met me at Schwaz station. I couldn't resist making a mock Nazi salute, saying 'Heil Hitler' in clipped tones. Jane was horrified. 'Idiot!' she said, 'don't do that here or you'll get us locked up.' I was still typically unwilling to take the jackboot image seriously, as were all too many of my countrymen. I was quite unaware that the Austrians were rightly fraught with anxiety about German intentions. The following year their fears were fully justified when Hitler accomplished what was euphemistically called the *Anschluss*.

We stayed at a guest-house called Hochbrunn, high above the Inn valley. There was a small terrace from which we could enjoy spectacular views and a pocket-size swimming-pool that was just in the process of being completed. Fed by water from a glacier it was unbelievably cold, and I only really enjoyed playing in it when it was empty. I would sometimes sweep it clean, relishing the delicious swoosh of stiff wet bristles on concrete. Our days would be spent rambling in the lush verdant meadows, occasionally descending into the neat and colourful streets of Schwaz to shop for fruit or biscuits and drink a glass of cool milk scooped up from a great churn. Not far out of the town, at the foot of the narrow road leading up to Hochbrunn, there were two houses, one on each side. In the upper one lived the Baroness von Schey, or Anni-Mutti as we all called her, an elegant and charming patrician with exquisite manners. I would sometimes spend the afternoon there. 'Play to me Tony,' she would murmur, stretching herself out on a chaise-longue by the window. I had the tiniest repertoire so I was forced to improvise or, if I was feeling courageous, to read the slow movements of sonatas of which she had copies stacked by the piano.

In the evenings we would descend as a party to the house opposite, occupied by two sisters in — I would guess — their early fifties whose aged semi-paralysed mother sat like a monument in one corner of a long room. There was an upright piano against one wall and every night there would be music — sonatas, duos, trios, quartets — played as chamber music should ideally be played with the windows open and the occasional sound of bird-song drifting in from outside. I would sit on the floor, knees pulled up in front of me, like the famous picture of the boyhood of Raleigh. Almost miraculously people would sit down and play *without music* for what seemed to be hours at a time, drawing on apparently limitless reserves of memory. I suppose I knew a few short pieces by heart but I could only keep going for any length of time by making it up as I went along. There, amongst professionals, I had the wit to realise I was quite outclassed, but I listened, absorbed, spellbound by the uncanny skills that I was witnessing at such close quarters. Of course we had sat through recitals at school, usually given by a pianist with the vaguely unconvincing name Ivan Phillipowsky; the performer in such concerts invariably seemed a remote figure, perched up on the high stage of the school hall, whose hollow acoustics jumbled the harmonies together in echoing confusion. Trapped in a sea of restless boys it was hard to surrender to the music; even to be seen enjoying it exposed one to derision from the Philistines. In Schwaz it was indeed a different world and all my latent enthusiasm for music could be tapped. Many years later I asked Jane what she could possibly have seen in me when I had achieved so little for my age. 'You saw the jokes in the music,' was her unexpected reply, by which she meant that I comprehended what I heard and knew by instinct when a composer had foiled expectation with a diverting twist of harmony.

If the weather was poor we would sit round a table and sing Palestrina or Bach. I had always loved singing and I have been told that I took to this choral initiation as the proverbial duck takes to water, though I trust more melodiously. Talk was endless with never a mention of a horse. Names of great contemporary musicians were tossed into the conversation with a casual ease that showed no trace of the awe I felt at their legendary status. Jane actually knew them and would entrance me with musicians' gossip such as I had never heard.

One night an Austrian pianist called Heinz Jolles sat down to play some Schubert, the Four Impromptus, Op. 90, as I later discovered. I need hardly say I had never heard them before, but as I listened I felt as though I was bewitched, helpless to resist the lure of great music. As I walked back up the mountain road to Hochbrunn my head seemed to reel with music. I paused to listen to the murmur of pine trees but heard only the memory of notes nimbly played rippling from the keyboard. It was a moment of considerable spiritual force, a literal conversion not all that different from a religious experience. Suddenly I knew that I really wanted to be a musician.

Inevitably the holiday had to end and we set out for England on the International Express. When we arrived at Munich there were cries of 'Everybody out!' and, to everyone's surprise, we were herded off the train and told there would be no further transport until the next day. The city was packed and we trudged from one hotel to another trying to find accommodation. In the end we found a room with one double bed in it and settled down to rest tired legs. I lay between Jane and Margaret and tried to derive some lecherous satisfaction from being on a bed with not one but two girls, a situation from which I felt I ought to be able to gain some credit when I subsequently narrated it at school. They were of course as safe as if they had bedded with the Pope under the gaze of a dozen Cardinals but I was sure I could embroider the tale to some of my credulous friends. Suddenly there was a knock on the door and an aggressive man in uniform came in. For reasons of morality I can only suppose, I was taken out and put in another room nearby which I had to share with several boys. In the middle of the night our fitful slumbers were disturbed by the relentless tread of marching feet. We went to the window and peered down at the cobbled street three stories below. A seemingly endless column of soldiers trampled by, iron helmets dully reflecting the light of the street-lamps. Even I, political innocent that I was, felt that there was something sinister about this; I knew the British Army would never march anywhere at that time of night. The next day we discovered that Hitler had ordered his troops into Czechoslovakia; it was for that momentous event in European history that our homeward journey had been interrupted.

Some twenty-five years later, returning from a holiday in Yugoslavia, I went by way of Schwaz to show my wife·where this oft-recounted episode had happened. We stopped for perhaps two minutes outside the house where all the music had been made. I was about to drive on up to Hochbrunn when a woman came down the path. 'Good Lord, aren't you Tony Hopkins?' 'Yes — who are you?' 'I'm Inge, don't you remember, Inge von Schey, the Baroness's daughter?' 'Oh, I'm sorry I didn't recognise you; you've changed a bit.' (She had; she had been about twelve when I'd last seen her.) I looked at her again trying to remember her as a child. 'So you've come back to live here after all,' I said. 'Oh no; I live in London. I'm having a holiday in Salzburg and I suddenly had this compulsion to come back here and see it again. I've just come for the day that's all. What about you — what are you doing here?' 'Oh, I'm just driving back from Yugoslavia and I suddenly had this compulsion to come back here and see it again ...' A strange convergence.

7
A Shortage of Legs

M y hopelessly inadequate technique precluded any serious thoughts of a career as a concert pianist; Jane therefore suggested that I should set my sights on becoming a music master at a public school. Having devoted his life to teaching, Major rightly regarded this as a worthy aim; with Jane as counsellor a plan of campaign was duly laid down. Since playing the organ is a fairly basic requirement for any potential Director of Music at a school it was decided that I should start to learn to cope with its fearsome demands forthwith. Shaken by my pianistic ineptitude, Jane further made a very strong recommendation that I should stop having lessons at school. They were clearly doing me no good; a private teacher in London might help to make up lost ground. When I finally left school I was to go to the Academy or the College to do organ as First Study for a year, at the end of which time I would unquestionably be so brilliant that I would gain an organ scholarship to Oxford, there to read for B.A. and B.Mus. degrees prior to being appointed music-master at Eton, Harrow or Winchester. It was a sound enough plan, had it not been for my remarkable incompetence on the organ. Doubtless I started with high hopes but I quickly found that all organs had a built-in malevolence towards me.

My first problem I firmly maintain was what I can only describe as a shortage of legs. I realise that there are organists who have managed to overcome this anatomical limitation but their success only bears out my contention that all organists are creatures from an alien planet. The complete independence of the lower portions from the upper is clear evidence that they possess two brains, the second one situated near the base of the spine. Lacking this essential adjunct I found the instrument presented almost insuperable problems. If I tried to play the extreme notes of the pedal-board, whether top or bottom, I would almost invariably fall off the stool. It may not be generally known that the Inland Revenue Department, not notable for liberal concessions, actually allows organists more trousers *per annum* than any other profession because of the sliding about that is involved. Now your pukka organist slides sideways, a skill I never mastered. I used to slide to and fro; 'fro' was quite acceptable but 'to' was fraught with disaster. Wrestling with the intricacies of a Bach fugue I would reach a crisis point when, in micro-simulation of the Big Bang theory of the expanding universe, my hands and feet would be moving outwards at ever increasing distances from the centre. Perched insecurely on the slippery edge I would realise that I was about to go over. In such perilous circumstances the human instinct is for survival at any cost. Desperate to save myself from (at the least) a broken ankle, I would clutch the nearest available keyboard, interrupting the tortured counterpoint with a massive dissonance such as nowadays one might find in Messiaen at his most orgasmic.

All too soon after my organ studies had begun I was expected to play for morning prayers in chapel. Incapable of playing anything in which I had to look at the music as well as my feet, I would improvise during the assembly of some five hundred boys. It was the only thing I could do with any confidence on the organ, since I could ensure that nothing took me unawares. With the grave solemnity appropriate to a religious ceremony I would embark on a richly harmonised version of the scale of D major, up an octave and back again before modulating into a related key and repeating the procedure. Since hardly anybody listened it didn't matter too much if I kept to the same formula, though one day, to my surprise, I found that my housemaster had rumbled me. 'Are you playing for prayers this morning?' he asked, as we extricated chunks of sausage from fast congealing pools of fat. 'Yes, Sir,' I said, not without a tinge of pride since even at my level it was a skill not universally possessed. 'Oh God,' he murmured, turning his eyes towards Heaven; for a moment I thought it was an expression of piety brought about by the beauty of my playing the previous week. Gratification was swiftly damped as he went on, 'That means that we'll have to listen to you playing scales again.' It was a cruelly perceptive remark; that day I based my improvisation on an arpeggio just to show that I could.

Once embarked upon the hymn one was expected to underline the context of the words with suitable changes of registration, soft for Jesus and loud for Glory. It was an added complexity that sometimes proved too much for me and on several occasions I managed to bring the entire school to a halt in mid-hymn. The Headmaster's voice would come booming across the chapel: 'Hopkins, I think we'd better start that verse again.' Sick with horror I would flick on a few stops to show that it was the organ's fault not mine and move to the relative security of the Great manual where there was less chance of disaster. My one accomplishment on the organ was something that I could scarcely display during Divine Service. By placing my left foot on the lowest two notes of the pedal-board (holding on to the stool with one hand) I was able to produce a passable imitation of the sound of an approaching aeroplane. It was a feat that even my less musical friends could appreciate, compared to which my laborious excursions through the thickets of Bach's counterpoint seemed painfully protracted.

Before the autumn term of 1937 began, Jane took me to Cleveland Square to meet Georg von Harten, the pianist to whom I was to be entrusted. He was a musician of great culture rather than a showy virtuoso. Bach was his favourite composer and I well remember attending a series of Bach concerts over which he presided at Londonderry House. I sometimes turned the pages for him, feeling immensely grand as I did so. Tall, quiet and serious, his was a temperament very different from mercurial Jane's, yet they were close friends. On arriving at his spacious flat we were ushered into the music-room by his delightful American wife. There, occupying pride of place, were two grand pianos side by side; a parquet floor ensured a beautifully live acoustic; everything was tidy, his music stowed neatly in shelves. It seemed so different from the cluttered little rooms in the music school at Berkhamsted and I felt quite awe-struck, the more so when Georg came into the room immaculately dressed, looking more like a distinguished diplomat than a musician. Encouraged by Jane I fumbled my way through a couple of pieces. I was then submitted to a test of musicianship which culminated with a performance by Georg of an obscure piece whose composer I was supposed to identify. When it was over I was able to say Schubert with some conviction since I had been astute enough to catch a quick glimpse of his name on the cover. The correctness of this attribution gave such pleasure to the assembled company that I refrained from bringing disillusion in its wake. I was accepted as a pupil and it was agreed that I would travel to London once a week for lessons. Such an arrangement was probably without precedent at the school; I became a valued messenger to the great outside world and was expected to smuggle back copies of a forbidden magazine called *Razzle*. After an hour's communion with Mozart I would make a swift sortie to Praed Street, there to purchase sealed copies of the unexpurgated tale of the Tribulations of Maria Monk. Such literary prizes raised my standing in School House until, in a Gestapo-like swoop by prefects, a copy of a girlie magazine was discovered in my locker. I received a severe reprimand from my housemaster and was told I must never bring back trophies from the wicked city again.

Meanwhile I naturally became involved in such musical activities as the school offered. In the winter there was the Glee Club, with weekly practices that led up to quite competent performances of *Merrie England, Hiawatha* or *Iolanthe* — these with an orchestra of staff, friends and professionals. There was a gramophone club which met on Sunday evenings, started by a science master. Most enjoyable of all were the school musicals, elaborate productions with a cast of a hundred or so, all of whom were somehow packed on to the small stage for a final tableau. Written by two of the classics masters with tuneful music composed by Forbes Milne they were the one outstanding creative effort in the school. Produced by a little human dynamo aptly known as 'Tubby' Rayfield they provided a valuable communal focus of activity.

Forbes Milne was a choleric Scotsman with a fearful smoker's cough that would leave him red-faced and gasping. Had he landed up in a university in charge of a small music department he would no doubt have been in his element; a public school was not a congenial environment for him and we could not help gaining the impression that he disliked boys. Doubtless we were a trial to him but his outbursts of rage during choral practice used to make music a less enjoyable experience than it might have been. Though he was genuinely kind to me at times, as for instance when he broke it to me in the nursing home that I wouldn't be able to sing the boy's solo in *Elijah*, he was more prone to frown on me. Many years later Miss Rogers (the violin mistress) told me that he would often say of me that I was too conceited. 'Don't praise him on any account,' he used to tell her, as though encouragement of a musical talent was to be deprecated in the music staff. Fortunately for me her enthusiasm for music was quite irrepressible, and although I no longer had lessons with her once I went into the senior school she was the one person with whom I could share the joy of musical discovery.

During the holidays I would often compose, proudly producing unsolicited manuscripts at the beginning of term. Fired by the excitement of my trip to Austria I wrote a Concertino for piano and orchestra, arranged for two pianos but with the orchestration indicated. Forbes looked at it with no great interest at my first 'harmony' lesson in the autumn term, possibly angered by the decision to let me learn the piano elsewhere. A month or so later he appeared to relent. 'You know the thing for piano and orchestra you produced at your first lesson,' he said; 'why not bring it along next week and we'll have another look at it.' I was naturally delighted at this renewed interest and the following Wednesday brought the black-bound score with me. There was a stranger in the room standing casually in the far corner. 'You don't mind if Mr So-and-so stays, do you?' said Forbes. If anything I was pleased to have an audience and on being asked to do so I sat down and played my piece. Forbes seemed to take an unusual interest and the lesson went swimmingly; only later did I discover that the visitor was one of His Majesty's Inspectors whom Forbes had sought to impress with my self-appointed holiday task. The following summer I wrote a far more ambitious work, a Fantasia for piano and orchestra written in full score and running to 120 pages or more. He perused it for one lesson; at the end of term my report read, 'While this boy has some musical talent he is not as yet equipped to write a major work.' I'm sure I wasn't, but it was a damning way to put it.

Each year the school would send a large party to support the local amateur operatic and dramatic society. In '37 they performed A Country Girl, an Edwardian musical comedy by Lionel Monckton. I was entranced by it, especially by the girl who played the title role. She epitomised everything that was glamorous about the theatre. Greatly daring I sent her a star-struck fan letter and to my huge delight received a reply that I carried around in my breast-pocket for the best part of a term. Her subsequent appearance as soprano soloist at a Glee Club concert confirmed my impression that here indeed was the beauty queen of the district, though her obvious sophistication was such as to put her in a quite different social class from mine. Had I known it, my instant infatuation with her stage presence was in its less spectacular way a replay of the romance of Berlioz and Harriet Smithson, he the penniless student, she the star. Although the cast was immeasurably more distinguished in the Berlioz affair, the plot was remarkably similar; against all odds the unknown schoolboy was to marry the girl who had earned his adoration from afar. It was a dénouement that neither of us could remotely have anticipated.

In the meantime my affection had been captured more realistically by an extremely attractive young violinist called Lina Tanner. Some time after my trip to Austria I had been invited to stay with Margaret Young's parents at their house in Maidenhead. There, on my arrival, I found that I was not the only guest. Lina, like Margaret a pupil of Adila Fachiri, sat demurely on a sofa wearing a pretty white blouse and a patterned skirt. Her soft blond hair hung loosely, shoulder-length, framing an angelic face whose fine-drawn features would crinkle into a delightful smile. Far less of an extrovert than Margaret, she was in some danger of being swamped by the forceful musical personalities surrounding us. However, her talent as a violinist was quite comparable to Margaret's and this, coupled with her physical charms, ensured that I quickly became devoted to her. One night a party of us went to the local cinema to see *Dawn Patrol*. As Errol Flynn (or was it one of his gallant comrades?) lay dying I noticed a tear or two trickling silently down her cheek. The desire to take advantage of her emotional state by sneaking an arm round her shoulder was almost irresistible, but the standards of gentlemanly conduct imposed by my upbringing proved to be even stronger and I held back. Major had brought me up to believe that women should at all times be put on a pedestal, a situation that inhibits contact even though it may concentrate one's gaze on their legs.

Lessons with Georg had been a weekly pleasure for nearly a year at the time of my Maidenhead visit. In the event he was not the ideal teacher for me since my greatest need was to develop some real technique. I should have been placed with a fierce martinet who would have kept me on a forced diet of scales and exercises. As it was, I squandered still more precious time by attempting to play works that were far beyond me. At the Youngs I was wrestling incompetently with the D minor concerto of Brahms, a pretentious choice which nourished my delusions of grandeur without doing anything much to improve my basic pianism. Mrs Young made no secret of her belief that the talent given to Margaret and Lina was far superior to mine, and my inept attempts to grapple with the Brahms supported her contention that I was nothing but an amateur. My compositions made more of an impression, especially the violin sonatas I dashed off for the two girls. Despite the derivative amalgam of Brahms, Franck and Vaughan Williams they did show signs of melodic invention, while the sheer facility with which I wrote suggested that there was some talent there.

School continued as an almost irrelevant background to these far more interesting events. I did not fit too easily into its confined society and had shown signs of rebellion ever since, at the age of fifteen, I had led a minor revolt against a well-established tradition. Between library and chapel was a paved walk decked with fragrant lavender bushes. It was, I knew, meant to be a small memorial to those who had died in the war, as in their more substantial way were the library and museum adjacent to it. It struck me as wrong that such a memorial should be exclusively used by prefects and staff; surely everyone should be allowed to pass through it. I went to ask the headmaster, Mr Cox, why the passage through this gap should be so restricted. To my utter astonishment he said that he didn't realise it was. 'By all means you can go through,' he went on. 'You are perfectly right — it should be open to everybody.' I decided to make my little demonstration the following Sunday when all the school prefects would by custom be standing in the quad close to the chapel doors. I had talked two friends into joining me even though they were sceptical of my claim that no harm would befall us. Boldly we marched through the forbidden area under the incredulous gaze of half a dozen prefects. The head boy himself yelled at me and grabbed me by the shoulder. 'What the hell do you think you're doing?' he asked indignantly. I told him that I was simply exercising my right to walk through a memorial garden that was open to all. 'It jolly well isn't,' he said and started to threaten me with some punishment. I demanded to be taken to the headmaster, an appeal that leapfrogged so dramatically through the echelons of the higher command that he felt compelled to gratify it. 'You two wait here,' he said angrily to my now thoroughly apprehensive friends. He stalked off across the quad towing me in his wake. The altercation had gathered a small crowd of spectators whose appetite for scandal had been deliciously whetted. Needless to say the head backed me up and a somewhat discomfited prefect accompanied me back to the expectant group still waiting in the quad. The point had been won, even though I believe the restriction was somehow re-established some years later.

Another happy memory stands out clearly from the muddled reminiscences of my four years as a senior boy. The occasion was a so-called Field Day for the OTC (Officers' Training Corps), an organisation which Major had done much to foster and which I had felt compelled to join largely to please him. I hated wearing the thick khaki uniform; it chafed my skin and was miserably hot in summer. The Field Day was a wide-flung war game played between several schools. Since I had a detailed knowledge of the surrounding countryside that was probably second to none, except for the odd poacher, I was appointed orderly and guide to the official referees. At that time we had a wonderfully eager little mare called Honey in our stables — 'a real go-er' as Tooley the groom used to say. The plan was that I would ride her while a few members of staff were to be mounted on some hacks of indifferent quality hired from a local riding-school. Bravely our little cavalcade set off with Honey snorting and curvetting to splendid effect as we rode past my envious friends, all left-righting up the hill beneath the considerable weight of rifle, pack and bayonet. My great moment came later in the day when the mock battle had extended to the region of Ivinghoe Beacon. For some of my 'officers' it was the sole equestrian exercise of the year and it was scarcely surprising that they were beginning to feel tired and sore. We had been on horseback for some five hours and it showed. I of course was in my element, fantasising a role somewhere between Prince Rupert and Tom Mix. We arrived at a ridge topping a small ravine, a wedge-shaped slice hewn from the earth by some glacial convulsion. 'Follow me,' I called and cantered Honey down the steep incline. There was a dry ditch at the bottom which she popped over as nimbly as a stag. I reined her in at the foot of the ascending slope and she pawed the earth impatiently at being thus checked. I looked back and to my intense delight saw them sitting in ashen-faced dismay at the prospect before them. 'We can't come down there,' one of them called. 'It's easy, Sir, honestly Sir, there's nothing to it!' I yelled back. 'Look, I'll show you how . . .' With more than a touch of impudence I urged Honey back across the ditch, swizzled her round and jumped it yet again. There was no response save for the stubborn look of mutiny, then, 'Isn't there another way?' 'Of course, Sir, but it's MILES further.' This was a gross exaggeration but worth saying to rub my psychological victory home.

Although I don't think I ever had any problems with impromptu speaking I was never good at memorising words. On one occasion I was required to learn a psalm by heart as a punishment for some minor offence. (Mr Cox had been enlightened enough to forbid prefects to use the cane and some ingenuity was exercised in devising alternatives.) I started to try to commit the lines to memory but soon realised that it would be a burden out of all proportion to the crime. It was then that I had a brilliant idea. I knew that in the organ loft there was a psalter with very large print, a helpful aid to short-sighted organists. The following day, having spent my allotted period floundering around on the organ, I smuggled this invaluable *aide-mémoire* out of the chapel. That evening I gave it to Sandy, instructing him to esconce himself in a strategic position at one of the communal reading-desks immediately alongside the prefect's dais. When I saw that he was in place I shambled up to the prefect muttering something about being ready to say the psalm. Sandy duly held the psalter up behind the prefect's head while I read off the verses, periodically looking at the floor or ceiling so as not to develop too fixed a gaze. The ruse worked perfectly; in fact without realising it I had invented Autocue, the television announcer's invaluable friend.

I think it must have been early in 1938 that School House was put into quarantine yet again. The weather must have been bad enough to keep us 'confined to barracks' for much of the time. We were hard put to it to keep ourselves amused until someone made the bright suggestion that we should start our own broadcasting service. Many of the boys enjoyed building radio sets as a hobby and welcomed this chance to show their expertise. A classroom in the School House wing was commandeered as a studio, loudspeakers were strung up in the main hall; regular transmission times were soon arranged. I remember doing a cod interview as a world-famous pianist, 'now in training for his next fight at the Queen's Hall where he will take on the London Symphony Orchestra'. It was my first broadcast.

Not until November '38 was I made a school prefect, a promotion whose tardiness must have caused Major some distress. Early the next morning, before anyone else was about, I went outside to the central grass quadrangle, a sizeable expanse of turf which only school prefects and staff were allowed to traverse. I stood at one corner, gratified to see that there had been a heavy white frost. With great deliberation I walked diagonally across, the grass crunching audibly beneath my shoes as though each blade had been dipped in icing sugar. It was a sweet moment to look back and see my footsteps firmly imprinted on the frosty lawn. It was my last term at Berkhamsted; in the New Year I was to go to another school, though to play a somewhat different role.

It may seem that I have painted a rather unflattering picture of the school that few of my contemporaries would endorse. Within the rough-and-tumble atmosphere of a strictly segregated boarding-house we managed for the most part to be fairly happy. Unfortunately my choice of career singled me out as a loner; the further I progressed the more isolated I became. In all fairness, the authorities did try to accommodate my special needs by allowing me a very unorthodox timetable once I had reached the sixth form. During my last term I was only supposed to do three subjects, English, History and Latin. By then fully aware of my woeful lack of pianistic technique I was adamant that I should not have to do the mountainous pile of homework expected of my classmates. Even so, I still felt that precious hours were being wasted preparing for exams I was not intending to take. Determined to gain more time to practise I told the history master that I could only manage to do Latin and English and the Latin master that I could only do history and English. By this ingenious stratagem I was able to reduce my schedule to three periods of English a week, leaving the rest of the time free for work in the Music School. At the end of the term Mr Wraith, my housemaster, summoned me to his study. 'There seem to be a lot of blanks on your report,' he said with a slightly mystified air; 'What on earth have you been doing?' I explained my plight, pointing out that I was ill-qualified to meet the requirements of a serious music student at the Royal College to which I was aiming to go. It was my fortune that he was an excellent amateur pianist whose playing had often delighted me; with a necessary show of reluctance he agreed that I had a point and the matter was allowed to rest.

8
It's Not Cricket

It was an unusual experience to leave one school as a boy in December and enter another as a member of staff in January. Mindful of my future, Major had decided that it would be sensible to let me have at least a taste of schoolmastering before I was finally committed to it. He had got in touch with Patrick Cory, who had been both boy and house-tutor at Berkhamsted, and asked him whether I could serve a sort of apprenticeship under him at Bromsgrove School, where he was then Director of Music. Pat agreed to take me on for two terms prior to my going to the Royal College, where, of course, I was supposedly to prepare myself for the consummation devoutly to be wished — the organ scholarship to Oxford. I doubt if I could have found a better mentor in the whole of the British Isles. Gifted pianist though he was, Pat's real *métier* was the teaching of musical appreciation. As a school, Bromsgrove would have been rated in much the same category as Berkhamsted; certainly it had no long-established musical tradition to build on. During his period as Director, Pat brought all his energy and enthusiasm to the task of converting boys to music. It was a revelation to me to hear him analysing Sibelius symphonies in his sixth-form class; to ensure genuine keenness he chose to make attendance voluntary, but virtually everyone came. I remember hearing a small group of boys singing a madrigal from memory as they walked down to the playing-fields, something I could scarcely have imagined at Berkhamsted. I entered into this new existence with a feeling of exhilaration, even though living conditions in the staff hostel were notable for their lack of comfort. I attended the piano lessons Pat gave, played for choir practices, stumbled through services at the organ and generally behaved with a glad irresponsibility that must have made me seem, from the schoolboy's viewpoint, an ideal master. Twice a week I would celebrate my new-found freedom by going to the cinema, regardless of the programme. (Visits to the 'flicks' had been strictly forbidden when I had been at school, a rule whose implicit challenge I was unable to resist. Of necessity it was not something one could boast about, but I believe I held the record for clandestine excursions to cinematic bliss. On one occasion I saw to my horror that my form master had settled himself down further along the very row in which I was sitting. As I rose to leave I remembered a phrase I'd read in Baden Powell's scouting book. If you are travelling in disguise as a spy, he advised, remember that you can easily be recognised by your walk; change it. I went down the aisle giving an impersonation of Quasimodo that Charles Laughton himself might have envied.)

That summer I used to supervise cricket among the junior boys. It was a game at which I had never excelled since I felt that the ball was far too hard for a musician's hands. Playing amongst ten-year-olds made all the difference to my enjoyment and by consistently putting myself in last and never getting out I managed to amass a creditable 'average' of 96. Dreams of cricketing glory were rudely shattered when I was asked to play for the masters against the school first eleven. I went in ninth with the score still in two figures. Taking guard I looked round the field with sure confidence that I could still save the day. Some distance away, in the outfield as I thought, stood a tall motionless figure of distinctly Teutonic mien, his fair hair damp with sweat in the heat of the afternoon. Suddenly he started to run towards me, gathering pace as he came. As his stride lengthened I could distinctly see the nails in his boots, lending additional menace to his rapid approach. When he reached the opposite wicket I began to wonder if he would be able to stop in time or whether his headlong rush would cause a violent and painful collision. His arm swung over viciously and with a speed that I was convinced Larwood himself could not have surpassed the ball hurtled towards me. I held the bat out with the helpless gesture of a duellist who finds his pistol has not been loaded. By pure chance the ball struck it and bounced off in the opposite direction. 'Yes!' I screamed to the other batsman and began to run as fast as a grotesquely large pair of pads would allow. Thankful still to be alive at the other end my fellow-sufferer was unwilling to swap places. The rattle of stumps behind me told me that my wicket had been thrown down. In a state of shock I made as if to leave for the sanctuary of the pavilion. 'No, I'll go,' he said, 'you stay and have a knock . . .' It was the sort of gesture that the English would naturally commend as sporting, though I fully sympathised with its tacit admission of sheer relief.

Since Bromsgrove was a mere thirty-minute drive from Birmingham it was relatively easy to make the journey to the City Hall. Concerts were given regularly by the CBSO under their excellent conductor Leslie Heward. I doubt if in my whole life up until then I had been to more than a dozen proper orchestral concerts and my ignorance of the standard repertoire was still alarming. However, the occasion that stands out most clearly in my memories of those few months was a piano recital by Rachmaninov. (I had totally succumbed to his music since I had heard Cyril Smith give a dazzling performance of the third concerto at a promenade concert the previous summer. I had written him an ardent fan-letter describing at length the overwhelming impact the music had had on me. I adored the work and had played the Horowitz recording time after time, conducting the imagined orchestra and singing the climaxes at the top of my voice.) The chance of hearing the master in person was not to be missed and Pat and I sat eagerly awaiting our first sight of him. Even his entrance was unforgettable. Immensely tall, walking with the grave demeanour of an undertaker at a Royal funeral, he came on stage without a trace of a smile, his face set in severe lines that belied the passion in his music. He began, as was the fashion in those days, with a transcription of a Bach organ work. His playing was magisterial, the extraordinary range of tone-colour seemingly achieved with an absolute minimum of effort. His hands were so enormous that one would have expected them to have been clumsy, yet his control was flawless. In response to the wild enthusiasm at the end of the concert he unbent sufficiently to murmur a few inaudible words to the front row; only then did he play anything of his own, the Prelude in C sharp minor that at the time was his best-known composition. (Its popularity ultimately killed it off and one seldom hears it played today.) I left the hall with a feeling of rare privilege, conscious that I had never before experienced such mastery at first hand.

Although paid no official salary I was given an honorarium of ten pounds for each of the two terms that I was at Bromsgrove. I had enjoyed the experience hugely and was entirely content to envisage a future as a music-master. Given the choice between the Academy and the College I had selected the latter on the unlikely grounds that Cyril Smith was listed as one of the piano professors. Since I was not intending to have any piano lessons this might seem an irrelevance; I simply felt that if he consented to teach there it was a warranty of excellence not to be disregarded. As I was to be a fee-paying pupil I don't think I had to take an entrance exam except for the purposes of grading. I was due to begin my studies in September 1939, a date of some importance in world affairs.

At the beginning of August I received a telephone call that was to have an infinitely greater significance than I could have dreamed at the time. I was asked if I would act as rehearsal accompanist for the local operatic society; the work was to be *Chu Chin Chow* and I was offered a fee of five shillings per evening. I thought for a moment, and then, remembering my goddess from *A Country Girl*, I said, 'Is Alison Purves going to be in it?' 'Oh yes,' was the reply; 'she'll be playing the soprano lead.' 'Right, I'll do it.' Date and time of the first rehearsal were agreed and I rang off feeling not merely that my career as a professional musician had at last begun but that the auguries were markedly favourable, coloured as they were by the prospect of meeting the girl whose very handwriting had thrilled my schoolboy heart.

A few days later I appeared for the first rehearsal in the familiar upstairs room of the Music School at Berkhamsted. The aura of glamour she brought in with her was something I had never experienced at close quarters. I was used to girls who wore not a trace of make-up; faced with someone who looked as though she'd come straight from a film-set I was overawed. Her singing was a bonus, a link that I realised might with luck be exploited. At the end of the rehearsal I haltingly offered my services as accompanist and to my delight was told that she'd be in touch if she needed me. I went home congratulating myself on the way I'd played my cards.

It must have been the following week that Hitler launched his *Blitzkrieg* on Poland. I remember clearly how at Woodyard we sat in the warm autumn sunshine listening to Neville Chamberlain's voice as he gravely announced that a state of war had been declared between Britain and Germany. For years I had been a devoted reader of the war books of Ian Hay and Siegfried Sassoon; although Major had been very reticent about his own war experiences, he had done everything possible to inspire me with patriotic pride. Naturally I wanted to join up straight away but it was a Sunday and we instinctively knew that everything would be closed. The wail of the sirens sounding the Alert soon after Chamberlain had finished impressed us with a sense of urgency. Even though it turned out to be a false alarm it made us feel that it might be only a matter of days before the Nazis were at the door. The next morning I took the train to London with the intention of joining up. The sergeant who saw me was somewhat put out by my premature arrival. I daresay he lacked the requisite forms. 'Not ready for you yet, lad,' he said cheerfully. 'Come back when we notify you; I've got your name and address.'

As it turned out, the cartilage operation from boyhood days was an effective bar to any thoughts of military service. I had already discovered that if I marched any distance wearing boots the knee joint would become water-logged. Since it was obviously impossible to fight Hitler wearing shoes I was consistently rejected on medical grounds, Grade IV, lowest form of animal life. 'Get on with your studies,' I was told, 'and help out how you can with voluntary work.'

For the next few days we were in a state of turmoil. Country folk like us were asked to take in evacuee children from London. Two girls arrived from the East End, excited by their sudden change of circumstances. With Machiavellian guile I managed to persuade Major and Signora that it would be a kindness to offer shelter to Lina. Her home was in Ruislip not far from Northolt aerodrome and her parents had nightmare visions of bombs exploding all around them. To my huge pleasure she duly came down, complete with violin case and the obligatory gas-mask. For a blissful ten days or so she stayed; hand in hand we would sit listening to the second concerto of Rachmaninov in a state of heady but still innocent romance. She was guarded by an aura of chastity and I was too hesitant to make any sort of move.

The production of Chu Chin Chow was cancelled in the initial panic of the war; I therefore assumed that I was unlikely to see Alison again. She had flown into sight like a brilliantly hued butterfly and would presumably fly out again. The thought of any sort of permanent relationship did not even enter my mind; not only did she move in a more exalted social circle, she was also married. I felt for her rather as later I was to feel towards Rita Hayworth or Marilyn Monroe; the fact that she happened to live in the district made her no more accessible than they were. I was more than happy to allow my feelings for Lina to develop, bashful courtier though I was. Unfortunately, once the initial panic had subsided, her parents summoned her home. Thinking it over, I came to the conclusion that, faced with a choice between the possibilities of death in Ruislip or worse than death at Woodyard, they had preferred the former. I began to feel that if ever I grew to love a girl she would be removed from me by circumstance or design. It was time to put any amorous thoughts behind me; I was due to begin my studies at the Royal College of Music.

9
Trial by Triad

On 19 September, 1939, I took my place as one of two hundred students in the great hall of the College to hear the Director's opening address. Dr George Dyson was slim and wiry in build with a somewhat pedantic manner that was emphasised by his dry tone of voice. He was an excellent administrator who steered the College through an unnaturally difficult period, but, although his qualifications were of the highest, he lacked charisma, displaying a typically English abhorrence of any emotional excess in music. There was a vague sense of unreality as we sat in the white-painted hall with the autumn sunshine streaming through the windows. The war had not as yet affected us greatly despite trenches in the parks and sandbags at the entrances of important buildings. Expecting the worst we were all relieved at the curious lack of drama as life went on with a semblance of normality. Not that the College timetable was to be normal. Until further notice things would be organised on a three-day basis, all teaching to stop by 4.00 pm and the building to be compulsorily cleared by 4.15. For me this meant the happy prospect of continuing to live at home since I was only due to have two lessons and two classes a week. I was put into Grade III for organ and Grade III for harmony; in addition I was expected to attend aural training class as well as some general lectures on psychology and music given by Percy Buck.

My organ tuition was entrusted to a dear kindly old man named Stanley Stubbs who had been organist at Holy Trinity Church just down the road since 1908. I conceived a great fondness for him though the singular lack of adventure in his existence confirmed my worst forebodings about life in the organ-loft. Slowly we would potter together down Prince Consort Road to the almost concealed church, he so respectable in his black Homburg hat, I babbling carelessly beside him. Once inside the dark interior, we would climb the narrow staircase that led to the organ. After a statutory pause for him to regain his breath we would settle into our cramped eyrie, there to endure an unproductive hour. I must have been his most depressing pupil; in a whole year I think I only learnt four pieces and those imperfectly. Even at the cost of hurting his feelings I made no secret of my lack of enthusiasm for the instrument. Opportunities for practice were severely limited by the restricted hours at College. I found no satisfaction in trying to produce music from the plain two-manual organs lodged high in the towers that give the building so castle-like an appearance. To my mind the greatest pleasure in playing a keyboard instrument is to cultivate the subtlest possible nuances of tone by sheer sensitivity of touch, something the organ does not allow. The relentless continuity of the sound of an eight-foot diapason was far from music to my ears and I would emerge from my practice sessions with aching head and hips, wondering how I would ever gain the scholarship upon which the thoughts of others were so firmly set.

The harmony class was altogether happier. Unlike dear Stanley Stubbs, whose whole tempo was distinctly tortoise-like, Dr Harold Darke was quite astonishingly nimble for his years. Bald as the proverbial coot, save for a tuft of white hair above each ear, he needed only a pixie-hat to pass for a gnome. Whereas Stanley was amply covered, Harold had not an ounce of spare flesh; his hands seemed unusually large and bony and he would crack his finger-joints in a disconcerting way as if to draw attention to these abnormal attributes. Of the eight or nine in the class I seemed to be the only one who had attempted to do any composition. My first appearance, armed with a bundle of manuscripts, was greeted with acclamation by the good Doctor. 'What's this — what's tnis?' he intoned in near-recitative. 'A violin sonata?, Your *third*? Well, well, I don't believe it, we must have a look at this.' Opening my 'Violin Sonata no. 3 in F sharp minor' with the enthusiasm of a small boy unwrapping a promising parcel, he sat down and, to my utter astonishment, proceeded to play it through with scarcely a blemish while I filled in the violin part at the top end of the piano. 'That's a very splendid work,' he said when he had concluded his bravura demonstration of sight-reading. 'How long did it take you to write?' 'Three days, Sir,' I replied with perfect truth since I was much smitten with Lina at the time and had found the creative juices flowing freely. 'Three *days?*' His eyebrows shot up and his jaw dropped, elongating his narrow face to such a degree that he looked like a caricature. 'That's ex-*straw*-dinary! You must write one for me . . .' I did try, but somehow it wasn't the same.

Walking along the corridors I could hear music on every side, most of it being performed with a dazzling proficiency that made my own relative incompetence cruelly evident. My piano technique was still almost rudimentary, my repertoire pathetically small. I was the perfect example of a 'Bitsa' pianist, able to play Bitsa this and Bitsa that but virtually nothing in its entirety. Having no piano lessons at all did not help my plight, while the frequent journeys to and fro on trains that seldom ran to time consumed precious hours that I desperately needed to spend in practical study. All the same I loved the College atmosphere and resolved to go to as many of the student concerts as I could. It was in every sense an education to sit in the concert hall listening to orchestral rehearsals; to this day I cannot hear the horn solo that comes at the beginning of Schubert's 'Great' C major symphony without remembering its first impact in those informal surroundings. At the final concert of that first term a slight figure in RAF blue gave a truly virtuoso performance of Weber's 'Konzertstück' that made me marvel. Afterwards I had the cheek to waylay the pianist on the stairs and start a conversation with him. His name was George Malcolm.

One day my guardian angel directed me to go up the right-hand staircase, possibly offering me the excuse of a visit to the students' common room. As I went up the first flight a trimly-suited man came nimbly down the stairs towards me. I was almost sure I recognised him; with a brashness that I often put on when I was actually feeling nervous I blurted out, 'Excuse me, but aren't you Cyril Smith?' Hand on banister he stopped, gave a quick smile and admitted that he was. We stood there for a moment or two while others pushed past us mumbling apologies. Haltingly I explained that I had written to him at length some two years previously. 'I don't expect you remember, Sir — it was about the third Rachmaninov — it was the greatest thing I'd ever heard, really . . .' 'I think I remember,' he said with characteristic charm, and went on to ask me what I was doing at College. I told him, touching on my discontent with the organ and my sadness at the lack of piano tuition. For no reason I can imagine other than pure politeness he suggested that I should go to his room and play something during the next few days. Taking him at his word, I duly appeared with my one show-piece, the Schubert Impromptu that had so excited me in Austria and which I had been working at off and on for two years or more. With quite remarkable kindness he offered to give me an occasional lesson at his home in East Sheen, a prospect that gave me a tremendous lift. From the crowded ranks of promenaders in Queen's Hall he had seemed a remote, almost god-like figure whom I could indeed idolise but would scarcely dare to approach. How could I have suspected that a chance encounter with him on a staircase would change the course of my life entirely? I am genuinely amazed that he should have taken any interest in me, since, whatever improvement I may have made subsequently, I was at the time far beneath the technical standard of his other pupils. My sole assets were intuitive musical perception and the ability to make a nice sound. This valuable gift had been developed largely because Major had bought me an elderly Broadwood grand whose metallic tone was so hideous that I never stopped trying to soften its edge.

Although the details have become hazy it seems clear that the occasional lessons Cyril so kindly gave me elicited a far more enthusiastic response than anything else College had to offer. Somehow I persuaded Major to agree to add piano to my official syllabus at the College, possibly using the imminent scholarship examination as an excuse.

New College was my target, and in the early summer of 1940 I went to Oxford for a single night, my aspirations unsupported by ability. There were perhaps half a dozen of us trying for the award, two of them friends from College whose ability greatly exceeded mine. We arrived at supper-time and spent the evening in fits of hysterical laughter brought on no doubt by communal nervousness. As is the custom the examination the following day was in several stages, both theoretical and practical. In an unforgettable half hour I found myself playing the César Franck Prelude, Chorale and Fugue to Sir Hugh Allen, a notorious musical eccentric who had been Dyson's predecessor at the College. (I had been warned that he had a fierce temper but hoped that the suitably deferential tones I adopted on entering his room would soften him up.) Having asked me a few questions about my background and future expectations he told me to play. As I began he started to stride around the room thumping a walking-stick on the floor at every other step. He began to sing so raucously that I was quickly reduced to the role of accompanist, following his wayward *rubato* as best as I could. Occasionally he would break off his wordless song with an interpolation such as, 'Real old College war-horse this, me boy — must have heard it dozens of times . . .' I felt it would be impudent to suggest that he could hardly be hearing it this time such was the racket he was making; it was a slight comfort to feel that the singing (and whistling) indicated a measure of enjoyment.

As might be expected the greater disaster came at the chapel organ. Totally different in lay-out and specification from the one in Holy Trinity, the instrument completely unnerved me. Miserably I struggled through a couple of pieces, surprising myself as much as my examiner by the unprecedented originality of my registration. When I had finished and wiped the cold sweat from hands and forehead, a large bound volume was placed in front of me. In the quietly soothing tones of a dentist about to commit a massive violation of one's oral sanctity, a voice said, 'I want you to read the voice parts from this score; you'll see they're in the C clef.' Sheer panic set in; the only C clef I knew of was used for viola parts; what on earth was he talking about? 'I'm sorry, Sir, I don't understand.' 'Haven't you seen a score like this before?' (*The quiet menace of the question*.) Sweat broke out again; I gulped. 'No, Sir . . . I mean, not with those clefs in the voice part.' Desperately I added, 'I can read the orchestral bit alright, at least I think so . . .' 'Ah, but I want you to read the voice parts.' As though speaking to the village idiot he explained that the soprano clef had middle C on its bottom line ('I didn't know that, Sir') and that the tenor clef had middle C on the second line from the top. 'Oh yes, Sir, like the trombone, Sir, but I haven't seen it used for voices.' 'Ah well, we live and learn. Now take your time to work out the first chord and then carry on from there.' The sounds that emerged bore only a slight resemblance to the Bach cantata he had confronted me with. I knew it was Bach because the upper orchestral parts were continuous semiquavers.

I came out into the light of day confident that I had failed, a surmise that proved to be entirely correct. A college friend, far more competent than I, properly gained the scholarship, duly to disappear from ken behind the veil of academic respectability.

Going through Major's desk after his death I discovered a letter written by William McKie, the organist at Magdalen, to a mutual friend, dated 22.iv.40.

... I didn't see enough of Antony to make my opinion by itself of any great value. When he came to see me here he played to me and showed me some of his compositions of no particular value except that they showed industry and some urge to write (the latter may or may not be a good thing). My general impression of him was judging by schoolboy standards, very good; by the standards of a Royal College of Music student the same age, moderate but promising.

There certainly is a great deal of promise, but I don't know enough of his character and disposition to guess how much the promise is likely to be fulfilled. From the rather superficial conversation we had I thought he was a little complacent and ready to be easily satisfied. But I think I was probably inclined to judge him too hardly as he spoke slightingly of the organ as a musical instrument!

... I find the opinions of Allen and Andrews are much the same as my own — and they tested him pretty thoroughly. They put him down as a good all-round musician, a promising pianist (not quite in the first class) but with the possibility of development. Allen's advice is that he should go for a school post rather than aim at being a pianist. The pianistic position nowadays is precarious. First-rate players are two a penny and the financial rewards are small except for a very few ....

The field of school posts is likely to be smaller than greater — our crack organ scholars in Oxford, who used to expect to step straightaway into directorships in the larger schools, are now very glad to get any sort of job at all. But at least schools must go on and there is some sort of security there.

I'm afraid this is not very helpful and decidedly on the gloomy side ... but I had better be absolutely truthful; anyway I always do my best to dissuade people from taking up music as a career if they can possibly keep away from it.

I really don't think I had ever thought of being a concert pianist except in flights of delusory fantasy, but it had possibly been mooted behind my back. At any rate I returned from my abortive trip to Oxford in some despair, convinced in my own mind that I had been following the wrong course. I turned to Cyril Smith for guidance. 'Why don't you try for a piano scholarship at the College?' he suggested. 'Because I haven't a hope of getting one,' I replied in all sincerity. He told me that if I really buckled down and practised for eight hours a day during the next six weeks I might have a chance. I didn't believe him but realised that the effort would at least give a much-needed boost to my piano-playing. Together we planned a programme built round the Brahms-Handel variations. I kept a notebook by the piano at home logging the hours each day; eight proved impractical with the travelling I still had to do but I certainly worked with a dedication I had never known before. I found the Brahms more than I could cope with technically although I could manage the first seven variations with reasonable conviction. (My tattered copy still bears scribbled comments in Cyril's hand of which my favourite is 'Good — why not before now?' in the margin of Variation I.)

I went into the examination room in a state of trepidation that I did my best to conceal. There was a jury of three chaired by Herbert Fryer, a teacher of high repute whom I regarded as a sort of musical grandparent since Cyril had been his pupil. I began with an extremely slow Prelude and Fugue by Bach (Book I, E flat minor), hoping to lull them into an uncritical stupor in which the Brahms might pass by almost unnoticed. Since they neither sang, whistled nor walked I felt that things were looking more promising than at Oxford; in tolerably good heart I struck into the Brahms. At the end of variation 7 I took an extra large breath, well aware of the perils ahead. Almost disbelieving my own ears I heard a quiet voice behind me say, 'Thank you very much, I think we've heard enough of that.' Filled with relief at this unforeseen delivery from potential disaster I shuffled out of the room dropping scores around me like rotting fruit. That evening a notice appeared asking three entrants to play again the following day to decide who should have the award; to my great surprise my name was on the list.

The next afternoon I had worked myself up into a considerable state of apprehension. It seemed highly unlikely that I would again be allowed to escape so lightly from the horrors of Brahms; they were sure to ask for the fugue, whose massive climax would expose all the shoddiness of my technique. To my consternation I saw as I entered the room that two members of the jury were new; any favourable impression I had managed to make on the previous day would be nullified.

'We have a very good report on your Brahms-Handel from yesterday; would you like to play something else?' For the second time I was incredulous. Trying not to show my inner joy at being thus spared I said, 'Would a Chopin Nocturne do?' and quickly sat down and started to play one before they changed their minds. Then as now I could play slow pieces really well, a somewhat limited accomplishment but better than nothing. It was enough to earn me my first major triumph, the Mathilde Verne scholarship. Stanley Stubbs congratulated me warmly at my next organ lesson, summing up my own reaction in a phrase, 'Well, I *am* surprised; I didn't think you had a chance!'

There was a nice postscript to the story for the following year I had to go through the whole grisly experience again. Feeling that Brahms had done me well even if I hadn't done particularly well for him, I took in his Rhapsody in B minor as my main offering. Sir George Dyson (as he had then become) was examining. 'We've got a lot of people in for scholarships as you can imagine,' he said. 'We like to spread them round as much as we can.' My heart sank; he was trying to break it nicely but obviously I'd failed. 'We've got a rather funny scholarship we don't seem to be able to give anybody; you play the organ don't you?' (*Oh God give me strength, surely he can't expect me to do that!*) 'Come on boy, do you or don't you?' 'Well, sort of, Sir . . . but I haven't had any lessons for nearly a year . . .' 'You can improvise, can't you?' 'Oh yes, Sir,' relief clearly showing in my voice. 'It's for improvising on the organ; would you like it?' 'You mean I wouldn't actually have to play the organ?' 'Oh no, we needn't bother with that; just improvise a bit on the middle section of the Brahms there.' I complied willingly, wondering as I did so whether other people experienced the same transition from apprehension to incredulity that seemed an inevitable concomitant to my College exams. In a way it seemed poetic justice that I should at last gain an organ scholarship of sorts, even if I won it by playing a Brahms Rhapsody on the piano.

* * *

'As for the future, it is no use even trying to see more than a day at a time.' So said Sir George at the start of the summer term, 1940. England was truly embattled, aerial combats scoring messy chalk-marks across a pale blue sky. Anti-aircraft guns reared their long snouts from London's garden squares; barrage balloons, incongruously elephantine in hue, strained at their umbilical wires. Looking back it seems strange that our musical activities continued at all. In spite of uniforms everywhere, in spite of the black news in the daily papers, it seemed as though the war receded into the background once we passed through the swing doors into the cool foyer of the College. To carry on making music was an act of defiance in its minor way, a gesture of determination that civilised values would be maintained. London's concert life was extraordinarily vigorous. In the early months of the war Myra Hess had launched the deservedly famous lunchtime concerts at the National Gallery. Admission prices were absurdly low and people flocked to them daily, hungering for spiritual sustenance as material conditions worsened. The atmosphere in the gallery was almost devotional, more like a church than a concert hall. The sense of life's impermanence was very strong, the concentration of the audience enhanced by the unspoken but ever-present thought that each concert could be the last of one's life.

Even more remarkable in a way were the promenade concerts in the Queen's Hall. Most nights the air-raid sirens would add their dismal wail to the music; a notice would be shown to inform those who had failed to realise that a raid was on, but scarcely a soul would move. After the concert had officially ended we would all stay in the hall, secure at least from falling shrapnel even if not a direct hit. Within days a splendid custom evolved, an impromptu extension of the concert that included community singing, solos from members of the orchestra, chamber music and, in due course, contributions from volunteers in the audience. A few tired soldiers might sleep stretched full-length on the floor, heads pillowed on their packs; for the most part, though, we enjoyed these improvised concerts almost more than the real thing. One classic story was circulated by the box-office staff. A woman appeared one morning to enquire about tickets for the evening performance.

'D'you think there'll be an air-raid tonight?' she asked with some urgency.

'I can't say, Madam, but I sincerely hope not.'

'Oh don't say that — I'm only coming if there's an air-raid . . .'

Two examples of this very English phenomenon come to mind. One was a brilliant conducting skit by an orchestral player called Ralph Nicholson. Announced as 'Sir Bombers Teach'em', he entered to huge applause, capturing Sir Thomas's every mannerism. He whisked the orchestra through a hilariously precipitate performance of the Overture to *The Marriage of Figaro*, followed by what he haughtily described as 'a piece of contemptible music'. The orchestra embarked on an improvised cacophony which might aptly have been named 'Stockhausen's Birthpangs'.

My other memory concerns Stiles Allen, a singer so well upholstered that she seemed to ripple on to the stage rather than walk. Earlier in the evening she had sung a Handel cantata with great beauty. During the 'Queen's Hall Night-Club' as it came to be known, she reappeared to our great delight and sang a group of solos. She finished with Roger Quilter's sentimental but touching setting of 'Now sleeps the crimson petal'. Leaning well forward, she delivered the final phrase in a way that Tennyson had clearly not envisaged — 'Slip into my bosom and be lost in me.'

Within a week from the start of the prom. season so many volunteers were clamouring to appear that a panel of orchestral players was formed to give auditions in the artists' room. Aspiring young music students even went to the concerts with the deliberate intention of playing if they possibly could; to have performed at the Queen's Hall was something to boast about, even if it was 'after hours'. In May 1940 the *Luftwaffe* put a stop to such dreams of glory by flattening the hall, fortunately on a Sunday night when there had been no concert. Somehow the Albert Hall did not lend itself to such informal japes and the delightful tradition died out. Orchestral managers worried by falling attendances might learn a lesson from history. Given even a slender chance of performing themselves audiences could not be deterred by bombs or blackout. A nightly lottery to fill a five-minute solo spot at the Festival Hall might do wonders for the box-office.

One of my greatest joys at College was choral class, a choir of perhaps a hundred singers conducted by Dr Reginald Jacques. I had never sung in a chorus of such quality and was exhilarated by the experience. The first major work we sang was Haydn's *Creation*, (totally new to me except for 'The Heavens are telling' which I'd played many times as a child; it had appeared in a large bound volume of Vocal Favourites, an almost nightly source of delight in the years at Incents). Jacques communicated a sheer joy in music that Dyson found impossible to convey; a string of bombs would not have kept me away from his rehearsals. One morning he welcomed a stocky uniformed figure to the class and asked the usual accompanist to stand down for a time to allow the newcomer to play. 'This lad used to play for me before he got called up,' said Jacques, 'and it's lovely to have him back, even for an hour.' On his instructions we turned to 'Achieved is the glorious work.' He flicked a precise upbeat towards the piano and our visitor started to play. The introduction is a mere five-and-a-bit bars long but it was performed with such marvellous crispness that instead of coming in we burst into spontaneous applause. Jacques roared with laughter, sharing our appreciation. 'What did he say his name was?' I muttered to my neighbour, a tenor who had been at College for several years. 'Charles Groves,' he replied. I doubt whether even in his distinguished career Sir Charles ever again received such acclamation for twenty seconds of music.

I cannot remember how I attained the enviable position of accompanist to the choral class. I think the regular player was called up and Jacques may well have asked for a volunteer. It must have happened in 1942, for in December of that year the College magazine records that I played the Vaughan Williams Benedicite with the choir. A few weeks previously I had made my pianistic début at College playing the third violin sonata of Delius and, surprisingly, the first movement of the Elgar violin concerto, both with a romantically inclined blonde called Betty Robay. Together we would play impassioned music far into the night, sublimating our sexual inhibitions in a welter of lush and decadent harmony.

Meanwhile, in December '41, I managed to scrape through the ARCM Performer's Diploma. Some five days or so before the exam I was practising the Brahms B minor Rhapsody in a college room. A friend came barging in and asked me why I was working so industriously at this particular piece. 'I'm doing it for A.R.,' I told him, a little peevish at the frivolous interruption. 'You won't pass then,' he said smartly. 'Why not?' 'It isn't on the list.' (The list was a substantial catalogue of works from which candidates were required to choose three contrasting works, one from each of three categories.) A tense argument ensued. I was sure I'd seen the

Brahms listed, he was adamant that it was not. Finally we made the trek downstairs to the office to check the syllabus. 'There!' I said, stabbing at the page with an indignant finger. 'That's not Rhapsody,' he crowed delightedly, 'it's *Ballade* in B minor, Op. 10 — silly!' 'My God, so it is ...' I was horror-struck. There didn't seem to be anything else I could brush up in the limited time left. I rushed up to the library. 'Brahms Ballades, Op. 10,' I gasped. A quick glance at the copy as I dashed back to my practice room confirmed my worst fears. It was quick *and* had semiquavers in the left hand — occasionally.

From my earliest days at the keyboard my left hand had obdurately refused to play as fast as my right, a grave disadvantage under pressure. I would like to feel that I had a legitimate excuse; perhaps, in those first traumatic months when only the brandy bottle stood between me and the Great Void, my brain had suffered some damage after all. The proposition cannot be supported by any evidence; I just didn't practise properly when it mattered. In some desperation I slogged away at the Ballade, arriving for the exam in an ill-prepared state. The examiners must have been in an indulgent mood to have let me pass even with a margin of two marks. I certainly wouldn't have passed myself had I been in their place.

To meet the genuine demand for live entertainment the Government established CEMA, the Council for the Encouragement of Music and the Arts, in 1940, followed by the more openly popular ENSA in '41. Despite the difficulties imposed by lack of transport, blackout, rationing and the call of duty, innumerable concerts were given all over the country, in barracks, camps, gunsites, factories, churches, village halls or hospitals. For the more advanced college students such concerts were a golden opportunity to gain experience. One afternoon I went to the Drury Lane theatre to audition for CEMA; I felt that my work with the choral class and sundry violinists qualified me for consideration as an accompanist. Alone on the vast stage with the piano sloping downhill alarmingly I felt hideously exposed. A voice from the outer darkness (later identified as Walter Legge's) commanded me to read a song by Richard Strauss. A copy was thrust in front of me, an equally unnerved singer smiled tautly at me and, unrehearsed, we started, staying in the same bar for most of the time.

'Now play it down a minor third,' called Mr Legge. For the life of me I couldn't see that I would ever have to perform such a feat unprepared in real life. Any singer who was incompetent enough to require such a transposition would hardly be likely to sing Strauss *Lieder*. I floundered nearly as badly as I had at New College and left the stage sorely humiliated. Another failure to chalk up.

Better news came one morning in the College canteen. 'You're wanted in the office,' someone called. I hurried upstairs. 'Could you go to Oxford to accompany Arthur Cranmer, the singer?' 'When?' 'Today; rehearsal at 4.00. There's a train at lunchtime. Have you got tails?' 'No.' 'Dinner-jacket?' 'No.' 'Oh well, I suppose a dark suit'll do.' Off I went to Oxford in a state of high excitement; I knew Cranmer's name though I had never heard him sing. The rehearsal, such as it was, stands out in my memory more clearly than the concert. It was the first time I had ever accompanied a singer while he was actually changing from everyday clothes to full evening dress.

'Give to me the life I love —
(*slightly muffled as shirt comes off over head*)
Let the lave go by me.
(*crackle of starched shirt front being shaken out*)
Give the jolly heaven above
And the byway nigh me;
Bed in the bush with stars to see
   (*disappearing into tent-like shirt and groping for sleeves*)
Bread I dip in the ri-ver —
   (*emerging into daylight again*)
There's the life for a man like me,
   (*attaching stiff collar at back*)
There's the life — for ever.'
   (*wrestling with front stud*)

This I supposed was the life of a man like *me*, this was how professionals worked — maybe not as glamorous as I had imagined but impressive in its dedication regardless of circumstance.

Such odd jobs began to come my way with increasing frequency during my last eighteen months at College. I did a short tour around the Salisbury plain area with Isolde Menges, travelling by bus in bitter cold. Her violin playing had been affected by arthritis but her musical insight was a revelation. She talked endlessly of Beethoven, who was her God. What small reputation I had at College was as an accompanist who could read tolerably well and I used to supplement my own tuition by sitting in at lessons given by Isolde, Albert Sammons or Frederick Thurston. It was one of the most beneficial aspects of College life, a rare initiation into the subtle delights of chamber music. Sometimes, of an evening, Sammons would walk me across the park to his house in Bayswater, there to share an informal read-through of unfamiliar repertoire. He and Isolde were extraordinarily kind and encouraging, accepting my inadequate technique with remarkable patience, perhaps because I was only too willing to spend time accompanying their pupils.

The most daunting job that I attempted during college days was to act briefly as rehearsal pianist for the International Ballet, a wartime venture run by Mona Inglesby. They were working at a ballet called Planetomania with music specially composed by Norman Demuth. It was no surprise to find it still in manuscript; what shook me was that it was arranged for two pianos and that I was expected to be able to read and condense four cluttered staves at a time. Barenboim himself would have been hard put to it to perform such a feat; it was literally beyond the scope of any two hands. I was paid five shillings a day and soon decided that they were welcome to find another mug; there had to be an easier way of earning such petty sums.

Having attained my ARCM, however unworthily, I thought it would be an additional asset to acquire the LRAM teacher's diploma. At a lesson one day in the summer term, '41, Cyril asked me what preparation I was making for the exam, then about three weeks away. 'Don't worry,' I said airily, 'there's nothing to it. After all, I've got A.R. performer's with the optional paperwork; I can coast through this one.' He looked faintly disapproving. 'If you say so . . . but if you fail you'd better have a jolly good excuse.' It was a phrase I remembered better than he.

I turned up for the exam in good spirits, oozing confidence. First came the aural. Having waited a short time at the end of a corridor, an usher showed me into a small, rather dark room whose occupant to my surprise was Forbes Milne, my old music-master from school days. 'I suppose it's all right for me to examine you,' he said rather dubiously, 'or would you prefer someone else? I can possibly arrange it . . .' 'Oh no, Sir, I'm quite happy.' The tests seemed absurdly easy, the sort of thing I had done with Miss Hedges when I was a small child. There was one hitch, a three-note chord known as an augmented triad which I was supposed to identify from its sound alone. 'D, F sharp and B flat,' I said without hesitation. 'Wrong I'm afraid,' said Forbes, 'I'll have to dock you two marks for that.' I was astonished; I was sure I'd named the notes correctly. 'I'm sorry, Sir, but what should it be then?' 'D, F sharp and A sharp,' he said. 'But that's the same thing, really,' I remonstrated. I realised I was treading into some academic quagmire. Applying the maxim, 'If you can't beat 'em, join 'em', I went on to produce what I felt to be a suitably arcane argument. 'As I see it, Sir, it's the first inversion of an augmented triad on B flat; in its root position it'd be B flat, D, F sharp, the first inversion would be D, F sharp, B flat. That's what I said.' He regarded me pensively for a second or two as if weighing my words with some care. 'True,' he said grudgingly, 'but if you'd read the syllabus properly you'd know you're only supposed to be able to recognise augmented triads in their root position. It's an A sharp, no question of it.' I left the room marvelling at the narrowness of the academic mind. Later in the day I went for the practical, a twenty-five-minute session in which one played three pieces and then answered questions on teaching matters. In addition one had to play scales to order, for which ordeal ten marks were allocated. I knew my scales were shoddy beyond belief, but since the passmark for the practical was seventy-five I felt that I could jettison all ten marks for the scales and still have a clear margin. I believe I even made the panel of three judges a sporting offer to that effect. 'Let's scrub the scales and save all of us a lot of suffering.' They failed to take the bait and I was forced to stagger up and down the keyboard a couple of times, left hand lagging well behind the right in its familiar fashion. As for the theory paper, it seemed relatively straightforward apart from a few silly questions in the rudiments section such as, 'How many augmented intervals are there in the scale of D minor?' I wanted to write, 'How long is the scale?' in the margin, visualising a keyboard that stretched into infinity.

A week or two later an official-looking envelope arrived in the post. I went upstairs to open it in privacy. The three sections of the exam were each marked out of 100 and I knew that the passmark overall was 225, 75 in each part. Quickly I scanned the figures.

Aural 98 (Well, he said he'd knock two marks off for that stupid triad . . .)

Practical 90 (Eighty-eight for the pieces and two for scales; what a lark!)

Theory

Harmony	34
Form	23
Rudiments	7
	64

Total: 252
Result: Fail

I shook my head in case there was something wrong with my eyes; how could I have failed with 252? In utter disbelief I read through the figures again. Thirty-four for harmony — why, that was the maximum possible, 100%. Form — well, twenty-three isn't bad I suppose . . . but Rudiments — *seven*!! Bloody rudiments! How can you get 252 out of 300 and not know the rudiments of a subject? I was flabbergasted at the stark injustice of it. How could I tell Major — even worse, how could I break it to Cyril after his expression of doubt? 'You'd better have a good excuse,' he'd said . . .

Somewhere I found a very official-looking piece of foolscap complete with lion and unicorn crest. Carefully I ruled some lines in Indian ink, giving it the appearance of an examiner's mark-sheet. I then devised what I though was a hilariously funny report, using various coloured inks and several different styles of handwriting. I was especially proud of 'Either this girl is tone-deaf or stone-deaf. R.V.W.' The marks were abysmally low, the remarks utterly damning except for the aural test, of which I wrote, 'Never in all my experience have I seen a paper with answers so percipient, exhibiting so profound a knowledge of the subject. D.F. Tovey.' I folded this patently phoney document up and placed it in an envelope with a letter that went something like this:

Dear Cyril,
    The results of the L.R. have just come through and very

puzzling they are. All my marks were good except for the rudiments. During the exam we sat in alphabetical order and guess what! — next to me was a gorgeous little blonde called Antonia Hopkins. (I've seen a *lot* of her since!!) Although she's enchanting to look at she's an absolute twit at music and felt she'd done appallingly badly in the exam, especially the rudiments which she messed up completely. The funny thing is she seems to have got maximum marks for this one section yet I only got 7. We both feel there must be some mistake. I enclose her report so that you can see for yourself. Love to Phyll. See you next week. Yrs.

Tony

Rather to my surprise I heard nothing from him in the following few days. The next time I was in London I phoned to enjoy his reaction to my joke, my 'good excuse'. Phyll answered.

'Did you get a letter from me about the L.R. results?'

'Yes, we sent it off to the Academy ...'

One of the most remarkable things about human physiology is the way that a simple sentence like that can provoke an instantaneous reaction of sweat, trembling at the knees and a feeling that an oversized cricket-ball has lodged itself in the lower intestinal tract.

'I'm sorry, Phyll, I don't think I heard that, would you repeat it please ...'

'We got your letter; we sent it off to the Academy. Naturally you're upset. It certainly looks as if —

'But it was a *joke*! Oh jeepers, what can I do? I made it all up. Cyril said I'd better have a good excuse if I failed and I *did* fail so I made up a good excuse, at least it seemed so at the time. I say I'm dreadfully sorry, what on earth shall I do? Surely, couldn't you *see* it wasn't real?'

With understandable chilliness Phyll explained that Cyril had arrived home from a concert at about 2.00 am after a *very* tiring journey, opened my letter, given it a cursory glance, muttered something about 'poor Tony' and bunged it back into the post.

Feeling distinctly *vomitoso* I had to ring the Registrar at the Academy and explain that it was a private joke that had badly misfired. Fortunately he took it in good part, though God punished me when I took the theory exam a second time and failed the harmony.

Harmony	18
Form	28
Rudiments	20
	66

Result: Fail

My efforts to pass this wretched theory paper became such a recurring event that it was almost worthwhile to buy a season ticket to Baker Street. The third time of asking I managed to achieve 31, 29, 23, Total 83, which combined with my still valid marks for the aural and practical made up the impressive sum of 271 out of a possible 300. I believe that my original 252 remains the highest 'Fail' mark in the history of the Academy. However, although my 'good excuse' fell disastrously flat, I feel I had the last laugh, for on 21 February 1980 I was given an Hon. RAM, the highest award the Academy can give to an outsider. I felt it was a proper compensation for the two clear miscarriages of justice!

My ARCM performer's diploma meant that I was automatically promoted to Grade V. While this was a boost to my morale it unfortunately meant that I was expected to go in for the top-grade prizes, competing against pianists who could whip through half a dozen Chopin studies without a trace of fear. The choice of pieces was free but one was supposed to give a short recital lasting some twenty minutes. Most of the candidates would choose virtuoso works to demonstrate their enviable mastery of the keyboard, something I could scarcely do with my extremely insecure technique. I decided to offer a programme which contained only one real technical challenge, the Prelude in B flat by Rachmaninov. I couldn't play it very accurately but I could give a reasonably convincing imitation of someone playing it well, tossing my head and growling at times in the manner of pianistic lions such as Moiseiwitsch. In addition to this I prepared a transcription of a Bourrée from a Bach cello suite, a Sonatine by the Belgian composer, Jongen, and a tiny gem by Chopin, the Prelude in B minor, the one with the tune in the left hand and the sadly throbbing repeated notes in the right. My College friends thought this a huge joke. 'You can't play *that* for the Chappell medal,' they would say scathingly, 'it's far too easy.' I couldn't deny that it was a cowardly choice; I was only entering because it was expected of me.

On the day of the grading exams the College fairly hummed with music, torrents of notes spilling out of the windows into the Kensington air. Everyone seemed to be able to play extraordinarily *fast*. I was so impressed as I sat waiting my turn that I nearly decided to withdraw quietly with a sudden onset of cholera. Then, 'Your turn', said the man, 'Good luck', and he ushered me in. Rather to my surprise there was just one judge instead of the usual panel of three. It was Irene Scharrer, a most sensitive and poetic pianist whose name was often coupled with that of Myra Hess. I told her what I was going to play and then sat down at the piano doing my 'imitating Cyril' act. I would slavishly copy any of his mannerisms I could, trying to pretend I was marvellously competent Him instead of madly *in*competent Me. Apart from the predictable splashes in the Rachmaninov it all went better than I had dared to hope. The next morning I saw a crowd of students gathered in front of the main notice-board. I eased my way in and gave a quick glance at the bottom of the prize-list, thinking that perhaps I might have earned myself a fiver and an obscure award of sorts. Nothing. I turned, slightly disappointed but not surprised, and began to go upstairs towards the library (now the senior common-room). Suddenly someone rushed after me and slapped me on the back. 'Marvellous — how did you do it?' he burbled. 'What do you mean — do what?' 'The Chappell, of course, don't you know you've won the Chappell?' 'Rubbish, you're having me on.' 'No, I'm not, go and see for yourself.' 'But I've just looked.' 'Well, look harder.'

I hurried back and shoved my way rudely through the tight-packed bunch. My God, it was true. There it was, right at the top of the list. The Chappell Gold Medal — Antony Hopkins. A thrill like an electric current whizzed through me. Avoiding the distinctly grumpy looks of some of the better pianists in the group, I tore out of College and ran at top speed to the nearby Albert Hall, leaping up the shallow steps four at a time. I knew Cyril was rehearsing for a prom. and I wanted to be the first to tell him. I had a breathless word with the man who guarded the artists' entrance and hurried down the familiar stone stairs to the catacomb-like tunnel that leads to the Green Room. At the first available moment I grabbed Cyril. 'I won! I won! I can't believe it — I won the Chappell.' 'I know,' he said, 'I was told last night.' 'Oh, you beast, why ever didn't you tell me?'

Although I am understandably proud of this small landmark in my student life, I should say in all fairness that I would never have won in normal times. The ranks of students had been considerably depleted by the demands of war, lessening the competition substantially. Furthermore I was extremely fortunate in having Irene Scharrer as judge; she, more than most, was the type of pianist who would appreciate those few virtues I had and take a charitable view of the deficiencies. Naturally my stock at College climbed a good deal higher after this unexpected victory. Thinking to compliment me, the Registrar, Hugo Anson, asked me to play one of the solo parts in his recently published concerto for two pianos. I took away the score and wrestled with it for a day or two. In all honesty it was quite beyond me and I had the humiliating experience of having to tell him that I simply couldn't play it.

On 11 May 1943, almost certainly as a result of winning the Chappell medal, I gave a solo recital at the National Gallery. I chose a programme that was within my very limited capabilities and arrived in Trafalgar Square at about 10.45 in order to have a good opportunity to accustom myself to the unfamiliar sensation of playing in so famous an environment. Wanting to emulate Cyril's always immaculate appearance I had used some precious clothing coupons to buy a new shirt, tie and shoes. In a state of high excitement I ran lightly up the steps outside, slipped and fell. It was the shiny new soles on my shoes that let me down. Instinctively I put out a hand to save myself. I caught the middle finger of my right hand on the edge of a step, bending it back so painfully that for an awful moment I thought I had broken the knuckle. I went into the gallery ooh-ing and aah-ing and rubbing my hand. I tried to play a little but soon realised that I would need some treatment if I was to manage the concert at all. I hurried away to Charing Cross Hospital, scuffing my shoes as I went. There wasn't a lot to show — no blood or bone splinters, and at a time when dust-caked bomb victims were rushed in at every dawn my injury must have seemed trifling to the nurses. They applied some sort of lotion but candidly admitted that it wouldn't do a lot of good. I was back at the piano by midday and managed to practise for some twenty minutes before the audience began to arrive. I felt slightly sick as I waited to go on but somehow I got through the programme despite an understandably nervous start. I had chosen a favourite Bach transcription to begin with, so aptly named 'Mortify us by thy grace'. It has a continuously circling pattern in the right hand which can easily go astray, the more so when one is forced to change the fingering on the spot. It should take about 2¼ minutes. My version wandered around for at least five so that I began to wonder if I would ever escape from the self-perpetuating chain of semi-quavers. I had visions of myself still playing the same piece an hour hence, while the audience quietly stole away leaving me and Bach in solitary communion. In fact I finished the concert with a finger the shape of a sausage, quite unable to bend. (It took sixteen weeks of therapy at the Middlesex Hospital to get it fully right again.) A couple of days later I had a postcard from Myra Hess saying, 'Sorry to hear of your accident. Glad you went on. Well done — that's the spirit!'

During my last eighteen months at College I played at quite a number of small concerts, usually for mere token fees; it was all experience though I very seldom did solo recitals. It reassured me to have someone else in the limelight, a cellist, violinist or singer. Although I played at the National Gallery some half a dozen times, once on my own was enough. The atmosphere for those wartime concerts was memorable, something I have only found matched in the Art Gallery at Belfast in recent years. It really does seem that music brings solace in times of violence and death.

I left the Royal College in 1943 after a somewhat aimless last term in which Cyril had left. An enlightened government had decided that pianists of his calibre could serve the country better by giving concerts than by serving in the forces. He was therefore honour bound to do as much playing as possible; teaching was a time-consuming commitment that could be dispensed with. I only studied with him for two years, not nearly enough for my needs. Years later I asked him why he had never taught me real technique, never made me settle down to the really necessary Czerny. He laughed and said, 'I knew you'd never make a concert pianist and I enjoyed your playing; I didn't want to listen to you hammering away at exercises. Mind you, when you played a Brahms Intermezzo I would sometimes go home and try to copy you.'

It was as high as compliment as I could wish for, but my technical insecurity remains and I have paid a heavy price for the wasted years of my youth. Even though I had acquired eight letters after my name I went out into the open world singularly unqualified to do anything. I couldn't play the organ well enough to be a music master at a public school, I couldn't play the piano well enough to be a concert pianist. I didn't know what I was going to do, but the precariousness of wartime life made any long-term future seem unreal; one lived a day-by-day existence. Anyway, I hadn't just been a student at the College; lots of other things had been happening. It was as though I was leading two lives each of which vied with the other for my attention. To explore my alter ego's story I need to turn back once more to the first period of the war.

10
Inglorious War

Although I was secretly relieved not to be called up I felt that I should try to do what I could for the war effort. As soon as a local unit was formed I joined the Home Guard, or LDV (Local Defence Volunteers) as it was originally called. Our exercises bore a close resemblance to the Field Days that I had participated in at school except that, rather surprisingly, we did not have the cavalry that romantically I yearned for. Nevertheless we of the Little Gaddesden Company travelled in considerable style, piling into a splendid open Bentley tourer of the type that had scored some famous victories at Le Mans. Maybe we couldn't halt the German armour if it appeared but we could at least outrun it. Concrete anti-tank traps were sited in strategic positions, plans for holding the Nazi hordes in check were seriously discussed. Our command base was the Ashridge Golf Clubhouse. It was generally felt that the long straight fairways might make convenient landing strips for troop-carrying gliders, while the bunkers could well have been chosen by the German High Command as suitably soft landing-places for paratroopers. Though not a golfer at the time I was fully ready to die in defence of the greens. It all seems rather foolish now, but the *Blitzkrieg* had been so overwhelmingly successful in Europe that invasion fever in the post-Dunkirk period was not in the least melodramatic. I used to have a recurring dream in which a heavily armed Nazi soldier would climb in through my bedroom window; I would keep on hitting him time after time but my blows would have no effect.

Keen though I was to repel the invader, my increasingly frequent trips to London created a problem I could not solve. One Sunday morning I was summoned urgently to the clubhouse.

Captain Gray, the Little Gaddesden Supreme Commander, sat tight-lipped behind his desk.

'There was an exercise here yesterday Hopkins, why weren't you here for it?'

'I was in London, Sir.'

'In London? That's no excuse. This is work of National Importance; you're in the King's Service now. These exercises have priority, do you understand?'

His hand, smartly gloved in brown leather, rapped the desk in time to the words.

'Nobody told me there was an exercise, Sir. I would have come if I'd kno . . .' 'Nobody *told* you? You must make arrangements to be told. You must arrange things better. Suppose we do have an invasion, eh? You'll be twiddling away on the piano in London and I'll be here having to waste time trying to get in touch. It's not good enough, Hopkins. It's not our job to tell you; it's your job to FIND OUT.'

'Yes, Sir.'

The image was so ludicrous that I could scarcely keep a straight face — the Little Gaddesden Company fighting to the death on the second fairway while I rang up from Kensington and asked if they'd like me to join them. By mutual agreement I was transferred to a London unit, but drilling on tarmac wrecked my knee and I was invalided out, a rare distinction.

Soon after the outbreak of war a number of prefabricated huts were hastily built on the fine green sward outside Ashridge House. The whole place was to be turned into a large emergency hospital. Since the Home Guard only really functioned in the evenings and at weekends I offered my services part-time to the hospital. I felt that my boyhood yen for the doctor's life might be satisfied in a practical way without the wearisome business of seven years' hard study. I saw myself as a sort of male Florence Nightingale, Fred Nightingale perhaps, standing by the operating table catching the limbs as they fell. The job I was actually given gave little scope for romantic daydreams; I was appointed Salvage Officer, a glorified dustman whose task it was to sort all the waste products of the hospital and take them down to the local sewage farm at Berkhamsted. Paper, scrap-metal, rags, bones and fat were my daily pickings. When half a dozen bins were full, we would load them into a little Commer van and cart them away. I suggested that it would save man-power if I did the ferrying myself. I acquired a provisional licence and started to learn to drive under the instruction of the hospital engineer, a Scotsman named, inevitably, Mac. One afternoon we were bowling along merrily with four dustbins full of bones and greasy fat in the van. As a crude gesture towards hygiene they had been heavily garnished with a pink antiseptic powder. I was happily imagining myself driving fearlessly through a hail of German bullets when Mac spoke: 'Some time I'll slap my leg like this — when I do I want you to slam the brakes on r-real hard and do an emer-r-gency stop. Got it?'

I nodded assent and continued my heroic drive through the ambush. Slap went his hand. I jammed on the brakes and there was a mighty metallic clang just behind us. Two large dustbins full of foul-smelling fat emptied themselves over our heads. The windscreen, the dashboard, Mac and I were covered with a vile mixture of pink powder and slime. We looked at each other, brushing gunge out of our hair. 'You cer-r-tainly stopped it,' he said with a broad grin.

With petrol-rationing being imposed with increasing severity we were glad to have a smart little pony-cart at home. It only took about twenty minutes to trot down to Berkhamsted. Most of the canal-side pubs had stabling for the big barge horses to stop in overnight. During the day the stables would be empty and it was a simple matter to clip-clop into the paved yard, unhitch the pony and leave him in a capacious stall. In those now distant days before commercial development ruined it the High Street had the rural charm one expects of a small country town. There was a smithy close to the Town Hall, a favourite haunt since my early childhood. One led the horses down to the glow of the forge, the clang of hammer on anvil and the sweet pungent smell of burnt hoof. 'Up you come my beauty,' the smith would say, lifting a fetlock and cradling the weighty leg between his knees. I used to gaze in disbelief as without a tremor he put the red-hot shoe in place. A thick crescent of smoke would encircle his capped head. 'Woa boy, woa boy,' he would soothe, but often as not the horse would never budge.

What with the Home Guard and my work at the hospital, music took up less of my time than it should have done. There always seemed to be distractions, wood to cut, lamps to fill, horses to exercise. As the autumn of 1940 chilled into winter I was again approached by the secretary of the local operatic society. It had been decided to put on a revue in aid of the Red Cross; would I act as rehearsal pianist, write any tunes that might be needed and play one of two pianos at the performances. I seem to think the magic sum of five shillings was mentioned again but I'm not sure. Naturally I jumped at the chance, not only for the musical experience but also because it would mean renewing my acquaintance with Alison.

For me each rehearsal had deeply romantic undertones of which she must have remained almost unaware. One evening I was pounding away at the battered old upright while the chorus went through their steps for yet another time. She, a star of the show, came and stood beside me, peeled a precious tangerine and fed me segments by hand as I played. It was a deliciously sensual experience that had me cycling home through the frosty night singing rhapsodies to the heedless forest. The winter that year was particularly severe. During the run of the show Woodyard was snowbound, the roads virtually impassable at night. Alison offered to put me up for the week at her home in Boxmoor, more accessible since the main road in the valley carried a lot more traffic. Her husband, a good amateur actor with a pleasing voice, was also involved in the production so that it was no inconvenience to take me to and fro. At the end of the week I could hardly bear to go home; I was completely under her spell, following her every move with calf-like eyes that expressed feelings I could not possibly put into words. The morning of my departure I made a little thank-you speech to her, she seated by windowsill, I removed at some distance across the room. I had prepared my peroration so carefully that it must have seemed as though I was reading it from notes.

'If I were to behave like a perfect gentleman,' I said with studied gallantry, 'I should walk out of your life now and never see you again. You see I know I've fallen terribly in love with you. I just think about you all the time. But I'm not going to behave like a gentleman because seeing you means too much to me. So I hope I can go on seeing you and perhaps when the weather's better you'll come up and ride one of our horses, and perhaps we could do some concerts together, and of course I'll rehearse with you as much as you like . . .' I broke off. It was an absurdly stilted speech delivered in such a gauche way that she had to laugh. Of course I could go on seeing her, she said; it had been a pleasure to have me stay for the week, and stop thinking silly thoughts.

It is quite understandable that she didn't take my protestation too seriously. I was a quite unsophisticated nineteen-year-old, a student several years her junior whose devotion she must have found flattering. Both her parents had died of cancer when she was in her 'teens and she had married very young. Though I had no inkling of it the marriage was even then beginning to show signs of fraying, as such early unions frequently do. She had been a student at the College before my time and sadly missed her music. The yoke of domesticity was irksome to her. In a matter of months we were doing a number of small concerts together, raising money for wartime charities or entertaining troops.

In March 1941 Jacques invited me to become rehearsal pianist to the Bach Choir. I was thrilled, and set about learning the accompaniments to all the choruses of the *St Matthew Passion*. It was a marvellous way to get to know the great choral masterpieces that I had never previously heard, even though my view of them was somewhat restricted since I got to know the choruses intimately but the solos not at all. For the performances I was usually displaced by Dr Thornton Lofthouse, although I did play at a carol concert the following December. It was the first time my name had appeared on a poster in London and I duly appreciated this rise to the giddy heights of fame.

Throughout that summer I welcomed every opportunity I could of being with Alison. Her husband had been called up and she was contemplating letting her house and moving to the outer fringe of London. She wanted to resume her singing studies, preferably at the Guildhall School of Music. My services as accompanist were much valued by her though I am sure she did not consider me as a potential lover. She often used to cycle up to Woodyard and we would saddle up the horses and go for long rides together, relishing every moment. One afternoon we were passing through a rich carpet of bluebells with shafts of sunlight falling sharp-edged between the enclosing trees. It was a scene of such breathtaking beauty that we stopped and dismounted. Standing there, with no sound but birdsong and the gentle swish of horses' tails, I felt an overpowering desire to cross the barrier that propriety had kept between us. Greatly daring I spoke: 'I would so much like to kiss you ...'

'Why don't you?'

'I'm not sure ... how ...'

Gently she took me and gave me a single kiss on the mouth. It was something that had never happened to me before. My pulse raced. It would be hard to imagine a more romantic setting. I knew it was a moment to be treasured; I felt that I could ask no more of life than this. 'We'd better go,' I said.

Having left the Home Guard I became a firewatcher at the College, living on the premises and sleeping (when I was able) on a small truckle-bed in the gents' cloakroom. It was something of a farce since we were never shown the way to the roof. Mostly we sat in the basement and played cards. There were four or five of us doing shifts. String and wind players with their own instruments could put in some useful hours practising, but for me it was a frustrating time. Shut up in a building with nearly a hundred pianos in it, I was forbidden to practise after six o'clock in case I wore them out! Each morning I used to walk down to Kensington High Street to breakfast at the Express Dairy. It was a proud time to be in London. One would pass a great tumble of rubble where a house had been hit in the night, but always would come the feeling that like some shambling giant the city would shake off the dust and rise to renew the struggle. I remember a very English moment during the buzz-bomb period. I was in Kensington Public Library. In the distance but then coming ever closer we heard the unmistakable sound of the horrid machine putt-putting through the sky like an angry pneumatic drill. Suddenly it cut out, sure indication that it was about to fall. A little shamefaced but with complete decorum we dipped on to one knee, as though paying homage to a benevolent sovereign. There was a moment's silence followed by a loud bang in the direction of Notting Hill. Not a word was said. We quietly stood up and resumed our browsing through the shelves.

One evening I took Alison into the College after we'd had a meal together at a marvellously cheap little restaurant near the Mercury Theatre. We behaved very properly, she sitting at one end of the bed, I at the other. Unfortunately we were observed by the caretaker, a shifty individual who had taken something of a dislike to me. The next day I was summoned to see the Director.

'Mr Devenish tells me you had a woman in your room last night,' he said abruptly, his tone expressing chilly disapproval.

'Not a woman, Sir,' I replied with some indignation; 'a close friend, a respectable married lady.'

Dyson gave me a challenging glance over his gold-rimmed spectacles, lips tightly pursed. I felt bitterly resentful at being thus paraded like a prisoner before the governor. What business was it of his?

He went on to rebuke me sharply and forbade me to bring her into the building again, even though she had been a former student who had acquired the Teacher's Diploma. His long term at Winchester College had made him very schoolmasterish, and the atmosphere was unnecessarily repressive.

In November 1941 Alison sang a composition of mine at the West Herts Music Festival. Heavily indebted to Vaughan Williams it was a wordless rhapsody called 'The Lonely Shepherd'. It was scored for voice, string quartet and piano and sounded well in the ultra-resonant hall. Maurice Jacobson, the adjudicator, was enthusiastic about it: 'A lovely little work. Enjoyed this enormously — the work itself and the performance.'

By that time Alison had established her independence by moving to a pleasant block of flats just over the road from Kew Gardens. Tired of my college cell I decided to share a room in Lansdowne Crescent with two fellow-students. There were only two beds but, since one or other of us was always on night-shift at the College, the accommodation was adequate if a trifle cramped. From there I moved on to an upstairs room in St Dunstan's Road, Baron's Court. My room-mate was Neville Marriner. For ten shillings a week we had bed and breakfast (baked beans on toast every morning), served in our beds by a perpetually moaning landlady called Mrs Coulton. We used to tease her mercilessly about Mr C. who, despite his withered-up appearance, had by some miracle given her a second daughter when she was all of fifty. 'What's he like in the nude?' we would ask, waiting in delighted anticipation for her invariable, almost ritual response.

'You dirty little buggers — fancy arskin' a fing like that. Course I never see'd 'im.'

'What, not even in the bath?'

'Naow, course not; don't be so disgustin'. Mr C. wouldn' dream of lettin' me see 'im wivout 'is coms. It ain't decent!'

The vision of Mr C. locked in a passionate embrace clad in his combinations struck us as hysterically funny and we would weep with laughter as she rose once again to the bait. I never saw her wear shoes. She shuffled round in a pair of battered bedroom slippers, even down to the shops and back. It was all so different from Woodyard.

As we wanted to share the pleasure of singing in a choir Alison and I enrolled at Morley College. There, for one evening each week, we would rehearse under the truly inspirational guidance of Michael Tippett. I certainly didn't realise that it was to be the start of one of the most significant relationships of my life, but from the first day I found the rehearsals an absolute joy. Apart from the very different location it was an experience rather comparable to my Austrian trip. In Schwaz I had been initiated into the delights of chamber music; in Lambeth it was the madrigals and anthems of Gibbons, Weelkes and Purcell, Monteverdi and Gesualdo. I had never dreamed that the choral music of more than three centuries ago could be so passionate. At the time, Monteverdi was known only to a privileged few; the performance of his 'Vespers' given by the Morley College choir was a revelation to all who took part.

If I were asked who taught me the most about music I would answer without hesitation, Michael Tippett. I was never a formal pupil nor did I ever pay for a lesson, but he was extraordinarily kind and encouraging to me. Sitting at a canteen table or walking briskly to Waterloo Station he would talk about music in so enlightening a way that I felt as if I had never really understood a note before. Occasionally I would go and stay for a weekend at his small modern cottage near Oxted, and there I would play him my latest composition. He would listen attentively as though it was actually of some value. His method of teaching was quite unusual but most illuminating. Instead of saying this harmony or that sequence was *wrong*, a type of criticism which would incur an instinctively protective reaction from any composer worth his salt, he would simply say, 'I think you could improve that; let's see how someone else coped with a similar problem.' He would go over to the bookcase and pull out a score — it could be Beethoven or Bach, Stravinsky or Hindemith. 'Ah, here it is ...' With that peculiarly intense gaze he would peer at the page, making little humming noises to himself, as though to check that he had indeed found the passage he wanted. 'Look — do you see how he avoided a cliché there? The obvious thing would have been to have gone da-bada-dah but he went da-bada-da bada — *deepa*-bada-dah. Makes all the difference, doesn't it?' The blue eyes would twinkle and he would burst into his infectious giggle. It was quite a new idea to me to discover that Bach or Stravinsky had ever had problems remotely similar to mine; I felt vastly flattered to be considered in the same breath and was only too willing to learn from them. Whereas Dr Darke had seemed to me to be obsessed with the academic proprieties of notation, Michael was only interested in content and construction. Perhaps most revealing of all were his explorations of his own music. In all honesty he was a pretty terrible pianist, but even with the handfuls of wrong notes, the blurred runs and the continual singing, one got a vivid impression of the musical substance. He carried the listener along on the tide of his own enthusiasm, creating the music anew rather than performing it.

His conducting was unorthodox to say the least. 'Quiet everybody. *From* the top. Right, GO!' His long arms would snake out in a wild gesture that was so different from Jacques' tidy beat, but our response made up in enthusiasm what we lacked in finesse. For months we worked towards the first performance of 'A Child Of Our Time', stumbling inaccurately through the Pogrom chorus, swooning at the spirituals. (He should have called it 'The Jung Idea',' whispered Stanley Etherton, the charming bearded schoolmaster who sat beside me in the small group of tenors.)

One Saturday afternoon, Malcolm Sargent, Walter Goehr, Michael and I gathered in a classroom at Morley to establish the correct metronome marks for the forthcoming published scores of 'Child'. I sat at a tinny upright, playing the opening bars of each number in turn while Walter, muttering imprecations, fumbled with a metronome, trying to adjust its soulless clacking to match my tempo. It was surprisingly difficult to do. In the event most of the indications were wrong since the proper tempi for an orchestra and chorus are unlikely to be the same as those suitable for a solo piano. The orchestra behaved badly at the rehearsal prior to the first performance, embarrassing us by their hostile reaction to the music and their tacit implication that Michael was incompetent.

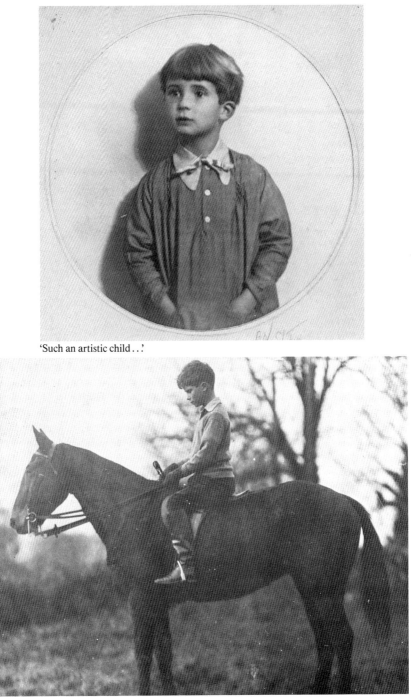

'Such an artistic child..'

Dancing Girl — not looking her best

Note the different shaped ears — one remodelled

The first XK

My lightweight E-type
(0-100 m.p.h. 11.5 secs!)

Blissful day at Goodwood

Alison helping me out

With Eric Delaney in 1963 on BBC's TV series *Let's Make Music*

Working for TV, Adelaide

'Come on sopranos — give me more!' (Japan)

Not another book . . .

'My "operatic frolic." ' *Lady Rohesia* at Sadler's Wells

Band of Hope and Glory...the Royal Albert Hall

Concerts at Morley were a disarming mixture of professional and amateur. Imagine a small string orchestra based on a few brilliant young refugees who were soon to form themselves into the Amadeus Quartet. Add a few more of Max Rostal's pupils and Walter Bergmann or Thurston Dart as continuo player. In the choir hardly a single professional singer except one bass from one of the great London churches. A perfect example of the blend was the occasion when I sang an elaborate Purcell duet for two countertenors with Alfred Deller. Afterwards Engel Lund, a much admired singer of folk music, came up to me radiating enjoyment. 'That was marvellous, Tony — I didn't know you were a countertenor. You're studying with Alfred?' I had to confess I wasn't and that I'd never had a singing lesson in my life.

For some reason, I can't think why, I once played the 'Michelangelo Sonnets' with Peter Pears even though Britten was at the concert; I must have been terrified. I also wrote three unaccompanied 'Songs from Cyprus' for the choir which, to my great excitement, were performed at the National Gallery in November 1943. Howard Ferguson wrote to Michael saying that I stood out too much in the tenor line, spoiling the blend of the choir. Suitably chastened I tried to become anonymous but my enthusiasm was so great that I found it hard not to 'lead' ostentatiously.

Although I certainly never gave the matter much thought, Morley proved to be the perfect bridge into my career as a professional musician. I taught the piano there, mostly to struggling amateurs; I took occasional rehearsals if Michael was unable to be present. Through him I became conductor of three women's choirs for the Royal Arsenal Co-operative Society, the Tooting, Balham and Clapham branches. It was all very humble but I felt that I had at least got a foot in the door. It was a considerable relief to discover that it didn't necessarily have to open on to a school quadrangle. My long-held ambition to be a schoolmaster (for which in my lackadaisical way I had supposedly trained) dwindled to nothing. I was enjoying myself far too much freelancing for petty sums that brought in an income of £3.00 a week. I had neither security nor prospects but it looked as though I had started a career of sorts, even if it totally lacked distinction. I had barely left the Royal College when events took a completely unexpected turn for which I had in no way been prepared. It was to prove a nettle worth grasping.

11
A Golden Ass

'Hang on after practice — I've got a job for you,' said Michael one evening at Morley as we took our places for the weekly choir rehearsal.

I can't remember the precise date, but it must have been in the spring of 1944. During the previous summer he had been given a sentence of three months' imprisonment for his conscientious objection to military service or even to directed labour. The very day he came out of Wormwood Scrubs he, John Amis, Alison and I took the train for Cornwall to have a recuperative holiday. It was a strange journey in a packed overnight train. The dim blue bulbs didn't give enough light to read by so we talked or dozed for most of the way. At Exeter (I think) we climbed out of the crowded carriage to stretch our legs. Trying to extricate herself from the baggage stacked between the seats, Alison lost a shoe. It fell between the train and platform, or so we guessed in the virtual darkness. (Stations were strategic targets for bombers and the blackout was strictly enforced.) To the accompaniment of ribald laughter I lay face down on the platform; John and Michael grabbed me by the legs and lowered me head first over the edge. 'Don't let the train start,' I called as I groped between the wheels searching for the elusive shoe. 'Got it!' Unceremoniously they hauled me up, filthy but triumphant; we piled back into the carriage as the whistle blew shrilly, sounding indignant at our breach of several bylaws. The train finished its journey at St Austell not long after daybreak. Far from rested, we limped stiffly out of the station. We had no rooms reserved, nor even a plan of action. 'Let's go to Mevagissey,' said Michael, his spirits still buoyant at his release from prison. 'A.L. Rowse lives there; he'll give us some breakfast. It's only five miles or so.' 'How do we get there?' 'Walk, of course.'

And so we did, arriving at Rowse's home unheralded. He took it remarkably well, behaving as though it was quite the normal thing for a friend to arrive direct from Wormwood Scrubs with three complete strangers in tow. He made a few phonecalls and fixed us up with lodgings; Alison and I were installed at the local baker's. The hollow clang of the oven door would wake us at a hideously early hour but we didn't mind, so appetising was the smell of newly-baked bread. It was a simple but happy holiday, mostly spent by the sea. The usual beaches were inaccessible because of the mines and barbed wire but we used to enjoy cliff walks, revelling in the peace and the freedom. One afternoon we climbed down a precipitous little path to a rocky cove whose position ensured (as we thought) absolute privacy. 'Let's have a bathe,' said Michael with the enthusiasm of a twelve-year-old. Needless to say, we had no bathing-costumes nor would we have dreamed of squandering precious clothing coupons on such inessentials. As a male I have always thought nude bathing an overrated pastime; I feel it is imprudent to offer such tasty morsels to invisible denizens of the deep. However, not wishing to reveal my innate cowardice, I joined in the general strip. Within moments we had all plunged in. For me, enough was enough very soon, and I scrambled out on to the unfriendly rocks to dry myself in the sun. The others soon joined me. We sat there for a while, talking, and, in the usual English manner, trying to convince ourselves that we weren't getting cold. Suddenly a small rowing boat appeared around the headland. It made fairly slow progress towards us, the sole occupant glancing over his shoulder from time to time to choose a suitable landing place. We lay there naiad-like, watching his laborious approach with some astonishment. It was a policeman, seeming curiously out of place in a dinghy. The last wave lifted the boat in an ungraceful lurch on to a small patch of shingle. Carefully the constable stowed the oars, stepped ashore and dragged the boat up a further yard. Heavy boots crunching, he came towards us, hand ferreting in breast-pocket. 'May I see your identity cards?' he said in a brook-no-nonsense tone. Stark naked as we were, we couldn't help laughing. It transpired that a coastguard had seen us from some distance away and, thinking that we might be a landing-party from an enemy submarine, had reported our presence to the police. Although the incident amused us all it was slightly embarrassing for Michael to have to admit that his 'previous residence' had been Wormwood Scrubs.

He returned from his native Cornwall refreshed, eager to prepare 'A Child of our Time' for its first performance in March 1944. It was to prove a significant landmark in his career, one in which I am pleased to have played a small part. I imagine that after so momentous an occasion the choir took it easy for a week or two, exploring music rather than polishing it. It was on such an evening that he asked me to stay behind. When he spoke of a 'job' my expectations were not very high; copying some Purcell string parts perhaps, or maybe a little proof-reading. Judge then of my delight when he said that he'd been asked to write incidental music for a production of Marlowe's play, *Dr Faustus*. 'Would you like to do the dirty work?' he asked — his exact phrase. 'What do you mean?' 'Well, making a full score — it'll only be for about nine players and I'll indicate everything on my rough copy. I thought you might enjoy going up to Liverpool and playing for the rehearsals — see that it's done properly ... What about it?

I was genuinely thrilled, flattered to become his amanuensis. I had done something of the sort the previous year for Britten when I had stood in for him at rehearsals of an epic radio play called *The Rescue*; this had been my first contact with the BBC. Now I was to be given even more responsibility and I discussed it excitedly with Alison as we went back to the basement flat in Drayton Gardens where we had recently set up our first home together.

I waited on the Master with growing impatience. At last, about three weeks before rehearsals were due to begin, I could stand it no longer. 'I must have something to go on with,' I said to Michael, 'I'll never get it done in time.' He gave me an amused glance. 'Oh, I can't be bothered; you do it instead!' 'What, write the music myself?' 'Yes, I'm sure you'll manage.' He rummaged about in his shabby old music-case. 'Here's a copy of the play — the cues are all marked up.'

I returned to the flat slightly dazed at the suddenness of the opportunity. (During my last term at the College I had studied orchestration with Gordon Jacob and, as an exercise, he had suggested that I should write short imaginary sequences for films. I had quite enjoyed doing it but never thought for a moment that I would actually be employed as a composer.) The next day I rushed out to buy a new stock of manuscript paper and half a dozen pencils. Feeling as though overnight I had become something more than a mere acolyte, I started work.

I duly arrived in Liverpool where I introduced myself to the producer, John Moody. He must have been disappointed to be landed with a completely unknown composer instead of Tippett but it was too late to complain. I settled in happily to the daily routine of rehearsals. The theatre, despite its shabbiness, seemed my natural environment; I could hardly keep away. The score was much more than 'a tucket within' and 'sound of drums afar'. There were several ballet sequences (arranged by Andrée Howard), while the decor by Tanya Moiseiwitsch, daughter of the pianist, was stunningly effective considering the limitations on materials brought about by the war. The company was known as the Liverpool Old Vic and contained a number of actors who were to become quite famous. My only worry was the orchestra, a group of old-age pensioners with many a long year in music-hall pits behind them. The conductor normally played in a piano trio during the intervals. He had 'Bitter Sweet' and *The Merry Widow* at his fingertips, but any confidence I might have had in him waned the moment I saw he was going to conduct with a knitting-needle.

The play opened on Tuesday, 15 May 1944. It was an awkward date for me as on the previous evening I was to play continuo at the Bach Choir's performance of *Messiah* in Westminster Abbey. I had to leave Knitting-needle to cope with the dress rehearsal on his own. With the strains of Handel still ringing in my ears I caught the train to Liverpool and arrived at the Playhouse stage-door about forty minutes early. I was met by the trumpeter, short and stout with a lifetime of honourable service in the Salvation Army. 'I've got a rather bad blister on my lip,' he said dolefully. 'Do you mind?' It's a hard question to answer since it sounds equally heartless whether one says, 'Yes I do' or, 'No I don't.' Avoiding the verbal trap, I said, 'I do hope it gets better.' 'That's all right then,' he mumbled, and drifted off to the nearby pub in search of the soothing touch of Guinness froth. (Perhaps he was a lapsed member of the 'Sally'.)

I sat in the circle, heart thumping. Westminster Abbey last night and now this; for someone whose original ambitions had been so limited it was almost too much. The houselights dimmed; footlights flooded the red curtain with a golden glow; the knitting-needle tapped peremptorily on the metal music-stand.

I had given considerable thought to the opening. How, in Marlowe's time, did they arrest the attention of the audience? A roll of drums perhaps? (Clearly impractical for me since everyone would get up, assuming it to be the National Anthem.) A fanfare then, brief but blood-tingling? That was it; that would grip them.

The knitting-needle flashed and out from the pit came a sort of brassy squeal, cousin twice removed to the notes I had written. Owing to the blister on the lip the Sallyman was playing the trumpet out of the corner of his mouth, rather as if it was a flute. Severe problems with the embouchure caused him to transpose most of the part down an approximate octave, sometimes more, sometimes less. As the evening wore on I shared his pain with increasing intensity, half expecting my lip to bleed in sympathy. I was certainly biting it hard enough. Towards the end of the play the knitting-needle wove ever more confusing patterns in the air. The strings, dogged to the last, would plough on righteously with cue forty-nine; the bassoon, quite out of touch, would try his luck with cue forty-seven while the brass, eager for a final pint, galloped ahead to number fifty-one. To this day I have not written a more 'modern' score than the closing scenes of *Dr Faustus*. 'Quite nice, but I thought the music was very strange,' said the lady in front of me as I slunk miserably out of the circle. She certainly didn't know who I was and I was thankful for the veil of anonymity. I went out into the dark shattered, my one chance ruined by the incompetence of others.

A career in music is often founded on chance as much as on ability. It was by lucky chance that I had met the influential music and literary critic Edward Sackville-West. Even more fortunate was my decision to show him my ill-fated *Faustus* score, graveyard of my hopes. It was as a direct result of this that one day at the end of October 1944 I received one of the most important telephone-calls of my life.

'Is that Antony Hopkins?'

'Yes' — a little guarded as I didn't recognise the voice.

'This is Louis Macneice.'

(*Must be someone pulling my leg; surely the real Macneice wouldn't ring me up?*)

'Yes?' — even more guarded, expecting a guffaw at my credulity.

'Eddie Sackville-West tells me you write incidental music . . .'

'Oh yes,' said I, composer of the great Liverpool disaster.

'I've tried eight other composers and they're all busy or ill. Time's getting a bit short now.'

'I'm sorry, I don't understand; what do you want me to do?'

'Write music for a radio play. Only actually it's two radio plays.'

'How long have I got?'

'About ten days . . . .'

'I'll come along straight away.'

I scribbled a brief message to Alison — HAVE GONE TO BBC!! — and dashed out of the mews house we rented in Linden Gardens. Rattling along in the tube to Oxford Circus I wondered what was in store for me, what subject, what size orchestra, how much music.

Louis' office was in an apartment-like building in New Cavendish Street. He was dark, with a thin rather pointed face and a hesitant way of speaking that revealed his intense shyness. His smile, rarely indulged, was a little wolfish, showing yellowish teeth, tobacco-stained. Seated behind a littered desk he produced, almost apologetically, two scripts, *The Golden Ass* and *Cupid and Psyche*. As I glanced through them I saw that there were a number of music-cues, some extending behind quite lengthy sequences of speech. It seemed a formidable assignment but the opportunity was too good to turn down. 'What sort of orchestra had you in mind?' I asked, expecting a dozen players at the most. 'Oh, full orchestra of course.' he said in a matter-of-fact way. 'It'll be the BBC Revue Orchestra, but you can augment it a bit if you like. Have what you want . . .'

I didn't know whether to thank him profusely for such an unimagined opportunity or to try to pass it off as though I was quite accustomed to such a situation. Apart from a short work for chorus and strings that had been performed in Berkhamsted I had never heard a note of mine played by an orchestra. (I don't count the nine good men and true in Liverpool since they hadn't got it right.) At my request Louis rang through to the orchestral manager to find precisely what instruments and how many were available; I noted them down and then glanced at the scripts again.

'Did you really mean ten days?' I asked. 'It looks like an awful lot of music . . .'

'Well' — a little embarrassed and avoiding my eye — 'it's just over three weeks to go but you've got to allow at least a week for copying the orchestral parts. You'd better aim at ten days for safety.'

I went home in an extraordinary state, half euphoric, half apprehensive. What if I made a frightful mess of it? I tried to arm myself against the possibility of disaster with the thought that time was so impossibly short that nobody could blame me if it didn't come off. At least there wouldn't be a knitting-needle to contend with. As I read through the scripts, music began to echo through the corridors of my mind, tantalising as a siren's song. The text was marvellously evocative, full of imagination, fantasy, poetry and humour. I decided to write a few pages at a time and then transcribe them on to the full score. In this way I could send the music to a copyist in instalments. With Gordon Jacob's helpful little book on orchestration at my side I settled down to tackle by far the most challenging task I had ever faced.

Ten days or perhaps a hundred hours later I had finished, 134 pages of full score in all. When the speech rehearsals began I played in the music where it was needed, partly to check the timing, but also so that the cast could become familiar with it. In those days there was no recording; actors and orchestra shared the same studio without the luxury of 're-takes', each very aware of the other's contribution. At the first appearance of the orchestra I felt like a child in a toyshop. My eyes must have sparkled at the sight of so many players, so many instruments, all seeming to shine extra bright in the lavish studio lighting. I could scarcely believe that they were all there for ME ... There was a hush. 'Cue One' said the conductor, and wafted music out of the air with his magic wand. I sat at a suitable distance, following my roughly pencilled short score and trying not to betray my naive excitement.

If, as I describe it now, it all seems a little too much like a fairy-tale, it should be remembered that it came out of nothing. Not in my wildest dreams had I ever visualised myself in such a situation. To hear my music played by a professional orchestra was thrill enough; for the experience to happen in a huge drama studio with a distinguished cast of actors and actresses was an immeasurable bonus.

Had I shown an ounce of prudence I would have turned the job down along with the 'eight other composers' Louis had mentioned. It was absurd with my inexperience to take on such an assignment. However, 'Fortune favours the brave' they say, and by some freak I succeeded. Laurence Gilliam, the head of drama, sent me a warmly complimentary letter about the music; Herbert Farjeon, reviewing the production in the Listener (16 November 1944), wrote: 'The legend was well and sensitively told, and the music of Mr Antony Hopkins conveyed the terranean, subterranean and superterranean atmospheres with unerring freshness.'

Suddenly, without premeditation or planning, I had a career as a composer. Before the year was out I had written music for four more radio productions, two of them Shakespearean. It was these perhaps that led to my first involvement in a London production, nothing less than Oedipus Rex with a cast that included Laurence Olivier, Ralph Richardson and Sybil Thorndike. I really found it very difficult to believe that I was moving in such illustrious circles. At the back of my mind I still saw myself as a failed organist, unsuited for schoolmastering and incompetent as a pianist, lucky to have scratched an uncertain living during my first year out of College.

The first night of Oedipus was a great theatrical occasion, notable even by the standards of the Old Vic company. There was a much larger orchestra than usual, for Grieg's benefit rather than mine since 'Peer Gynt' was also in the repertory for that season. Naturally I took advantage of the extra resources available and, since music played a considerable part in the production, I felt that I had made a significant contribution to the evening. After it was all over, the bows on stage, the mutual congratulations, the lightning tour of the dressing-rooms to prolong the ecstasy for a few moments further, I left by the stage-door. There was a crowd of at least eighty packed tightly round the exit. As I stood briefly silhouetted against the light they eased back a foot or so to let me pass. A disgusted voice muttered, 'Oh, 'e's NOBODY!' They surged around again, waiting for a real star to appear.

12
Cathedral Capers

A notable element in this very attractive production was the music by Antony Hopkins. He is, to my mind, the most radio-minded of all who write music for wireless features, for he evidently regards himself as a collaborator and not as an accompanist. There were moments in 'Enemy of Cant' when he seemed to take over a word or situation which had baffled the ingenuity of Macneice, and there were other occasions when he invented noises off so cunning as to send (I hope) the BBC sound-effects boys back to school to learn the ABC of aural association.

Thus wrote W.E. Williams, radio critic of the *Observer* in 1946. By then I had become securely established as a prolific composer of music for broadcast drama with nineteen scores to my credit in less than three years. One of these was an ambitious production of *Moby Dick* for which I wrote some forty-five minutes of music for large orchestra. No longer so incredulous at the turn of events, I like to think that I had become fully professional, able to meet the requirements of author and producer without fuss.

In the course of my association with the Old Vic I had had the good fortune to meet Tyrone Guthrie. He was so tall that I felt distinctly uncomfortable trying to converse with him standing up; it seemed as though he was addressing a gathering some way behind me. In spite of this gross discrepancy in stature we got on tolerably well, though I was a little surprised to be invited to his home for a meal. Over dinner he broached the subject of an opera based on the tale of the Sleeping Beauty. He had done a libretto; would I like to do the music? I argued as politely as I could that the subject was too familiar, but he contended that it was an advantage for opera audiences to know the plot. The upshot of a long evening was that I agreed to try my hand at it. I took the neatly typed libretto home and put it on the piano to take its place in the positive queue of enterprises in which I was involved.

Between projects I worked at it quite industriously and within a couple of months had finished the first act. Guthrie was delighted with it and urged me to go on. My own view was rather less optimistic. I didn't like to say so but I felt that his treatment of the story was somewhat dated; I jibbed at writing any more without a reasonably firm prospect of production. Through his influence I arranged an audition at Sadler's Wells. There one afternoon I played and sang the whole of Act I to an audience consisting of Norman Tucker, James Robertson, Michael Mudie and (as an independent listener) Muir Mathieson. It was a slightly daunting experience but they paid me the compliment of listening to the end, even asking for a repeat of one section. Afterwards there was a long discussion centred mostly on such practicalities as expense. It was the general opinion (with which I wholly agreed) that the conception was too extravagant for a composer taking his first step into opera. 'Why don't you try your hand at a one-acter with a small cast?' said James Robertson. There were murmurs of approval and I went home by no means disheartened. A seed had been planted in my mind.

Although composition occupied the bulk of my time I continued to attempt to play the piano in public. Owing to my still feeble technique my repertoire was very limited. I therefore wrote three piano sonatas in the hope that one or other would provide a centrepiece to a recital programme. Unfortunately, vaulting ambition o'er-leaped itself and I found my own works too much of a handful to play accurately. I could put up a convincing bluff, though, and earned myself some flattering notices such as this one in the *Yorkshire Post*:

His Sonata in D minor (No. 1) proved to be an immediately acceptable work to which heart and mind had evidently made that fairly divided contribution without which music ... does not fulfill its function as a medium for entertainment. The treatment of the subject matter throughout is clear cut, the piano is used essentially as a lyrical instrument ... and one admired especially not only some exquisite touches of counterpoint, but the marked simplicity, in the slow movement, of the melodic line and the ease and straightforwardness with which it was brought to rest. In this work Mr Hopkins's playing was at its best, and he left us in no doubt that his superlative quality is well worth listening to.

They don't write notices like that nowadays, a nine-inch column to review a solo recital in Harrogate by an unknown. Hindsight tells me that words such as 'lyrical', 'simplicity', 'melodic', 'ease' and 'straightforwardness' were nails in my artistic coffin, a hymn of praise to obsolescent virtues. However, even the London press frequently lauded me during this period; the *Daily Mail* proclaimed EXCEPTIONAL MR HOPKINS in a headline above a Ralph Hill notice, praising a cantata that had been performed at the Wigmore Hall.

'This is not music for posterity, still less for critics,' says the most recent edition of Grove concerning my compositions. I rather thankfully agree but feel it is worth recording that I was extremely well received by a number of reputable critics when I was still in my twenties. It was enough to turn my head. It didn't, largely because I felt that it all belonged to the land of make-believe. I knew better than anyone how insecure were the foundations of my career. Naturally I enjoyed successes when they came, but I realised perfectly well that while the newspapers might bandy names, my talent was not to be compared with real composers such as Tippett, Britten, Rawsthorne or Berkeley. I used to describe myself as a musical carpenter, an odd-job man who could knock up anything to order. It was not an idle boast since I have been required to write music suitable for the fourth century BC and the twenty-first century AD as well as most of the centuries in between. I loved to write pastiche, putting on musical fancy-dress. Such eclecticism is suspect, but it proved to be a useful gift.

In June 1946 I spent a month up at Lichfield. To celebrate the seven-hundred-and-fiftieth anniversary of the cathedral, the Dean and Chapter decided to commission a religious drama from Dorothy L. Sayers. I was asked to write the music for choir, strings and organ. Having read all the Peter Wimsey stories I was greatly intrigued at the chance of meeting the authoress. She turned out to be something of an eccentric, even though the possessor of a formidable intellect. Her daily garb in the cathedral was a woolly tam-o'-shanter of rainbow hue, gym shoes and a fur coat that Flanagan would have envied. She, the cast and I were lodged in the Theological College in the Close, an environment which I found depressingly austere. I did my best to rise to her intellectual level but was ill-equipped to argue; she was fond of the last word in all conversations and would thump her points home with unanswerable vigour.

Some months before the first performance I had gone to Lichfield to play the music for 'The Just Vengeance' to the choir. It was poorly received since it sounded quite unlike the usual cathedral fare. 'It's very *modern*,' said an elderly choirman in disgust, while the organist, a Pickwickian figure if I ever saw one, prophesied disaster with considerable relish, piqued no doubt that he had not been asked to write it himself. The final rehearsals converted the unbelievers, giving me reassurance that the choir would at least bring some enthusiasm to their task. The problems of synchronisation were immense with the organ a nave's length away. I kept my foot on an electric button connected by at least fifty yards of flex to a green light in the organ loft. I would give 'a bar for nothing', blipping the light in time and hoping that no one had accidentally severed the connection.

Major and Signora travelled up from Berkhamsted for the occasion, their first long car journey since 1939. They arrived at the Angel Croft hotel just in time to see the Queen drive in state from the station to the Bishop's palace. The royal party, together with the Archbishop of York and the local cathedral dignitaries, sat in the front row. The performance was on a Wagnerian time-scale, nearly three hours without a break. Afterwards I was presented to the Queen who was, I felt, sincerely complimentary. Almost exactly thirty years later I was again presented to her, when she was the Queen Mother. 'Do you know,' she said, 'I've seen so many things in my life but that Lichfield occasion stands out quite clearly in my mind.'

It's as well she didn't come on the fourth night. I had been feeling very unwell all day and arrived at the cathedral looking green. I conducted the first chorus with black spots floating with increasing rapidity through my gaze. As soon as it ended I was enormously, comprehensively sick. Jacket, trousers and shoes were smothered and I collapsed, gasping, at the foot of the pillar that fortunately had concealed most of the misadventure from the public. Two St John's ambulance men tiptoed forward, as hastily as dignity would allow, their moment of glory upon them. With handfuls of cotton-wool they rubbed vigorously at my clothes. As I sat there on the cold stone floor I suddenly felt remarkably recovered. I was aware that the leading tenor had stepped gallantly on to my podium; baton in hand he was all ready to lead the choir into action. 'No you don't,' I muttered, and rose to my feet, tufts of cotton-wool clinging to my garments so that I resembled a sort of manic Santa Claus. 'Wish I'd known how you felt,' said Dorothy gruffly after the performance. 'I'd have shoved a finger down your throat this afternoon — that or a good strong dose of salt and water. Bring it all up, no trouble ...'

13
No Ring on her Finger

After what might be described as a five-year rehearsal Alison and I were finally married, a gesture towards convention largely prompted by the need for our passports to match. We had been extremely happy together and she had established quite a satisfactory career for herself teaching the piano at Morley and singing in a professional madrigal group of six voices known as The London Singers. She had a true clear voice of appealing quality but was bedevilled by nerves when she sang on her own. We did a Wigmore Hall recital together in a lunchtime series. Though she sang admirably and was well received, I almost had to frogmarch her on to the stage. In the end she decided that the preliminary agonies made the prospect of solo recitals seem hardly worthwhile. She was altogether less nervous working with a group and derived great enjoyment from the concerts they gave.

Her first involvement in matrimony had not been as successful as she must have hoped. I was reluctant to ensnare her in the marriage trap a second time since we were extremely contented as we were. We decided to have a sort of anti-wedding. It was a bitterly cold morning in February 1947 when we set out for Kensington Registry Office. Scorning the lures of Moss Bros I wore a duffel coat, a rather grubby white polo-neck sweater and thick corduroy trousers, while she was wrapped up as warmly as coupons would allow. We sat in a corridor for about quarter of an hour before being shown into a small office where the registrar sat behind a desk. I first began to feel sorry for him when we both gave the same address. He was clearly embarrassed by this breach of propriety.

'Have you got the ring?' he asked me, anxious, as it were, to change the subject.

'No,' I replied. 'Symbol of servitude; I don't believe in it. I never want her to wear one.'

'But you've got to have a ring,' he protested in some distress.

'Why? We're not in church. This is simply a legal ceremony. Surely you can marry us without a ring?'

We argued the matter for a few moments until, with considerable reluctance, he agreed that we *could* actually get married in spite of my strange attitude.

'Well now,' he said, 'who have you brought with you? Presumably you have some relatives or friends out there ...'

'Actually not. We prefer to keep it private. As you see we're already' — I was going to say 'living together' but I thought it might upset him — 'we're already sharing the same house. It seemed silly to bother to make a fuss about it.'

His face became quite stern. He cleared his throat a mite aggressively. 'If I may say so, you don't appear to be taking this wedding in a proper spirit. Marriage is a serious matter not to be taken on in this, er, frivolous state of mind. You have responsibilities towards each other and to society ...'

He warmed to the topic, beginning to enjoy this departure from the normal script. ... 'but we must have witnesses, be clear on that. Do without the ring if you will, but witnesses there must be.'

An exploration of the corridors produced two chars who willingly put aside buckets and mops to come and have a little sit-down. In their presence our union was endorsed by the State. I tipped them ten shillings between them and we went out into the winter air legal.

'We must have a wedding breakfast,' I said as we hurried past Barker's. 'Let's go to the Majestic.' It was a slightly posh café opposite Derry and Toms, grander than Lyons or a milk bar but not ruinous. We sat down, the sole customers since it was barely midday. There was no heating. The waitress came to us unwillingly, hunched with cold.

'Coffee, with lots of milk,' I said cheerily. 'I like mine very white.'

'No milk,' she said. 'Sorry.'

I looked at Alison. 'Do you mind it black?' 'No, that's alright; anything, so long as it's warm.'

'Right. Black coffee for the lady and tea for me; no, on second thoughts I'll have a glass of water.' (I couldn't stand tea without milk.) 'And could we have some nice biscuits ...'

'We got no biscuits, not sweet ones that is. We got some cheese biscuits, you know, the square ones.'

It was truly Austerity Britain; even so, not many can claim to have had a glass of water and a dry biscuit as a wedding feast.

The following month I began a tour that was to take me to thirteen towns in France and Switzerland. I was to accompany Sophie Wyss, the soprano for whom Britten wrote 'Les Illuminations'; I was also to play some English music. I had read my way through pages of Bax, Ireland, Rawsthorne and the like but had found it all beyond me — too many notes and too fast! Fortunately I had my first two piano sonatas to fall back on. We travelled mostly by train, long arduous journeys through a countryside still heavily scarred by war. One letter survives:

March 25th '47

Dear Folks,

Thank you for the letters which I got last Thursday at Dijon. All goes remarkably well: concerts a great success and my stock has never been higher. Today was our first free day and I must say it was very welcome, even if I was so tired that I slept like the dead in the afternoon.

All the towns are lovely and interesting and full of beautiful old houses: people are very kind to us and show us round, and at Dijon on my birthday after the concert (which was an absolute riot!) we had a 'vin d'honneur' which means that all the bigwigs of the town, mayors and suchlike, gather round an enormous table and drink our health in champagne and make speeches and things. As we had already had a banquet at lunchtime I had quite a birthday!

We were driven up from Grenoble to Dijon — a wonderful drive through the Jura mountains along the most marvellous wild gorges with swift-flowing rivers at the bottom. We were held up by a bridge which was still blown up from the war, and had to go 12 miles out of our way and cross the river by a dam. I'm thankful we did because it gave us the best scenery of all . . .

Tomorrow is the last concert in France then we go over the border. I heard from Alison that the bookings for our holidays are alright, so we will be staying at 'Der Schiff', Ascona, Lac Maggiore, Switzerland. I shall be there from the 4th of April till the 16th. A. is hoping to come out earlier than she had intended. I hope she does as I miss her terribly and even with all the excitement am awfully lonely.

The tour, sponsored by the British Council, had begun in Paris at the Salle Gaveau. The pedal squeaked irritatingly on the piano and during the interval a porter in blue overalls and a beret knelt beneath the instrument, squirting oil into its vitals. In spite of this I seem to have scored a critical success.

Antony Hopkins, âgé de 25 ans seulement, est destiné . . . à prendre la tête de la jeune école anglaise, aux côtés d'un Benjamin Britten. Sa 'Sonate en ré mineur' manifeste un très beau tempérament musical: tourmentée, expressive, prenante, elle a un accent intensément personnel qui ne s'oublie pas. L'auteur est de plus un pianiste de grand classe: sonorité, veloutée jusque dans la puissance, poésie ensorceleuse, jeu extraordinairement nuancé, vivant, jamais mécanique ou statique, changeant comme les formes des nuages.

They were very pro-British at the time. My 'tormented expressive' sonata has disappeared from even my repertoire, though I like to think that my bewitching poetry is still extraordinarily nuanced.

Switzerland seemed like a literal fairyland, the shop-windows stacked with almost forgotten delights. I used to stand in a daze taking in a visual feast of chocolates, glacé fruits, richly iced cakes and fruit tarts, my tummy rumbling its appreciation. Instinctively one felt for a ration-book before trying to buy anything. Staying in a monstrously grand hotel in Geneva, I went early to the dining-room for a light supper before the concert. Clad in tails, I was the only guest in the lofty restaurant. Four waiters converged on me, bearing menus or wheeling huge trollies of *hors d'oeuvre*, but I simply wanted an omelette and an icecream. I looked at the unwieldy menu, bewildered by the columns of gastronomic French. On the right hand page I saw the word '*Omelette*', a welcome beacon amidst a vocabulary that school had never prepared me for. Nervously I pointed to it. '*Omelette Surprise, et puis un glace, s'il vous plaît.*' The waiter babbled something incomprehensible, so I repeated my order more firmly. Again a stream of incoherent French. Seeing that I was nonplussed, he summoned yet another colleague who explained in English that an *Omelette Surprise* was an icecream; surely I did not want icecream twice? I was unnerved. The following night I rashly made an announcement in French which I had carefully prepared. 'I have played my first piano sonata at every concert I have given in the last ten days,' I said. 'Tonight I would like to play my second sonata for a change.' I thought the reaction a little strange, but went to it with a will. Sophie was laughing in the wings as I came off.

'Do you know what you said?'

'No.'

'— that you'd played your first sonata at every concert you'd given in the last ten *years*!'

At the end of the tour I went on to Ascona on my own and spent the weekend at 'Der Schiff', at that time the perfect small hotel which is now virtually impossible to find. Situated at the north end of the lake it offered a picture-postcard view of the island where Toscanini had a villa. The village was drowsy, unspoilt by tourism, an ideal spot for a long delayed honeymoon. The hotel staff were slightly mystified by the bridegroom's solo arrival though I felt that it harmonised well with the unorthodoxy of our wedding. On the Monday I took the bus to Bellinzona, aiming to surprise Alison and to help her change from the express to the little local train. Concealed behind a pillar I watched the huge transcontinental engine ease its bulk along the platform, brakes squealing in protest. Doors opened, voices called, porters hurried. Bandbox-neat she descended the awkwardly high steps, the large suitcase thumping down beside her. I circled and came up behind her.

'Helpa la signora witha da baggagio,' I carolled in the phoniest Italian accent.

'No thank you,' she said in tones calculated to chill the ardour of Casanova himself. 'I can manage quite well . . .'

She was so busy tossing her head and protesting her virtue that she had not given me a glance; then suddenly she realised that the voice had been faintly familiar. She turned; the pain of a month apart melted as the train wolf-whistled at our embrace.

It was a blissful honeymoon, free from the awkward skirmishing and unaccustomed intimacy that must often seem an embarrassment to newly-weds. After the long war years and the routine privations we had grown to accept, even the simplest pleasures seemed a luxury. We were like children let loose in a story-book world.

During my absence the builders had been at work in Campden Street. Alison had bought a small house there, its top floor not too severely damaged by an incendiary bomb. We planned to knock four small rooms into two large ones, a major alteration that took some time. We moved in soon after our return from Switzerland. The holiday was over and I settled down to a hard summer's work.

June '47

Dear Folks

Nothing much to report here except great heat and a lot of music-copying . . .

Some of my 'works' are being broadcast about July 21st — I can't remember the exact date but look out in that week: 3rd programme 6.30 I think . . .

Great excitement this week. British Council had urgent enquiry for my music for *Oedipus* to be done in Istanbul. Nobody could find the score for two days, but all is now well and it has been sent to Turkey. What with the 'Just Vengeance' being done in Buenos Aires and *Oedipus* in Istanbul the works of A.H. are getting propagated fairly widely.

I now have to kill myself getting the film done in time as Peter Ustinov gets back from America tomorrow. I have been unable to do much until his return. Unfortunately the date for recording music is fixed for July 28th. Would it amuse you to come to the studios to hear a recording session? You could drive across to Denham fairly easily . . .

The film was *Vice Versa*, the first feature that I had been asked to do. My initiation into the film world had been so strange that it is worth making a diversion to recount the experience. I cannot remember exactly how the contact was made, but having earned quite a reputation as a composer of incidental music for radio, I was not surprised to be asked if I would be interested in 'assisting' a film composer. Scenting big money and happy to prostitute my art if the price was right I agreed to meet the great man. His name was Brodsky. He lived in a surprisingly squalid flat in The White House, Albany Street. I arrived by appointment at midday; I was slightly taken aback by his appearance, unshaven and wearing blue and white striped pyjamas, no dressing-gown. It seemed to worry him less than it did me and the conversation quickly turned to business.

'Zis ees a littul love t'eme zat I wrote yestoday,' he said with a Soho waiter's accent; 'mebbe you stretch heem out to tree minnits, yes?'

He handed me a single sheet of manuscript paper on which about twelve bars of music had been inscribed in a spidery hand.

'You mean you want me to use this as a starting-point and then develop it into a three-minute piece?'

'Zassa right — lak I said, stretch heem out. Amma too busy; writa so much myself.'

'Do you want me to orchestrate it?'

'Oh no-a, joost indicate . . .'

'Just indicate the instruments?'

'Yes.' A pause to show the burden of creativity. 'When-a ze horns come in, you know . . .'

A few days later I returned with a satisfactorily stretched-out love t'eme, (TH was a grave problem for him) and was given another fragment in exchange. Over a month or so the weird ritual continued, each piece earning me a fiver. I soon noticed that his handwriting changed week by week. It seemed that he was acting as a sort of musical sorting office, passing off others' work as his own and circulating it among a group of minions. My final contribution was a splendid Elgarian march of which I was quite proud. ('I want-a sumsing very Eenglish. Amma not Eenglish — you do heem better.') He told me it was to be used for the opening titles of a film called *Demi-Paradise*, starring Laurence Olivier as a Russian engineer over here on some wartime mission.

Months later I took a few friends to the Fulham Forum to see this epic. The newsreel ended, the curtains swished down decoratively and then opened again as the man whammed the gong. The titles came up to unrecognisable music. After a moment or two my friends made thumbs up signs. 'Very good,' they mouthed in a hoarse whisper. 'Not mine,' I whispered back, indignant at having been put in such a false position. Towards the end of the film there was a typically 'Eenglish' fête in the grounds of a stately home. A comic village band in ill-fitting uniforms assembled, honking ineptly. The conductor tapped his stand. 'My God,' I thought, the Knitting-needle strikes again. Out of tune and time the band launched into my march, its *nobilmente* strains reduced to a travesty. I stood up, gesticulating in anguish. 'My music, my music!' I cried. An angry usherette flashed her torch at me and I subsided miserably as a storm broke, the heavens opened and the band played on, rain pouring down their instruments, their music flapping in the gale. I resolved that if I were to write for films I would do it on my own.

Vice Versa was an altogether happier experience. Peter Ustinov and I shared a similar sense of humour. The score was full of parody and at the première the opening titles were generously applauded, some compensation for the Fulham débâcle. (A touch of neatness was added to my untidy career by the coincidence that both my first feature film and my last — *Billy Budd* — involved Peter. We collaborated on several projects over the years.)

1947 was especially productive. In addition to the wedding, the foreign tour, the honeymoon and the first film, I wrote a ballet, initially arranged for two pianos, and my one-act opera, *Lady Rohesia*. Encouraged by the reception I had been given at Sadler's Wells, I had been keeping an eye open for a likely subject. I knew that I hadn't the musical stature for a big drama; comedy was more my line. Someone suggested that I should try the Ingoldsby Legends and there I found a story that seemed to me entirely suitable for operatic treatment. Set in the early sixteenth century, it was a farcical death-bed scene in which Lady Rohesia, about to breathe her last, beats a hasty retreat from Death's embrace when she realises that her husband is on the point of proposing to the seductive little serving-maid, Beatrice Grey. As their lips meet in a loving kiss, she rises like the Angel of Wrath and whacks him on the head with a warming-pan.

It was enough for a scene but not an act. I decided to invent a second part in which the situations would be reversed, the husband on the death-bed, the wife getting off with the priest. In this way I would be remaining true to the essential features of Barham's original. So far as I could I retained every word of his dialogue but expansion was still necessary. Ever since I had become involved in the theatre I had been fascinated by that aspect which had also so intrigued Pirandello, the actor *behind* the role. What is he thinking as he speaks words from another's mind, wears clothes that are foreign to him, performs acts that he would not dream of in real life? I thought that it might be amusing to let the concealed self come to the surface at times. Aware of that strange operatic personage, the prompter, who from within his shell steers the singers through the score, I devised a part for him. Germanic, humourless, hating the irreverence of my treatment of the subject, sceptical of anything remotely modern, he represented the deadweight of tradition at its worst. Yet, although he supposedly hated the opera, his professional conscience forced him to try to do it justice. Stepping through the curtains, he interrupted the orchestral prelude with an *apologia*, sung as an accompanied recitative:

If the composer knew that I was making this announcement he would be mad at me; but I feel we owe it to ourselves in self-defence. The opera you now are going to hear is another of these modern works. For my taste give me the classics, but there — I'm old-fashioned ... We've been rehearsing this for months now, but still we aren't safe, at least not what I would call safe. So if during the performance anything comes unstuck, kindly give us your indulgences. Thank you, thank you. All right Jack, get on with the overture.

Thus spoke not Zarathustra but 'Herr Kochenocker', setting my operatic frolic on its irreverent way. Periodically things were supposed to go wrong and he, in desperation, would rush on stage to get the opera back on course. The humour was at times surrealistic, influenced no doubt by my many collaborations with Louis Macneice.

Having completed the rough score, I went off to Sadler's Wells to play it through to the directors. It was accepted, to my great delight; I quickly settled down to the finger-cramping back-aching labour of making a full score, 377 pages written fair in three weeks.

Rehearsals began the following February. For six weeks I worked in the theatre nearly every day, teaching the cast their notes and involving myself in all aspects of the production. Geoffrey Dunn was the witty and inventive producer, Tanya Moiseiwitsch (from *Dr Faustus* days) designed the set and costumes. We had some hilarious sessions dreaming up 'business' to keep the action bubbling along. Many years later, Kate Jackson, who

played the title role, told me she had enjoyed it more than anything she'd ever done at the Wells. 'We had such *fun!*' she said,
and laughed out loud at the memory. The management offered
me every support, in particular James Robertson who gave me
wonderfully helpful advice about operatic conducting, a rather
different skill from concert work.

As I groped my way into the pit on the first night I felt once
again a quick spasm of incredulity. In no way had my College days
prepared me for this. What suddenly frightened me was the
number of other people involved apart from me — the orchestra,
the seven singers, the scene painters, the carpenters, the stage-
hands, a professional team to whom I owed a quite unpayable
debt of gratitude. Up to that moment I had always been one of
such a team myself, a contributor to the overall effect but certainly not the star. Now, as a composer, librettist and conductor I
was perched on the apex of a pyramid, uncertain of my hold.
With something of a gulp I acknowledged the friendly welcome of
a full house.

> The first-night house at the Wells laughed its head off. People
> barked. They bellowed. They choked. They mopped the happy
> tears from their eyes . . .

So wrote Charles Reid, the music critic, in a long article in a
magazine of the day. He went on to express his misgivings about
the 'snook-cocking' in the opera, the iconoclasm.

> . . . English opera is too tender and vulnerable to be guyed with
> safety. It is the business of Sadler's Wells, surely, to persuade
> people to take it seriously. Why encourage people to laugh at it?

Although Reid was disturbed by my lack of reverence, he paid the
music some handsome compliments, as did that doyen of music
critics, Ernest Newman.

> More ingenuity than is perhaps apparent on the surface has
> gone to the making of *Lady Rohesia*, of which Sadler's Wells
> gave us a first performance on Wednesday. When I heard that
> Antony Hopkins was making an 'operatic frolic' out of the well-
> known story in the Ingoldsby Legends I wondered how that
> would be possible; the theme seemed too slight for the stage. Mr

Hopkins, however, has made short work of that little problem: he takes Barham over intact for his first scene, and then contrives another, equally delightful, by the simple process of reversing the motivation of the first. It is astonishing, by the way, how easily the original adapts itself to a stage action: Mr Hopkins has been able, as he says in his programme note, to use 'almost every word of the original dialogue'. The technique of construction is in general that made familiar to us by Sheridan in *The Critic*; a glorious piece of fooling is made still funnier by the constant intervention of a worried producer.

My own grievance was that too many of the words were unintelligible, partly because of the continuous laughter of the audience, partly because some of the lines are written at a pitch too high for clear enunciation. I found myself next day with only a general impression of the music; one will be able to see it in clearer detail when one can concentrate on it more exclusively, taking the situations and the words more for granted that one could do at a first hearing. The little work as a whole is the most riotous fun imaginable. The performance was very good throughout, with an exceptionally fine-fingered piece of comedy in Rose Hill's Beatrice Gray.

Critical opinion was divided though, and Desmond Shawe-Taylor dismissed the opera in a single, witheringly contemptuous sentence. At the end of the season, the governors took Charles Reid's point and decided that the piece was not really suitable for the theatre. There were no hard feelings, since the following year they put on quite a lengthy ballet to my music. Originally performed for the Ballet Club on a Sunday night with two pianos under the title 'Mirages', it was subsequently renamed 'Etude' and performed with full orchestra. I again conducted all the performances, by then feeling quite an old hand.

A vivid memory comes back from that initial Sunday. The young company had rehearsed three ballets all day with only two short breaks. After the performance there was a birthday-party for one of the dancers on stage. Tired though we were, we all attended, the girls wearing their prettiest dresses, the boys dandily Bohemian. At around eleven at night some malicious soul put on a record of the dances from 'The Bartered Bride'. There were squeals of dismay followed by a mad rush to shove trestle-tables and chairs into the wings. In what seemed a matter of seconds, the whole company took up formation and whirled into the dance with quite unbelievable exuberance. I stood at the side of the stage spellbound, wondering at the precision and agility they displayed after so exhausting a day.

Although both works have long disappeared from the repertory, my two ventures at Sadler's Wells were an experience to be treasured, possibly the most valuable of my professional life. It is perhaps better to have had a brief taste of such glories than to have them dulled by repetition.

VIC — WELLS ASSOCIATION BULLETIN
Feb. 1948

(Extract)
Twelfth Night Party

... Mr Wright first presented Antony Hopkins, whose new opera *Lady Rohesia* was soon to be produced. He explained that Mr Hopkins was anxious to sing the title-role himself, but Sadler's Wells never accepted anyone, however well qualified, without giving them an audition.

Antony Hopkins appeared, wearing complete *Madam Butterfly* costume, and sang 'One Fine Day'* in a beautiful falsetto voice, with certain deviations from the score.

* A mere semitone down!

14
A Service Faulted

'Did we tell you we're going to get married?' said Debbie half-way through the meal. 'No; congratulations, well done.' A starry look came into her eyes and she suddenly pointed at me across the table. 'I've had a *marvellous* idea — you could play for the wedding.' My hand halted on its mouthward path and then returned unsteadily to the plate. 'Please not,' I said, 'I haven't touched the organ for five years and I was always lousy at it.'

'Oh, come on,' said Colin, the groom-to-be. 'Anyone who can play the piano can play the organ —'

'They jolly well can't; that's a typical string-player's remark.' (Colin and I had been close friends since College days; he was a good violinist but lost on a keyboard.) Debbie put on her most appealing look.

'You must, Tony. We've both known you so long; you're almost like one of the family. Anyway,' (giggling mischievously) 'you wouldn't *charge* us anthing would you . . .'

'When you've heard me play you wouldn't want to *pay* me anything.'

My protests were useless in the face of their combined appeal. Then and there she reached out for the menu-card with its frugal choice of three main dishes, turned it over and started to make a list of pieces she would like me to play. With the ruthlessness of wartime waiter I went through it striking off each item in turn.

'If you want a menu,' I said firmly, 'it's got to be Table d'hôte; you'll have what I can play and lump it. During the gathering of the clans I'll improvise —'

'Funk!' said Colin, knowing that I was probably the only

student in the history of the College who'd had the cheek to improvise at a grading exam, *and* passed!

'Funk you. Debbie, you may enter to the 'Trumpet Voluntary' . . .'

'That's OK, I like that.'

I went on, 'Hymns I don't mind; I can cope with them. They're all in minims so they don't frighten me.'

'Are we having any hymns?' said Colin to Debbie.

'I should think so; I don't know — haven't thought really.'

'Shut up both of you. You know that bit where everyone goes off and signs the Visitors' Book —'

'Register, silly!'

'Well, how do I know? None of my relatives has ever been married . . . Anyway, during that bit I am prepared to offer you what Malcolm Sargent calls "Please be kind to me". I hummed the opening phrase of the famous minuet from the 'Water Music'. 'Afterwards you may emerge radiant and transformed to the strains of Mendelssohn's "Wedding March". I can just about manage that even after five years.'

We finished the meal in high spirits and I jotted down the date of the wedding in my diary.

It was due to take place at Holy Trinity, Brompton Road, one of London's most fashionable churches. (I knew the organist well since Alison sang professionally in the choir.) The evening before the nuptials, I took a bus to Knightsbridge and went into the church. Confronted with the organ I saw at a glance that it was a Formula One job with more power than I could ever handle. With a sinking heart I switched on and slid into place. There seemed to be hundreds of stops. Experimentally I jabbed at a few thumb-pistons. Lights flicked on to either side of me; I felt as if I was on a flare path, ready for take-off. I engaged the starboard engine and a gigantic chord of D minor roared into life.

I practised for about an hour and a half, not excessive considering that I was bewildered by the instrument's gadgetry. It kept on doing things I didn't ask it to, but I felt I had it more or less under control. The next day I arrived sharp at 2.00 for 2.15. There didn't seem to be many people about; indeed the church itself appeared to be completely empty.

'Have I come on the right day?' I asked the verger anxiously, 'or is it three o'clock, not two?'

'No, it's two-fifteen alright,' he said reassuringly, 'but they don't seem to have asked anybody.'

It was surprising in so grand a church, but I presumed it was because the bride's parents were very upper-class, the groom's rather lower. Perhaps neither family wished anyone to witness this gross betrayal of the English class system. At any rate there they sat in the choir stalls looking a little glumly at each other and from time to time surveying the rows of empty pews. I was about to take my place at the instrument Dryden so rightly called the 'wondrous machine' when the verger grabbed my sleeve and said, 'Excuse me, there is no choir today, but the vicar does rather like a played Amen at the end of the prayers. Could you oblige?'

'My dear chap,' I replied, 'you can have any one of three,' and hummed him a going-up one, a coming-down one and a staying-on-the-same-note one — all from memory . . . (Not for nothing had I acquired those diplomas.)

'Whichever you like,' he whispered. 'Nobody'll sing them anyway.'

I felt somehow comforted at this opportunity for free enterprise. Discreetly, I made my way along the side aisle to the console, halfway down the church. I pressed the little red button marked ON and the mighty organ came to life. With memories of school chapel floating through my mind I began to improvise in D.

In due course a buzzer buzzed, a tiny red light winked — she was without! Boldly I launched into the 'Trumpet Voluntary', trying to ensure that I didn't accidentally drift into the theme of the Brahms-Handel Variations which it initially resembles. In the middle of the piece comes a rather dull bit where Jeremiah Clarke stopped trying. I thought this would be a good moment to have a look round to see what progress the bride and her father were making through the virtually empty church; was she hastening to the altar or proceeding with dignity? Straining at an awkward angle to peer over my right shoulder without losing touch with Jeremiah, I inadvertently raised my right knee. Beneath the lowest manual was a secret device about which nobody had ever warned me. It was a sort of trip-rod whose sole function was to cancel, beyond recall, the trumpet stop. I felt as if the starboard engine had failed; we were in dire peril. Panic set in as I dabbed feverishly at the nearest (and then the furthest) stops, trying to bring my trumpet-player back to life. The wretched trip-rod had scuppered him for keeps and my efforts were in vain. Meanwhile left hand and feet ploughed on, ill-co-ordinated but relentless.

Brides are supposed to weep at their weddings, but not with laughter. She was brought to the altar in no fit condition for so important an occasion. As for me, I was sincerely hoping that earthquake, fire or flood would cut short the proceedings and permit a re-play on another day. Somehow I laid the trumpeter's remains to rest. The service began.

Owing to the extreme paucity of the congregation the vicar decided to conduct the ceremony in unusually intimate tones. 'Dearly beloved brethren ...' he began, or so I imagined. I couldn't actually *hear* a word, just a faint ecclesiastical murmur without the slightest definition to it. With my hand cupped to my ear, like Beethoven trying to hear a late quartet, I strained to catch some clue that would tell me how things were going in the invisible chancel. Nothing. From time to time there appeared to be a complete silence so I would drop in a tentative Amen for luck.

Alison arrived quarter of an hour late for the wedding, having mistaken the time. A lone figure, she sat in the unpopulated pews, mute witness to the distant spectacle. Experienced chorister that she was, she knew the marriage service by heart. 'You did three Amens too many,' she said mockingly afterwards. I still don't know where.

15
Speed Unlimited

Although I had learnt to drive in wartime, first in the Commer van and then (rather more dashingly) in Alison's Ford Popular, I did not own a car until 1950. During the war years we made a number of forays into Kent in an estate car whose rear had been converted into a miniature concert platform, complete with upright piano. It was a dangerously tail-happy vehicle and on one occasion I frightened Alison considerably by dodging to avoid a chicken. The piano took over and we proceeded down the road in a series of graceful zig-zags, clipping the verges on either side with metronomic precision. We arrived at the gun-site to give our concert with a more than usually nervous soprano, but I had enjoyed the experience, the screech of tyres music to my ears. However, for six years I never sat behind a steering-wheel. Severe petrol-rationing had put a stop to virtually all private motoring, and once we were living in London a car seemed unnecessary.

Then, one June morning in 1950, WAR IN KOREA screamed the headlines. I sat in bed reading the paper. 'Here we go again,' I said to Alison. 'We'll all be in it within a year and do you realise — I'll never have had a car of my own. I really think I'll buy one before it's too late!' That very day I bought an evening paper and started to scan the advertisements with some thoroughness. Within a week I had become the proud owner of a 2½-litre MG drophead coupé, black, with a long slim bonnet and wire wheels. GHT 222 was its number and I called 'her' Ger-Her-Trude. I would imagine I was the third or fourth owner but I felt no end of a fellow drivin' round in such a snazzy bus. My first trip out of town was to the Bryanston Summer School; there, on two miles of private road, I practised racing gear changes, blipping the throttle to get the revs just right, and terrorising wandering students.

It so happened that at the time I was involved in a group called Opera Trio. With two singers to illustrate the points, I used to give a fairly lighthearted talk on opera, culminating in a performance of Wolf-Ferrari's 'Susanna's Secret' or Menotti's 'The Telephone'. The need to ferry two passengers plus operatic costumes to numerous music clubs gave me an excuse to go in for a grander style of motoring. Within a year Ger-Her-Trude had been replaced by BWidGet, a seductive Jaguar drophead, the handsome pre-Mark V model that looked like a Bentley — well, nearly. It was the beginning of a love affair with the marque that was to last for many years.

I still remember the instant, love-at-first-sight thrill of the first XK 120 at the Motor Show. It was bronze, not my favourite colour, but its lines were so exquisite, so clearly designed for speed that I wanted one more than any single object I had ever seen. Of course, it was a hopeless dream since they were made for export only. However, a two-seater with minimal luggage-space was quite impractical for my needs; sadly I resigned myself to the fact that I would never be able to have one.

One day, in Malvern, I saw a scarlet XK in a Jaguar dealer's showroom window. I kept returning to look at it, utterly seduced by its beauty. Finally, as though under a spell, I went in. Dry-mouthed, scarcely daring to speak, I asked whether it was for sale.

'No, Sir, I'm afraid not; demonstration only. Of course we'll be happy to order one for you, Sir. About two years' delivery for the home market.'

Two years . . . it was an unreal period in which anything might happen. I could become rich. Even if not . . . Hypnotised by the gleaming metal I signed a form, wondering how I would break the news of such irresponsible extravagance to Alison. (She was Scottish on both sides of her family, perpetually worried by my profligate attitude to money.) It is hard to make a wife see reason over such matters but after some argument she agreed that if I managed to save up two thousand pounds I could buy one. Incredible though it may seem nowadays, the XK was originally priced at £988, plus purchase tax· of course. £1263 in all still seemed a bargain.

By the autumn of 1952 I had acquired the magic sum. A few of my dream cars had begun to filter on to the home market, 571 in all, 8% of the production, were sold at home between 1950 and 1953, and I started to search the advertisements eagerly for a second-hand one since my man in Malvern was pessimistic about delivery. I don't think Alison took it seriously. Then, one day when I had been babbling away about 'my' XK, she said, 'What are you going to do about touring with Opera Trio? You don't imagine you can get two singers and their luggage into a sports car, do you?'

'Oh, I'll keep the drophead. The XK's for me — well, for us.' Diplomatic, that.

'You're not going to have *two* Jaguars?'

'Yes.'

She crumpled visibly under this mortal blow to rationality. With eminent logic she pointed out the folly of buying an open two-seater at the onset of winter; if I was determined to persist in this madness, at least postpone it till the spring; my birthday was due in March; why not wait until then, and so on. I felt she was going back on her word. Here was I, a model husband, non-drinker, non-smoker, passable cook, thrifty enough to save the almost unthinkable sum of two thousand pounds, and she was objecting to a simple little proposal that I should have two Jaguars. It seemed so unreasonable that I retired to bed with a temperature, and lay there racked with psychosomatic pains for three days. Then the phone rang. It was Roy from the garage in Bayswater where BWidGet was serviced.

'I hear there's an XK for sale at Inwards' in Ruislip,' he said helpfully. 'It's Mr Inwards' demonstrator; only got 3000 miles on the clock. Sounds a good buy. Better hurry though; sure to be lots of people after it.'

Feverishly (I did have a temperature of 101) I took down the address, begged him to ask Inwards to fend off buyers for an hour, flung on some clothes and tore out of the house. Within thirty minutes I arrived in Ruislip. O wondrous sight! There it was in the window, virginal white with red tartan seats and a number plate that had a gloriously onomatopoeic sound, WMF 338. 'It spells Woo-mm-ff!' I thought to myself, and growled like an open exhaust. Ten minutes later they had wheeled it out and I was in the driving seat, caressing the steering wheel with loving fingers. I started it up. It was better than any organ; indeed, if organs could make a comparable sound I would have practised enough to worry Thalben Ball himself. (Years later, my eighth choice on 'Desert Island Discs' was the sound of Jaguars accelerating up the Mulsanne straight at Le Mans; it greatly upset some of my more spiritual listeners.) With Mr Inwards' minion palely clutching, I was soon roaring down the Denham bypass with 110 on the clock, my sickness miraculously cured. I duly wrote out a cheque for something like fifteen hundred pounds (Jaguars were at a premium) and arranged for delivery the next day.

Concerts and lecture-recitals took me all over the British Isles. Twenty-six to thirty thousand miles a year was my normal stint; I would therefore trade in my car every year in exchange for a new one. I never kept an exact record but between 1951 and 1966 I must have had at least fourteen Jaguars, culminating in an alarmingly fast lightweight E-type with a full D-type engine, 5-speed box, aluminium body, wide wheels and the ability to go from 0-100 m.p.h. in under twelve seconds.

Although I loved them all, ordering each new model as soon as it was announced, they were not the luckiest of cars when it came to travelling abroad. I had several curious slow-speed accidents of which the strangest happened north of Poitiers as we were returning from a holiday in Portugal. The amount of money we were allowed to take abroad was severely limited but even so we had managed to go to the extreme south and back. On the penultimate day we were having a picnic lunch by the roadside. Lying on a rug behind the car I noticed that the tyres were completely bald. There was no question of buying new ones since we only had about twelve pounds between us. I wondered whether I should get out the spare wheel and stick it on but decided against it for two reasons; first, it might be better to have matching tyres, however poor, rather than a new one on one side and a bald one on the other; second, it would be an awful fag to unload the tight-packed boot and then reload it. We tidied up, put up the hood (as there were some threatening clouds about), climbed in and resumed our homeward journey. It was a Bank Holiday Saturday and, as we emerged from Poitiers, traffic was a continuous stream, flowing rather sluggishly. A few kilometres further north we were diverted on to a minor road whose edges were frayed like nibbled pastry round a pie. 'Route glissée' warned the sign, complete with little pictograph. We crossed a dark bar on the tarmac showing where rain had fallen a minute or two earlier. We were in a line of traffic ambling along at not more than thirty-five miles an hour. The rear end twitched, fighting for grip on the shiny black surface. Alison gasped. 'Careful,' she said, 'it's very skiddy.' 'It's alright,' I reassured her, 'nothing I can't control.' With which oft-quoted words I gave a Moss-like flick of the wheel to correct the incipient slide. As though stung in the bum by a bee, the car shot right and waltzed on to the grass verge. Nose-first we struck a slim and flexible sapling; like a spring it lifted us into the air, rolling us over and spinning us round, so that we landed upside down in the ditch, facing the way we had come. There was a near silence, broken by the sound of wheels spinning to a halt above us. Voices shouting excitedly in French, running feet.

'Are you alright?'

'Yes ... Are you?'

'Yes.'

We sat inverted, maintaining a very English calm. Eager hands clutched at Alison, dragging her through the window. I came out the other side, a tiny cut on my scalp bleeding spectacularly even though it was no bigger than a fingernail. We had hit a freak stretch of road. Within minutes there were five crashes involving thirteen cars, all in a space of two hundred metres.

Two English lads pulled up on a motorbike. 'Nasty,' said one, peering with interest at the underside of the XK. 'Didn't I see you with your Opera Trio?' It was the sort of occasion when one would have preferred not to have been recognised. Soon the drizzle began to turn to rain and a gendarme suggested that we should take shelter in a farm cottage on the other side of the road. With Gallic courtesy he stepped into the middle of the road and held up an authoritative hand to enable us to cross over. The car nearest him stopped; the one behind didn't. There was a clang, a tinkle of breaking glass and shouted imprecations from the indignant driver. 'Imbécile! Que faites-vous ...' His wife began to scream fluent but incomprehensible abuse at the shaken occupants of the offending vehicle. Taking Alison by the arm I crossed the road, giving a restrained Royal Salute to express our appreciation.

The cottage had no telephone so I went out into the rain again, my face dramatically streaked with blood, my hair bright purple with mercurochrome, daubed on by an enthusiastic first-aider. I began to flag down British cars, with the simple idea of getting a message to a garage in Poitiers. Perhaps because all eyes were on the considerable wreckage along the road, I was unsuccessful at first. I didn't like to ask the gendarme again for fear of provoking yet another accident. Seeing a Rolls-Royce approach at a crawl, I stepped almost in front of its stately radiator and brought it to a halt.

'Excuse me, but we've had a bit of a prang — you see the XK over there; I wonder if you'd mind stopping at a garage and getting them to send . . .'

'Terribly sorry, old boy, we're in a bit of a hurry. Got to get down South, you know. You really ought to go and clean yourself up a bit. Why don't you go and have a good wash, eh? You've quite upset the wife.'

The Rolls glided away into the murk, exuding disapproval.

A few moments later a beautiful coach-built Bristol drew up without any signal from me. A cheerful voice called out, 'Had a spot of trouble, eh? Anything we can do to help?'

I explained about getting a message through to a breakdown crew.

'Of course; easily done. How are you off for funds?'

'Not too good, actually. We're on our way home; got about a tenner between us.'

'I can spare you . . . let's have a look — oooh, about twelve quid if you like. Can you give me a cheque?'

This was handsome indeed. The sums sound absurd nowadays but back in the early nineteen-fifties one could go a long way on ten pounds. Heartened by the Bristol-owner's Samaritan-like behaviour I went back into the cottage to await the arrival of the breakdown truck.

(Several months later I was performing at a music club in Somerset and the Samaritan came round to see me afterwards. I was thankful the cheque hadn't bounced.)

We were stranded in Poitiers for the weekend. The garage foreman told me he could do nothing for the time being but that he himself would check over the Jaguar on the Monday. The body was hideously crumpled but the chassis and engine might well be undamaged. We had been amazingly lucky; had we not landed in the fairly wide ditch we would surely have broken our necks. He drove us round the town, calling at every hotel in search of a room. There seemed to be nothing available. At last, in some desperation, he took us to the Café Terminus, opposite the railway station. It was a typical French bar, complete with coffee machine, wall mirror and a multitude of obscure alcoholic drinks.

'There is one room here,' said the good-looking young proprietor, 'but it is not very desirable.'

Damp and weary we trudged up the wooden stair. He was right. It wasn't very desirable. Pale green paper, heavily stained, peeled off the walls; a single unshaded light-bulb hung fly-blown from a flex; a hideous double bed sagged so wearily that it looked on the point of collapse.

'Tomorrow I will give you a nice room,' he said with an apologetic smile. 'I show you. In the courtyard, with balcony.'

We stayed, dispirited but, I suppose, glad to be alive.

No guests could have been treated with greater kindness. On Sunday the owner and his wife took us for a memorable picnic by a little stream. There he told us of his wartime experiences. He had escaped to England on a fishing-boat and enlisted with de Gaulle. The café was the realisation of a long-cherished dream, a dream whose fulfilment he felt he owed in large part to the English. The next evening he cooked us a special meal in the courtyard, barbecue fashion. We left early on the Tuesday morning in a very battered Jaguar. 'The bill,' I said, 'what about the bill?' 'You are my guests,' he replied with a warm smile; 'a small repayment for English hospitality.'

On the boat a fellow-passenger gaped in horror at the XK. 'Cor, that looks bad — whatever did you do?' 'I dropped it,' I replied.

The most unnerving of all my experiences with cars seemed to be a genuine case of haunting. As usual, when the new XK 150 model was announced I ordered one, resigned to the habitual long wait before any would be allowed to reach the home market. One afternoon, driving down Holland Park towards Brook Green (where we then lived) I saw a white hardtop 150 in Chipstead Motors. It was the first I'd seen except for pictures in the motoring magazines. I turned sharply into Norland Square, parked my 140 drophead, and hurried round to have a look. I'd always had a preference for open cars, but here was a genuine 150, apparently for sale with a mere 200 miles or so on the clock. Fixed head or not, I had to know more.

'Sad story, Sir. It was ordered by an American customer,

husband of —' He mentioned the name of a well-known English film star. 'Apparently the car was delivered to him one morning. He drove it round the block, said he was delighted with it and then went in for lunch. Before he could take it out again he had a heart-attack and died. The executors have instructed us to sell it; that explains why it's got delivery mileage only, Sir.'

The following day I bought it and became possibly the first private British owner of an XK 150. My first long journey came a couple of days later, a trip to Oldham in Lancashire. Arriving there in near darkness I saw to my dismay that the oil pressure had dropped to zero. Not wanting to damage a brand new engine I left the car on the forecourt of the first available garage, explained the problem, and carted my suitcase to my hotel. Examining the car the next morning they found that the drainage-plug at the bottom of the sump was nearly unscrewed; all the oil had leaked out. I swore mildly but dismissed the accident as bad assembly, no more.

The following night I had a long drive back to London, with little hope of arriving home until midnight. About fifteen miles from the outskirts of London the brakes failed completely. I crawled through the fortunately deserted streets with only a rather inefficient handbrake to check my progress. I left the car outside Chipstead's and took a taxi home. The foreman was mystified. The hydraulic fluid in the braking system had dribbled away, leaving pink snail-tracks all along the underside of the car. I was furious, accusing them of criminal carelessness; he was adamant that the car had been thoroughly checked.

My next journey out of town was to Stratford where I was in-volved in rehearsals of a play for which I had written some music. I had just escaped from the built-up area and was zooming happily down the hill towards Northolt when there was a sudden thump and the bonnet opened, completely blocking the windscreen. It was a nasty moment, but I stopped without coming to any further harm. I got out and surveyed the damage; the bonnet had been bent back so sharply that there was a sizeable dent in the roof. There was no way that the catch could have been left unfastened since, if the lock failed to shut properly, there was a secondary catch. If this was engaged, the bonnet would stay closed but loose enough to rattle about, something I could never have missed.

A week or two later I was down at Bournemouth, doing a

concert at the Winter Gardens. I left the car locked in the artists' car-park. After the rehearsal I started to drive off to have a meal; as I eased my way into the road, the passenger door opened. I couldn't believe it as I hadn't touched it since I had locked the car up on my arrival. I got out, shut the door firmly and locked it from the outside. I drove slowly down the hill, puzzling over the event. Less than a hundred yards along the road, the door opened again, smacking against a lamp-post with a nasty metallic thud. It was distinctly creepy.

'We can get it straightened out for you,' said Roy, running an expert hand over the damage, 'but no chance of getting it sprayed for the weekend.'

With the door painted with pale pink primer, Alison and I set off for Goodwood to watch the Easter Bank Holiday motor-racing, a regular jaunt that we both enjoyed. We stayed at a little hotel nearby and had a pleasant three-day break. The following Wednesday at about ten o'clock at night there was a knock at the door. A rather senior-looking policeman stood outside.

'Are you Mr Hopkins?'

'Yes.'

'Do you own a white Jaguar?'

'Yes?'

'Is there any damage on it?'

'As a matter of face there is; the near-side door was damaged. It's not properly repaired yet.'

'Have you been in the vicinity of Gerrards Cross recently?'

'Yes.' I had, twice that day, driving to and from Stratford.

'May I come inside, Sir; I'm afraid this is going to take rather a long time.'

'Of course, sorry, I should have thought of it.'

Alison came into the hall. 'Whatever's the matter? You look as white as a sheet . . .'

'I think I'd better speak to your husband alone, Madam.'

I was beginning to feel thoroughly guilty, though what of I didn't know. I ushered him into the sitting-room and closed the door.

'What's this all about, officer?' I said, uncertain of his rank.

'Well, Sir, there's been a fatal accident on the A40 near Gerrards Cross and it is alleged that your car was involved.'

I felt slightly sick. 'But I haven't been in an accident,' I protested. 'I couldn't have an accident without knowing ...'

'This was a rather unusual accident, Sir. It is alleged that this white Jaguar overtook another car and then cut in sharply in front of it — *so* sharply that the driver of the other car swerved, mounted the footpath and killed a pedestrian.' He paused for a moment, looked at me with an unblinking gaze. 'So you could have done it without knowing, couldn't you, Sir. Do you recall the incident at all?'

I was completely at a loss. Although I love to drive fast I always try to extend courtesy to other road-users. Cutting in sharply didn't sound like me; anyway, surely I'd have seen the accident in my mirror.

'When did this happen?' I asked, fearing the worst.

'Easter Monday, Sir.'

'But I was at Goodwood then; I was nowhere near Gerrards Cross.'

'Can you prove that, Sir?'

'Yes I can. I was at the BARC meeting. I can describe all the races to you — and we stayed at a hotel. How could my car have been involved?'

'*Alleged* to have been involved. It was a white Jaguar alright; we've got witnesses to that. Then one of our men saw you going through Gerrards Cross this morning, took your number and ... well, that's why I'm here, Sir. Sorry to have taken up your time.' He rose as if to leave. 'You don't mind if we just check with that hotel do you, Sir — purely for the record of course ...'

'No, of course not.'

Thinking it over I came to the conclusion that the car was haunted by its late owner, and that this catalogue of uncanny misfortunes could be attributed to his posthumous resentment that somebody else was enjoying the Jaguar which Fate had so unkindly denied him. I sold it back to Chipstead's. Curiously enough, although Jaguars were much in demand, they had some difficulty in selling it; it sat in the showroom window for about six months before it finally went.

My first trip to Le Mans for the twenty-four-hour race was in a coach party, the first and only time I've taken part in such an outing. We had splendid seats opposite the pits thanks to Thomas Cook's. On the day of the race we left Paris at about 6 am after a night in which I'd barely slept for an hour, so noisy was the traffic round the hotel. Though fatigue made me feel disoriented in the early hours of the next morning, the end of the race was intensely exciting. Conditions were appallingly wet, but we all stood and cheered the Rolt-Hamilton D-type Jaguar during its thrilling chase of the Gonzales Ferrari.

I cannot remember how I managed it but in the following year, 1955, I somehow became a very junior assistant to the BBC team covering the race. I travelled out on the Thursday with Raymond Baxter, arriving in time to watch the cars practising. I was as excited as a schoolboy, delighted to run errands or help in any way I could. Well after nightfall we went to a crowded restaurant bar in the main square of the town. As the only member of the party guaranteed to stay sober I began to feel boringly responsible at around one o'clock in the morning, suggesting to Raymond that it really was time we headed for the *château* where the BBC had arranged accommodation for us. It was supposedly a dozen miles away and we had not as yet communicated with the owner. A good half an hour after I had started to act as nanny, we left in a noisy convoy. 'Damn,' said Raymond, stabbing the brakes, 'I've lost the map.' We stopped in rather ragged formation. 'Has anyone got the map?' I asked, going from car to car. Nobody had. With only a vague idea of our destination we began a crazy rally-type exploration of the minor roads around Le Mans. At around two o'clock we stopped by a signal-box, the railway lines gleaming like silver in the clear moonlight. I ran up the steps and asked the signal-man the whereabouts of the *château*. He gave me detailed instructions which I tried to commit to memory. 'All's well,' I said to Raymond as I climbed back into the car. After a few kilometres we came to an imposing gateway. 'This is it,' I called out in triumph. We turned into the drive, prompting an enormous dog to bark ferociously at us. As we approached the house, lights came on on the first floor, curtains were flung back. To our astonishment a man clad in a red smoking-jacket appeared on the balcony, glass in hand. He was as surprised to see us as we were to see him. We were at the wrong *château*; we wanted the *château* of his cousin, so he informed us.

With friendly farewells we set off into the night once more. Successful at last we pulled up in the gravel courtyard as quietly as we could and unloaded our luggage. There was a handwritten notice on the door: '*Messieurs du BBC: vous trouverez vos chambres au premier étage, numeros 8-11.*'

The door was firmly locked. 'Let's try the back,' said Raymond with the authority of a born leader of men. We crunched our way round to the rear of the silent building, only to be confronted by another enormous dog, fortunately chained to its kennel.

'There's a window open up there,' said Raymond, pointing towards what seemed to be a first-floor corridor. 'Perhaps I could climb up to it.'

Together we manhandled a huge pole towards the window and rested the top end on the sill. Hand over hand, monkey fashion, he started to clamber up it, causing the dog to fling itself repeatedly at him, barking hysterically. Just out of range, our intrepid hero clung on. Progress was slow since the further he climbed the more the pole sagged. In spite of the canine clamour there was still no sign of life in the house. I began to wonder which would break first, the pole or the dog's chain. Relief came in the person of Robin Richards who hurried round the corner towards us, proudly announcing that he'd picked the lock. We groped our way inside, using cigarette lighters to locate the light-switches.

Later that morning, at about ten, I went into John Bolster's room with a cup of coffee. 'Morning John,' I said, rather too brightly. 'How do you feel today?'

Bleary-eyed, he made a classic reply: 'I don't feel myself at all; I feel like some other poor bugger and I think he's going to die ...'

Le Mans became an annual trip for as long as Jaguars and Astons were showing the flag. It was both fun and a privilege to be involved in such an active way. One year I took my own E-type; with Eric Tobitt as passenger I did a few laps of the circuit while he took a series of photographs. My favourite shows my hands in the approved ten-to-two position on the wheel; one can just see the speedometer registering 140 miles per hour.

(My car mania has cost me extravagant sums, but I do not begrudge a pound, such is my enjoyment of driving. I have never kept a precise list but as far as I can remember I have owned three MGs, fourteen Jaguars, two Lotuses, one Ferrari, a Gordon-Keeble, a modified Triumph Herald, an Austin-Healey, a Heinkel bubble-car, a Gilbern, an Alfa-Romeo GTV, a VW Scirocco, two Bagheeras, five Datsuns (240 or 260) and two turbo-charged Mazda Rx7s. Not bad for a late starter!)

16
Words before Music

L ast week brought Antony Hopkins's 'Studies in musical taste' to an end. He concluded this lively and highly instructive series with what I can only describe as a pyrotechnic display, by which I mean not flashy but brilliant . . . . The analysis of a fugue — in this case Bach's E major from Book 2 — interesting and instructive though it might prove to be, did not seem to promise amusing entertainment, yet this is what Mr Hopkins's half-hour analysis was. Step by step he expounded and built up the structure of a fugue, and finally presented it complete on the piano. It was a fascinating performance.

Martin Armstrong, the *Listener*, 12 Nov. 1953

It was after such a programme that the producer, Roger Fiske asked me, 'If you had *carte blanche* on the radio, what would you like to do?' I had never given any thought to the matter so I gave the first answer that came into my head.

'Oh, I don't know. I suppose it'd be nice to have a half-hour programme on Sunday evenings talking about a work that was being broadcast that week.'

'Would you really like to do that?'

'Yes, why not? Would you pass the sugar . . .' — and I took it no more seriously than that. The casual remark bore surprising fruit and in due course a contract arrived to do an initial series of six programmes; six became twelve, twelve became eighteen and so on. 'Talking about Music' had been launched and has continued for the greater part of each year ever since. Once more I found myself doing something I had never visualised, something I had certainly never been trained for.

Ever since I had first shattered the speech barrier with 'Bumble-bee', talking had come easily to me. My voracious reading as a child had equipped me with a good vocabulary, while my lack of academic background kept my mind clear of the obscure jargon that all too often stands in the way of comprehension. I imagine that I first gave lectures at Morley College although I cannot remember the reason I was asked to do so. However, I must have gained some reputation quite early in my career, for in 1947 I was sent on a lecture-tour in Germany by the Foreign Office with the idea that I should tell the Germans what had been happening musically in the great outside world during the Nazi regime. I was ill-equipped for such a task but managed to bluff my way through with the help of earnest interpreters. Soon I had taken over from Herbert Howells as lecturer on general musical topics at the Royal College. The whole first-year intake was supposed to attend, and I would chat away informally on any subject that took my fancy. I think the lectures were enjoyed because they were the only ones that made the students laugh.

In all truth, lecturing was an expedient I had been forced to devise as a cover-up for my abysmally insecure technique. It enabled me to skip all the bits I was incapable of playing, or else to play them in slow motion under the pretext of analysis. I have never felt that much credit should be attached to the lecturing itself since I mostly work from intuition rather than scholarship. Music is so stimulating that I always find I have something to say about it; it is almost a reflex action.

Although I continued to compose a great deal of incidental music during the 'fifties I also acted as adjudicator at a number of music festivals. It is very dishonest work since the generally accepted marking system is absurdly inflated. As I have sometimes put it, 'You get 69 for walking on.' If marks have to be given (and I would much prefer to dispense with them) they should mean something; to give 70 for performances that are shoddy, inaccurate and ill-conceived is farcical, yet the convention amongst adjudicators is that 70 is the lowest mark.

I once served as a co-adjudicator at a delightful if slightly pretentious International Choral Festival in Cork. Robert Irwin, a fine baritone, represented Ireland, I represented England and a diminutive Spaniard represented Europe. He came at the last minute as a substitute for a Frenchman who had fallen ill; he was a choral conductor himself but spoke not a word of any other language than his own. Each morning we three would sign on at the festival office and be given the mark-sheets. They were the largest I have ever seen with the names of the choirs in heavy Gothic type at the top of each page. Two sheets of carbon, interleaved, ensured that the reports were made out in triplicate, one for the choir, one for the press and one for the record. It was all very grand.

Our Spanish colleague needed an interpreter so we were joined by an immensely distinguished-looking man, tall and thin with a little white goatee beard, gold-rimmed spectacles and a walking-stick embossed with silver. On the very first day, Robert and I had to explain the facts of adjudicating life (via the interpreter) as the Spaniard had been naive enough to start giving forty marks to choirs that only deserved forty marks. 'Seventy,' we said, brooking no opposition; 'seventy is the lowest mark.' Apart from this disagreement about fundamentals all went well until the Thursday evening session. I arrived a little ahead of the others and to my surprise found an absolutely gorgeous girl sitting at our table. She was dressed in a low-cut gown in white; her hair, stylishly flowing down to her shoulders, was shiny black, her eyes violet. She could have been a stand-in for Elizabeth Taylor. My pulse rate quickened perceptibly as I asked her what she was doing.

'I'm the interpreter,' she answered in tones so soft and seductive that I had hurriedly to sit, lest I fainted dead away.

'And what happened to that nice Mr O'Leary,' I enquired.

'Oh, he's not feelin' so good tonight; he's me teacher and he asked me to come along to help out. I only hope I'll manage . . .'

'I'm sure you will,' I said, incestuously paternal. 'You just sit right by me and I'll tell you anything you want to know.' (Like my address, my telephone number and my urgent desire to sweep you off your pretty feet in an irresistible embrace cried the wolf that has lurked so long behind my sheep's clothing.)

At that moment, as hot passion threatened to engulf me, Robert and Carlos arrived. The dark Spanish eyes opened wide at the delectable sight, and when she spoke to him in husky Castilian his smile was oleaginous and sickening. He insisted that she should sit at the far end of the table where he could have her to himself.

The evening's proceedings began. Choir after choir tramped on or off, their singing interspersed with somewhat inaudible solos on the Irish harp. From time to time I would hear her darlin' voice cooing and lisping into his ear while he oozed Mediterranean charm at her. At last I could stand it no longer; between choirs, I scribbled her a note. I cannot remember the exact text but it was pretty romantic stuff. Calculated to make her realise that as bright a flame could burn in an Anglo-Saxon breast as in any swarthy Spaniard's.

Beloved stranger — (or words to that effect)
'Tis too cruel that my instant love for you should thus be thwarted by circumstances. I positively *must* see you again, you are too lovely to lose so soon, especially to that oily dago. *Please* can we not meet at some trysting place before the midnight hour; a blasted oak perhaps, or at least a local hostelry?
Yours in smitten devotion
A.H.

I folded it carefully, signalled to her and gave it to Robert to pass along. She opened it, eyes widening in delicious astonishment as she read. My heartfelt words were rewarded with a melting smile, a slight flutter of the lashes. Romance, like a heady perfume, filled the encircling air. Suddenly Robert went into a scarlet-faced convulsion, nearly falling out of his chair. 'What is it?' I said, anxiously wondering if I knew how to cope with a coronary. 'You forgot about the *carbon*,' he spluttered, suppressing his mirth with a handkerchief. The whole of my lunatic missive had come out on a Welsh male voice choir's marksheet. I had to borrow a 6B pencil and write a report of five hundred crowded words to conceal the evidence of my misplaced ardour. Destiny was not with me that night and I never saw her again.

While it is true that I have heard many excellent, even memorable performances at festivals, I am thankful to have discontinued adjudicating. So often the constructive purpose of criticism is misinterpreted by entrants who are only interested in winning, or at least in gaining a high mark. I will quote two examples. Years ago I was adjudicating a festival in Yorkshire in which there was a well-patronised class for amateur operatic singers. By the rules of the competition, operatic costume was not permitted, nor were the singers to indulge in stage movement. Ambition was not lacking, and for most of the afternoon I listened to a selection of the best-known operatic arias being sung with varying degrees of success. One lady made a fair shot at *Ritorna vincitor* from *Aida*. I have always tried to give helpful and encouraging criticisms. In her case I drew attention to a point, which, I said, *all* the entrants should heed. 'I know you're not allowed operatic costume,' I went on to say, 'but there's nothing to stop you wearing something in keeping with the aria. The great singers have a way of creating the mood of a song before they utter a note, by the way they stand, by their expression, by the position of the hands. To do this successfully demands a good deal of experience, perhaps more than any of you have had. Clothes can help, though, and if you are going to sing a big dramatic aria from (say) *Aida*, a pretty little blue two-piece suit topped by a pill-box hat with flowers and cherries on it is not going to help your cause. It's a lovely suit; I'm not saying it isn't. But save it for Mignon or Micaela; for an aria like this wear a black frock, perhaps with a gold belt and sandals.'

It seemed like good advice to me but she was furious. When the class was over she came up to me scarlet with rage. I thought she was about to strike me with her handbag. 'I've never been so insulted, so humiliated,' she said with savage intensity. 'You're here to criticise my voice, not my clothes. What right have you to make a mock of me in front of my friends? I bought that suit specially for the festival I did and now you . . .' Words momentarily failed her. 'I'll see that you never adjudicate a festival in this part of the world again, I tell you that.' And she stamped off, cherries bobbing in indignation. I was sorry to have upset her so but I truly meant to be helpful to everyone. I had given the advice with a very light touch; I also gave her about eighty-four marks, which made her sixth overall. What amuses me is that they do so pride themselves on speaking plain truths in Yorkshire.

My other example of the less happy aspect of festivals was more distressing because of the effect it had on innocent parties. It was in Holywood, a small town not far from Belfast. The festival was due to last for a week, and on the first afternoon there was a class for under-sixteen vocal duets. I gave first place to two schoolgirls who sang a Mendelssohn duet with considerable charm. Second place went to two boys, trebles, with true, pure voices, beautifully in tune. They sang a Latin duo by Mozart, a glorious but very difficult piece which they could not really do justice to. They took it a lot too fast and had little idea of Mozartean style. I gave them a very high mark to encourage them and made a point of talking to them afterwards, explaining to them why I had put them second. The next morning their diploma was returned by their teacher (a booking clerk at the railway station) with a message to the effect that they were the best two boy singers in Ireland; any adjudicator who failed to recognise this clearly knew nothing about music. He would therefore withdraw all his pupils from the festival in protest at my incompetence. More than fifty children were deprived of the chance to sing in the event as a result of his warped attitude. One wonders how such people would stand up to being professional, having to read scathing criticisms in the national press rather than in a private handwritten report.

Adjudication at the highest level is a different matter and I recall with pleasure such occasions as the Grand Prix Marguerite Long in Paris or the National Piano Competition of Canada, held in Toronto. In recent years I have served on each of the juries for the Rupert Foundation Young Conductor's Awards, a truly fascinating event that attracts entries from all over the world. I am not likely to forget one day in Barking Town Hall where we heard ten performances of the closing scene of 'The Rite of Spring'. From our vantage-point immediately behind the percussion we watched ten young aspirants steering the BBC Symphony Orchestra through this challenging work. My admiration for the percussion players was unstinted as they banged, thumped and crashed their way through the Stravinskyan maze with scarcely a glance at the copy, let alone the conductor. They were even able to talk among themselves, commenting on the merits of the beat as they struck the next blow. After the fourth shattering performance Malcolm Williamson (beside me) had turned ashy pale and was lighting his eighth cigarette. 'I don't think I can stand this again,' he muttered, wilting under fire. It was a resonant hall and the sound was truly tremendous.

Of the several varied and unforeseen careers I seem to have pursued since I left College, conducting has brought me the greatest joy and the greatest frustration — joy because I find it immensely satisfying, frustration because of the label 'Children's Concerts' that has been irrevocably attached to me. I suppose I should be grateful to have had the chance to conduct each of the great London orchestras in the Festival Hall, but the more often one does it, the more irritating it becomes not to be allowed to do it after dark. I have conducted innumerable concerts for the Robert Mayer or Ernest Read organisations, invariably being offered a return booking for the following year, yet to be accepted as a Conductor rather than a Talking Conductor seems almost impossible. I cannot believe that it is due to any lack of competence since the orchestral players themselves are often very complimentary. Ironically enough I am treated as a *maestro* in Japan, Yugoslavia or Australia but not in my home country.

During my first tour of Japan I was invited to conduct several very good students' orchestras attached to universities. At the University of Fine Arts in Tokyo I was asked if I could take the rehearsal in French as no member of the music staff was competent to translate into English. I said I would love to, and was duly introduced to a Japanese cellist who had studied in Paris for seven years. He sat beside me during the rehearsal. Much of the time I managed perfectly well by singing a phrase the way I wanted it to go and by using my hands. From time to time though, I would want to elaborate a point; I would speak French to the cellist who passed it on in Japanese to the orchestra who were playing German music under an English conductor. A fine example of the shrinking world.

One of the disadvantages of being a guest conductor is a shortage of rehearsal time. I seldom have more than one three-hour session to rehearse for a whole concert. On one occasion, for a young people's concert in the Festival Hall, I did the following programme to illustrate the way that different composers will exploit identical note-patterns.

An extract from Bach's Third Brandenburg.
A movement from Stravinsky's Concerto in D for strings.
The first movement of Brahms' Second Symphony.
The first of the Two Portraits for Orchestra Op. 5 by Bartok.
The slow movement of Rachmaninov's Second Symphony.

This was asking a great deal, even of an orchestra as excellent as the Royal Philharmonic. In fact they played superbly, though the Brahms I had to leave completely unrehearsed. Under the contractual arrangement for children's concerts, I was only allowed an hour and a quarter; we could easily have spent that on the Stravinsky alone.

On the whole I have the greatest admiration for professional orchestral musicians. They have an unenviable job in many ways, overworked and undervalued. Taking great pride in what they do they are marvellously competent, maintaining standards of performance that are far too easily taken for granted by the listener. Even so they can be fallible. One year at the Norwich Festival I was conducting one of the best-known string orchestras in the world. The final work in the programme was Stravinsky's 'Apollon Musagête'. It had (for once!) been adequately rehearsed and the whole concert had gone so well that morale was high. The orchestra was one of such excellence that the players really preferred to work without a conductor. In deference to this I was conducting extremely economically, not allowing myself to indulge in the romantic gestures that catch the public eye. The penultimate section of 'Apollon' begins with an eleven-bar flourish followed by a single silent bar. Cellos and basses then set a rumti-tumti rhythm going before violas, second and first violins enter in turn. I marked the silent bar and then gave the cellos the nod. Suddenly the violas came in with all the confidence in the world, a bar *early*. In such situations the conductor must think very quickly how to put things right. I brought the seconds in a bar early, likewise the firsts. The top three parts were now at least together; all that I had to do was to persuade the lower strings to skip a bar. 'Seventy-four,' I mouthed at them, giving them a bar number. 'Jump one ...' There was a slight kerfuffle before everything slotted into place. I don't think that anybody in the audience knew that we had had a little crisis. After a positively rapturous reception — they had played superbly — I made my way backstage. The leading viola player came up to me. 'Terribly sorry,' he said with genuine contrition, 'all my fault.' I am not often angry but on this occasion I felt I was justified. 'You all admitted at rehearsal that you didn't know the piece. I know you don't like being conducted but you can't say I was having any sort of an ego-trip. I was being bloody meticulous; why the hell couldn't you wait for a lead from me instead of crashing in like that?' His expression froze. 'I *never* take leads from conductors,' he said icily.

While I naturally prefer to conduct professionals I have inevitably worked a great deal with amateurs, especially the young. One of my most ambitious works, 'A Time for Growing', was written specifically for young performers apart from a few adult soloists. Telling the story of the evolution of the world, of man and of faith, it had two opposing choruses presenting respectively the scientific and the biblical views of creation. A central protagonist represented a young man of today looking for something to believe in at a time when the bedrock of orthodox faith has been severely eroded. It was first performed at the Norwich Festival with some five hundred children from more than thirty schools taking part. Subsequently it was done in the Albert Hall (1969) with seven hundred and fifty performers. When planning the production it was rather fun to be able to stand on the stage of that vast place and say, 'It's no use; it's too small . . .' What I meant of course was that one couldn't have cast and orchestra on the platform. In the event it was acted out in the arena, with a choir of five hundred youngsters massed behind an orchestra of over a hundred. Only on the day of the performance did we manage to fit it all together, since we had never before had a hall big enough to accommodate all the forces involved.

I was very anxious that the impact of the opening should not be spoiled by conventional applause. The work began with a completely unaccompanied recitative for solo tenor; the part was brilliantly sung by Bernard Dickerson. While the audience was still gathering, he went and fiddled about with a sort of cage — very symbolic — which was placed in the arena not far from the platform. He then settled down inside the cage without drawing attention to himself. At a given moment all the lights went out except for a single harsh spotlight focussed on him. Meanwhile I had come on unobtrusively as a member of the orchestra, sitting among the second violins. During Bernard's opening recitative I sneaked quietly to the rostrum and stood facing the players in virtual darkness. Exactly on cue the orchestral lights were switched on with just an upbeat to spare. It was a genuinely dramatic moment that gripped the six-thousand-plus in the audience.

While the emotional response of the young is very gratifying, I grow tired at times of having so often to accept amateur

standards. I had a particularly harrowing time with the first performance of an operatic treatment of the life of St Francis that I
wrote for the Stroud Festival of Religious Drama. I was invited to
a meeting of the Festival committee and asked if I would be prepared to accept the commission. I told them that the only
religious subject I could think of offhand was St Francis; at some
length we discussed possible librettists, ending with a shortlist of
about four. Two days later I received a small parcel through the
post. It was a little book of poems about the Chilterns written by a
Methodist minister called David Nixon. The accompanying letter
told me that as a boy he'd worked at the farm up the road from
Woodyard and that he had often brought hay or turnips down for
our horses. He asked me if I would mind writing a short preface to
his book. I thought the style perfect for the required libretto, the
completely coincidental appearance of his poems seeming to be a
singularly auspicious omen.

The church where the opera was to be performed presented
almost insoluble problems. There seemed to be nowhere to put an
orchestra. In the end they were lodged in the back of the gallery; I
was therefore at the opposite end of the church, facing away from
the stage that had been erected over the choirstalls. Behind me, in
the gallery seats, sat the 'commentary' choir, unable to see my
beat. An assistant conductor was supposed to follow me slavishly,
passing on my beat to the choir. There was really hardly any need
for him to look at the score so long as he watched me closely. A
letter to a friend describes the first-night agonies as they were
recollected the following morning.

I was in such despair: it *could* have been so good and yet it was
wrecked by the conductor of the chorus. His *only* job was to
watch me and faithfully relay my beat to the choir. He decided
to take his own speeds practically throughout, kept his head
down in the copy — as though that would make the choir sing!
— and when he did bring them in, did so with a gesture of bene-
diction that ensured they were at least one beat late if not two. I
nearly walked out half-way through Act II and let him get on
with it at his own speed. The Orch. did its best, even to picking
up (rather insecurely) after Francis's father had had a memory
lapse and jumped about 30 bars. The voice of God failed to
materialise when F. had his first vision, and after waiting an age,

I decided to speak it myself .... The producer, who should have been saying it through a mike, was out in the street and heard me inside the church. He clapped his hand to his forehead and said, 'Oh my God — it's God!'

The girl who played Clare panicked and sang dreadfully out of tune much of the time. But it *looked* gorgeous and the kids rose to the occasion magnificently.

I was so furious with the stupid conductor that I could hardly bring myself to go to the reception afterwards. The Italian consul-general was there, plus cultural attaché, Arts Council rep., Sir Edward Boyle etc. etc. and I felt that I couldn't face them after such a shambles. But people were kind and understanding though I don't want charity from my audiences. If Britten had written it he'd have had Heather Harper, John Shirley-Quirk, the English Chamber Orch. and so on for 3 weeks non-stop rehearsals off printed copies and everyone would still have marvelled. I had to work with 98% amateurs, mostly incompetent, who even a week before had no clue how it went.

Here indeed is a cry from the heart. Although I feel that such works have a genuinely useful function to fulfil it would be nice, just once, to hear them really well done. Bernard Dickerson, for whom I created the role of Francis, was again superb, but he could not carry the whole show on his own.

Later the opera was done in the Theatre Royal at Norwich. The double basses and all the percussion were placed in line along the gangway at the side of the stalls, extending to the middle of the house; my beat was conveyed to them by closed-circuit television, not the ideal way to establish confidence between players and conductor. I do not wish to seem ungrateful to the many people who worked enthusiastically in a number of such productions, but merely to establish what music in the raw can be like.

I think that the nicest amateur group I have ever worked with was a women's choir formed from members of the Women's Institutes. Chosen by audition from thirteen counties, they were originally intended to give a demonstration of what a W.I. choir could do, given the chance. After two performances they were officially disbanded, an edict which they refused to obey. Having given a number of concerts over several years, we decided to splash out and do an evening at the Purcell Room on the South Bank.

The rehearsal in the afternoon went very promisingly and everyone was on their mettle. Backstage was chaos though, with forty-five women trying to change into evening dress in space designed for a string quartet at most. I put my suitcase in a corner and, trying to avert my gaze from the unprecedented display of undergarments, began as modestly as I could to exchange my grubby cords for a respectable dinner jacket. I started to unpack. Jacket, shirt, tie, socks, shoes ... shirt, tie, socks, shoes ... Oh no, I can't believe it. NO TROUSERS! In blind panic I rushed half-dressed to the house phone and rang the stage door.

'Have you got a spare pair of black trousers I could borrow; I'm conducting the choir in the Purcell Room.'

An agonised pause while the chatter in the room gradually died and recriminatory glances began to home in on me.

'You're in luck, Sir; we do have one pair down here.'

'What size?'

'Oh, large-ish; about a forty-two-inch waist I'd say at a guess ...'

'Sorry, that's hopeless.'

I rang off despairingly, aware that we had a mere quarter of an hour before we were due to begin. In a flash of inspiration I remembered that one of my keenest singers had been wearing black slacks and a jersey all day.

'Ros,' I called to her; 'I'll have to wear your trousers. Can I try them on?'

Heedless of modesty I removed my own (in the great tradition of Robertson Hare) and, as quickly as I could, struggled into hers. Waist and hips not too bad; legs far too long. In such circumstances a W.I. choir is probably the best any conductor could wish for. Within seconds needles were produced and as swiftly threaded. For the first and, I would imagine, only time in my life I had two women kneeling at my feet, tacking up hems with nimble fingers. Meanwhile I stripped my manly torso and donned my fancy gear. At the stroke of 7.30 the choir filed on to the platform, leaving me to make the final adjustments to my unorthodox garb. Looking at myself in the mirror I saw that for some reason which psychologists could doubtless explain, there was a very visible bright chrome zip drawing attention to those parts men's trousers are supposed to conceal. I took my bows very demurely that night, hands folded in front of me to hide my shame.

The following week we did a concert at Reading University. I sensed that something was afoot as soon as I came on stage for the rehearsal. There, on the music stand, was an unbelievably shabby pair of jeans sawn off jaggedly above the knee. A neatly written notice was attached:

FOR EMERGENCY USE ONLY.

That time I had to borrow shoes from the caretaker.

The choir seemed to have a curious effect on me, for soon afterwards we converged on Denman College for a weekend residential course. 'Guess what I've left behind this time,' I said to Janet, my indefatigable accompanist and assistant; 'my *pyjamas* . . .'

17
Trips and Travels

Travel is an inevitable part of a musician's life, certainly something that schoolmastering would never have provided in such abundance. For years it gave me great delight to have a valid excuse to leap into an open Jaguar and set off on a two-hundred mile journey. Those contradictory features of modern driving, motorways and speed limits, have destroyed a lot of the fun, though trips through the wilds of Scotland or Wales can still be thoroughly enjoyable. On one occasion, years ago, I remember going to a city in the North Midlands on a glorious summer day. I arrived at the hotel looking as though I had just driven a stage of the *Mille Miglia*, my face streaked with dust, hair in a tangle, shirt stuck to my back. A wash and brush-up would not be adequate to make me platform-presentable; it would have to be a bath. The hotel had been expensively refurbished downstairs with a wide selection of multi-coloured wallpapers clamouring for attention. Upstairs was not so good and my room had no bathroom attached. Gathering clean shirt, pants, socks, trousers and toilet things together I padded down the corridor, found a large but spartan bathroom, turned on the taps, dumped my clothes and went into the adjacent loo. For some reason nature failed to function as smoothly as usual and I remained there longer than I would have wished. Mission accomplished, I hurried back to the bathroom. To my dismay I found it flooded to a depth of two inches, water cascading over the edges of the bath. Feeling like the Sorcerer's Apprentice I splashed across the room, turned off the taps and plunged my arm in, shoulder-deep, to pull out the plug. With dripping feet I went in search of a chambermaid.

'I'm in a spot of trouble,' I explained awkwardly. 'The bath has overflown — I mean overflowed. I was sort of taken *ill* in the gents' down the way, couldn't get out . . .' (Inspiration struck.) 'The lock jammed.'

'That's alright dear; I'll come an 'ave a look.'

'I think you'll need a mop and bucket.'

Together we returned to the scene of the crime. The level seemed to have subsided a little. I stood in the doorway watching her splosh up water with the mop. Out of the corner of my eye I saw the top of the chef's hat rising into view as he ascended the stairs.

'What the bloody 'ell's goin' on,' he called loudly. 'There's water pourin' through the bloody ceiling and me pastry's covered with bits o' plaster.' I slipped quietly into my room and locked the door. I never did manage to wash my hair that evening and arrived at the concert a red-nosed scarecrow.

I have already mentioned my first postwar trip to France and Switzerland. The following year I went to Holland for a small festival of contemporary music at a place called Bilthoven It was there that I first met a recurring problem on foreign tours, food. Perhaps because of the traumas of my infancy I have a dislike for anything with a strong flavour. How people drink black coffee, beer, spirits or stewed tea I don't know, nor can I comprehend a liking for curries, cheeses, garlic or mulligatawny soup. Breakfast at Bilthoven consisted of black bread that reminded me of the sole of a patent leather shoe and a large selection of smoked meats and potent cheeses. I felt ungrateful to my host who had obviously scoured the market for so prodigal a choice of Dutch delicacies. I would soothe the pangs of hunger with a glass of milk and pray that the lunch would not be too aggressive.

Although my travels bear no comparison with the international artists who give concerts between airports, I have usually been abroad once or twice in each year, nearly always on my own. Alison would be left to hold the fort, continuing to teach huge numbers of adult beginners with more patience and tolerance than I could ever muster.

I returned from one of my trips to find the garden at Brook Green covered almost knee-deep in manure. Two men had turned up with a cartload of the stuff saying that the Guv'nor had ordered it. They'd spent the best part of an hour trailing sackloads through the house, dumping them all over the small garden. 'The manure's come,' she said brightly when I came back, 'but did you need to order quite so much?' 'I never ordered any,' I said; 'it's the first I've heard of it.' It was a 'right con'.

In November 1957 I went to Jamaica for the first time to adjudicate a festival. I was there for a month and adored it, even though the standard of performance, with two very notable exceptions, was rather low. Discussing the quality of the teaching with Mrs Manley, sister of the Prime Minister, I suggested that I should return the following summer to give a fortnight's intensive course for music teachers on the island. She was enthusiastic and managed to find government support for the scheme.

Since Alison had a profound distrust of the theory of aerodynamics we decided to go out by sea. We duly embarked from Tilbury on a Norwegian banana boat with only nine other passengers, not counting the racehorse that was stabled on deck. Our accommodation was magnificent, a huge cabin with a large private bathroom; it would have cost a fortune on any of the big passenger liners. At our first meal, gliding almost silently out of the Thames estuary in the soft evening light, I ordered Alison a bottle of wine, thinking that we would inevitably have something of a party. It seemed to take rather a long time to appear but once it did arrive I offered a glass to the Captain, who seemed to be in a state of deep Scandinavian gloom. He grunted and said that he didn't drink, nor did he approve of drinking. Somewhat put out by this contradiction of all my preconceived notions about mariners, I proceeded to offer a glass all round the table. To Alison's visible dismay, our fellow voyagers all turned out to be devout members of the sterner religious sects. In even uncorking the bottle I had allowed the devil to gain a foothold on board. Alison sipped half a glass as though she really preferred Ribena, while I placed the offending bottle near the chair. It was the biggest disappointment of the voyage as her frugal spirit had looked forward to the prospect of duty-free for eleven days. In desperation she resorted to gin and coke when we were in public view, but owing to the number of strict teetotallers aboard, the ship ran out of coke in mid-Atlantic, a sorry plight.

On the first Sunday at sea I was subjected to some pressure by the brethren and sisters — *Alleluia!* — since it was generally felt that to have the maestro at the mighty harmonium would add a touch of class to the service. I was mean, and took revenge upon their sanctimonious attitude by going to the sharp end and reading *Doctor in the House*.

As we came into warmer waters I would sit in the bows for hours at a time, watching the perpetually changing colours of the sea and counting the flying fish skimming the waves ahead of us. On our arrival at Kingston we were met by several friends from my previous visit and driven off through the sweltering heat to the enchantingly beautiful Mona Hotel, just over the road from the university grounds. For the duration of the course we worked very hard, the tropical August heat sapping our energies. Alison passed on her ideas about teaching piano in classes, a method she had initiated very successfully at the City Literary Institute, while I lectured on everything I could think of. Each evening, at about ten o'clock, I would give a short recital on a small upright piano. One night I was more than usually disturbed by the continuous peep-peep ... peep-peep ... peep-peep of a little tree frog who had found a perch close to the open windows. He only had the one note, a high A flat, but he kept on pumping away at it, shrill as a piccolo. His performance was so beautifully rhythmic that I decided to join him in a duet. To the absolute delight of the audience I began to improvise a waltz, incorporating his paired notes into the music. I think it meant more to them than all my gems from the classics. Afterwards they were bubbling over with excitement — 'That duet with the frog, MAN, that was *really* something!'

After the course was over we went up to the north coast to have a week's holiday at a small hotel that had once been a private house. The beauty of the island in those days surpassed belief, though I believe it has been ruined by tourism in recent years. In the last two days of our stay there was considerable anxiety about a hurricane that threatened the coast. First-aid posts were set up, windows boarded, anything moveable lashed down with ropes. I greatly upset the owner of the hotel by lending a willing hand to help prepare for the emergency. His objection was not that I was a guest but that I was white. It is such people that cause revolutions. I was almost sorry that the hurricane passed by; I enjoy a bit of drama.

The holiday over, we flew up to New York, Alison resolutely refusing to move from her seat lest she upset the precarious balance of the plane. We travelled back on a Cunarder, the

Saxonia. After our banana boat it was a nightmare voyage. With only about twenty per cent of the cabin crew on board — the rest were on strike — the service was abysmal. Only one restaurant was open and long queues were the typical manifestation of the British way of life. Even Alison's enthusiasm for the sea became muted in our cold cramped cabin, whose stark discomfort seemed the more hideous after our idyllic stay in the Caribbean.

Another and happier Atlantic crossing took us to Canada for a six-week music camp organised by *Jeunesses Musicales*. The long cautious trip up the St Lawrence River made a strange contrast to the vast expanses of the open sea. We were met in Quebec and driven down to Mt. Orford by car, arriving late at night. The camp was situated around a small lake, barely visible at that hour but occasionally mirroring the headlights of a passing car. A barn-like wooden building housed the administration, the girls' dormitory, the main classroom and a common room. Boys slept in a row of tents at the lakeside. 'Come,' said Gilles, the organiser, 'you must be tired. I will take you to your . . . room.' He seemed to hesitate about the choice of word; we soon discovered why. Armed with a single torch he led the way, scrambling up a tortuous path through dense and rain-soaked pines. The lower boughs slashed at us, showering us with raindrops. At last, after what seemed like a quarter of a mile, we arrived at a tiny log cabin, it's sharply angled roof making an inverted V against the night sky. More than slightly incredulous, I lugged the heavy suitcase on to the miniature verandah. The camp was completely obscured by the forest; not a light was to be seen. Gilles groped around inside and found a lamp, pumped it energetically to arouse the dormant vapour, and lit it. It hissed and flared, instantly attracting a kamikaze moth that hurled itself at the glass. Two small camp-beds occupied most of the floor-space; creature comforts were notably absent. He bade us goodnight and disappeared into the darkness, leaving us to fend for ourselves.

The next morning I awoke to the sounds of the forest. I looked out into the small grass clearing in front of our cabin. There was a creature about the size of a plump otter sitting up outside, twitching his whiskers. I shook Alison's shoulder. 'Wake up,' I said urgently, 'there's a coypu outside.' 'A what?' she mumbled. 'A coypu — at least I think it is.' 'What on earth is a coypu?' 'Look, look, you can see one right on our doorstep.' The creature vanished into the trees. Wearily she sat up. 'What are you talking about?' 'It was there, a coypu, I promise you; he was sitting up doing his morning toilet, cleaning his whiskers.' 'I can't see him.' 'You've missed him now.' She sank back into her narrow little bed and closed her eyes again.

Filled with the pioneering spirit I strode down the footpath towards the camp, stripped to the waist, with a towel slung casually over my shoulder (we had no washing facilities in our forest home). The place seemed deserted except for one man sitting outside the main building reading a newspaper.

'Are you Antony Hopkins?' he asked as I looked for a sign to direct me to the washrooms.

'Yes, that's right.'

'I'm Walter Joachim.' He stood up, folding the newspaper. 'Don't mind if I give you a tip . . .'

'Of course not.'

'Gilles is very strict on morals; you mustn't walk around the camp like that. You have to wear a shirt at all times.'

'You're not serious —'

'But I am.'

He laughed and shook his finger at me. 'You don't want to upset these French-Canadians as soon as you arrive.'

I went back to our hut mystified by this unlikely revelation. It was true though; we may have been camping in the wild but the atmosphere was extraordinarily puritanical. I even got into trouble for sunbathing below a sheltering bank on a day when the camp was virtually empty.

Walter Joachim turned out to be the leading cellist of the CBC orchestra. He was a wonderful musician and I learned a lot by listening to him coaching chamber music. The other great master there was Vlado Perlemuter. A French musicologist (whom I thought a pompous bore) gave a long series of lectures on the history of keyboard music. Perlemuter sat silent and patient through the streams of oratory.

'*Et maintenant mon collègue jouera la sonate dont j'ai parlé,*' would come the cue, and he would play like an angel. In six weeks he went through the major part of the piano repertoire without a note in front of him. I marvelled at his artistry and humility and sat in on his classes whenever I had the opportunity.

The following year I went to Canada again. Alison decided that it wasn't quite the life for her and sensibly stayed at home. I took the long homeward flight in a Constellation, fifteen hours into a head wind. After we had been in the air for about four hours, a noisily obstreperous drunk insisted that he wanted to lie in one of the four sleeping berths that were primarily intended for invalids. At the cost of £80 he was stowed aloft, to everybody's relief. As we crossed the West Country the next morning he decided that it was time to get up. He was a big man, well over six feet tall. Without warning he jumped down from the berth into the central gangway. I expected him to go straight through the floor. Instead he fell right across me, cutting the bridge of his nose and both cheeks on the edge of my glass of orange juice. Blood spurted all over me as he lay groaning with his head in my lap. Stewardesses rushed forward with towels to stem the flow but my trousers were ruined and I arrived home looking as if I'd been in a major accident. To cap it all, we had been kept waiting in the plane for an extra ten minutes while an ambulance came to fetch him. I hope the stitches hurt!

My longest trip abroad was to Australia where, for six months, I was the visiting professor of composition at the University of Adelaide. While I have no fear of flying, I do object to flying over places I would love to visit. I decided therefore to fly but to take twelve days. I went first to Beirut; this was in 1964, before any of the present strife. My prime purpose in doing so was to enable me to go to Baalbek where I had heard there were Roman ruins finer than anything in Europe. I was not disappointed. I took a car up there and spent the day wandering around the magnificent site. I had the place to myself, apart from a solitary Arab sitting on the ground by a placid donkey. I like to dispense with the boring chatter of guides, churning out their catalogue of names and dates parrot-fashion; it is enough to sit and look and listen, imagining that I can hear the voices and everyday sounds of that long distant time when Rome ruled the known world.

My next stop was Jerusalem, from whose narrow overcrowded streets I sought refuge in the desert by making the trip to Petra. The road stopped at a line of rocky foothills of no great height but whose harsh and jagged peaks made a formidable barrier. A party of about six gathered in the shadow of the rocks. Ponies were led forward, gaunt and listless as they shuffled over the arid stones. I

climbed into the sun-cracked saddle, wanting to show the grizzled
Arab beside me that I was at least able to ride, though the inane
shrieks of my fellow-travellers made me feel ashamed of the whole
tribe of tourists. We entered an extraordinary narrow defile, a
channel carved through the rock by some age-old stream long
dried up. At times the edges of the canyon seemed almost to meet
above us, cutting out all but a tiny slit of sky. I pushed on a little,
trying to distance myself from the voices of my companions,
wanting to savour the silence and the isolation of this magic place.
Ahead the path narrowed still further, giving the impression that
we had reached a cul-de-sac. Just when one had the illusion that
only a hand's breadth separated one rockface from the other,
there was a fleeting glimpse of a rose pink pillar, perfectly carved.
It was so unexpected that it was like a mirage. We emerged into
the bright sunlight of a sharply defined valley, not a hundred
yards across. Directly opposite was the most breathtaking
building I have ever seen, its elegant façade carved out of the cliff-
face itself. Inside, it was nothing but a dark box, a veritable hole in
the wall; but the exterior, its exquisite pillars marvellously preserved by a freak of nature, was an amazing testament to the
creative spirit of man. I count myself fortunate not only to have
visited this unique wonder but also to have been there at a time
when it was almost deserted (it was easy to shake off the other
members of the small party). I suppose that now it has been
opened up to pestilential coaches carrying hordes of trippers
whose noisy babble breaks the desert spell.

I moved on to Cairo, realising a long-held ambition. Unfortunately I hadn't the time to go south to Luxor, but I spent a day
and a half in the great museum, which again, by amazing good
fortune, I had almost to myself. I climbed to the top of the Great
Pyramid in the heat of the midday sun and imagined that I heard
the lash of the whip cutting across the shoulders of sweating
slaves. If my emotions had been stirred by the beauty of Petra I
was moved in a different way by the implicit cruelty of the
Pyramids, the sheer size of whose blocks cannot be imagined. To
shape and then to stack such massive stones to make a single
monument seemed a monstrous perversion of labour, and yet
there were many aspects of Egyptian culture which I found haunt-
ingly beautiful, evoking a deeper response than anything I had
seen in Greece or Rome. Those unforgettable eyes, dark-rimmed

ovals, stared out at me from the walls as though desperate to communicate some secret from the past.

From the contemplation of ancient wonders I went on to the agonies of today, Karachi and Bombay, cities of indescribable poverty. One could not escape the matchstick hands of beggars, thrust even into the little motorised rickshaws in which one chugged through the overcrowded streets. If one were as rich as Rockefeller and pressed a pound into every hand, it could make no conceivable difference to the human desolation one sees on every side. It was a relief to escape briefly to Ceylon and thence to Australia.

18
I Delayed in Adelaide

I arrived in Sydney at about 8.30 on the morning of 17 March 1964. Within half an hour I was sitting in the airport restaurant searching the advertisement columns of the daily paper for a second-hand sports car. With the prospect of a six-month stay in front of me it was unthinkable that I should be without transport. I took a taxi up to the street where most of the traders seemed to be and started to prowl around the used car lots. There wasn't a great deal of choice — mostly American saloons which had no appeal for me. After wandering up and down a few times I decided to try out a rather dashing Austin-Healey in scarlet. With the salesman commending my choice I drove it round the block. It chugged and chuffed in an unconvincing way, but he assured me that the carburettors merely needed the magic touch of his head mechanic's hand. Looking under the bonnet, I saw that it had two double-choke Webers, a very non-standard conversion that promised a lively performance. I emphasised that I would only be staying for six months and asked whether he would buy it back from me. 'Can't get enough of stock like this,' the man said, patting its curved flank approvingly. Having arranged for it to be delivered to Adelaide by transporter, I returned to the airport and took the midday plane to my destination.

Although I was in Australia primarily at the university's request, the first month of my stay was more occupied by the festival, an Antipodean rival to Edinburgh that was truly impressive in its programme. John Bishop, the organiser, was also head of the music department at the university; he was a man of great vision and energy, determined to put Adelaide on the cultural map. Over dinner that evening he gave me an elaborate schedule in which I saw that I would be conducting some concerts with a specially formed string orchestra, giving a number of public lectures, and supervising rehearsals of my little opera *Three's Company*. I was to stay in half a house owned by the mother of Max Worthly, the tenor. 'There's quite a decent piano, there,' said John. 'She's very deaf so you can practise all night if you want to.'

The city was truly *en fête* with gorgeous flower arrangements on every side and loudspeakers at the street corners feeding 'classical' music to the passers-by. All the same I felt a mite desolate on the morning of my birthday, wandering down the main street looking at the shops. It was a Saturday and things seemed surprisingly quiet. I was trying to find a pleasant eating-house so that I could have a special lunch to celebrate my coming of greater age. After rejecting several burger-bars, I descended rather unwillingly into the basement of a men's outfitters. The restaurant there was deserted, but I sat down in the dim light and picked up the menu. IS IT YOUR BIRTHDAY? it said right across the top of the page; IF SO, HAVE A MEAL ON US! I didn't have the nerve to say it was; I think one was supposed to bring a party of at least twelve witnesses to qualify for the free treat.

Three weeks later the Healey arrived. I collected it from the freight depot, feeling that I now had a companion to share my experiences with. I headed back for town but the top mechanic had lost his magic touch and it lurched along like a lame dog. Disgusted, I left it at a garage near to my lodgings. They rang up the next day saying that there was nothing much they could do. The conversion had been completely botched; the carburettors were ineptly placed directly over the exhaust manifold so that petrol was evaporating as fast as it was fed in. Furious, I drove the asthmatic machine back to the freight-yard and told them to return it to Sydney.

After an angry and expensive telephone conversation, I arranged a straight swap. The festival was over and I was supposed to be teaching every day but John allowed me to finish a day before the end of term. The Wednesday before Easter I flew back to Sydney and collected what I frankly considered to be a rather tattier-looking model, this time in a light metallic blue. The next day, having given myself a bit of a sight-seeing tour, I set out on the long drive back, first heading for Canberra, which I felt I ought to visit. Bright and early on Good Friday morning I drove out of the capital, the hood down, happy to be at the wheel with the prospect of a major journey ahead. It wasn't long before I was out of the city and humming along a gently undulating road lined with the handsome eucalyptus trees that are such a feature of the Australian landscape. The roads seemed curiously quiet. With slight unease I became increasingly aware that every filling station I passed was closed. My worries mounted when the car coughed and spluttered to a halt. I may love cars but I am no sort of a mechanic and I felt singularly helpless stranded somewhere in the Murrumbidgee valley. I let it rest awhile, the soft crackle of cooling metal giving me a faint reassurance that there was still life of a sort beneath the bonnet. No traffic passed, no helpful patrol. I climbed out and laid healing hands upon the creature, offering silent prayers as I did so. Inexplicably it seemed to do the trick and I got her started again. We staggered on, hiccuping and misfiring until we came to the forecourt of a garage. Closed, of course, but there was a bungalow next door. With some diffidence I rang the bell. The owner, bald as Kojak and stripped to the waist, laughed merrily when I told him my problems. 'There ain't a g'rardge in Austreyelier open on Good Friday,' he said, enjoying my predicament to the full.

"Spect it's dirt in the fuel pump. Try stickin' some more juice in 'er.'

'There's nobody on the pumps,' I said rather desperately.

'Ain't you got coins then? Ain't you got florins?'

I was innocent of Australian customs and hadn't realised that one could feed florins into the pumps in exchange for petrol. Pitying my Pommy ignorance he produced a great bag of the precious coins and changed me a few pounds' worth. The life-giving transfusion seemed to do wonders for the Healey and I roared off down the road in better heart. Within fifty miles it had another temperament . . . and then another . . . and another. At last, in mid-afternoon, I was prepared to give up. I entered a small town called Echuca and coasted into a lay-by in the main street. It was totally deserted. I half expected Gary Cooper to walk slowly down the road, hand poised over his holster ready for the big shoot-out. All Australia seemed to be asleep. I walked aimlessly down the street for perhaps fifteen paces. One door only in the line of shops was open, above it a sign saying LUCAS. I went inside. Somewhere in the dark interior I could hear movement, scraping, the chink of metal on metal.

'Anybody there? Hello . . . is there somebody there, please?'

A man came into the shop, hands black with oil. 'We're closed,' he said, defying the logic of the open door.

I explained my plight and asked if he could recommend somewhere I could put up for the night. Perhaps I could find a garage the following day . . .?

'Find a bed on Good Friday — impossible. There ain't a hotel in Aussie-land that's got a room goin' spare; booked up months ahead they are. I'll come out and take a look at yer motor though, seein' yer stuck.'

He came out into the empty street and looked disparagingly at the Healey. I pulled the bonnet-release and opened her up. He fiddled around for a moment or two, whistling quietly through his teeth, then he straightened up, looking at me with an amused grin.

'Are you in luck sport; d'you realise I'm the only guy in five hundred miles that's got the right spare part for this?'

It was the strangest of coincidences. In less than fifteen minutes I was on my way once more, the car purring along smooth as a dream. He was right about the beds, too; I tried my luck at several motels but was always told that I'd never get a room on Good Friday. I drove on, prudently changing pounds for florins whenever I could and keeping the tank topped up. The roads turned to red dust so that every now and then the car would weave gently from side to side as though the tyres were feeling for a firmer grip. Night fell, and huge moths met a sudden and messy death on the windscreen. Once I drove through a dense cloud of flies whose multitudinous corpses completely blocked my vision. I had to stop a hundred yards further on and scrape the glass clear. Occasionally giant kangaroos, looking white in the glare of the headlights lolloped across the track, heedless of danger. Shortly after midnight I came to the South Australian border, a pool of brilliant light in the black landscape. Customs officers greeted the Healey with some enthusiasm. 'Ain't she a little beaut! Don't see many of them round this way. Got any fruit on you?' It seemed an unlikely request though I felt that I was the one in greatest need. Seeing my puzzled look the men explained that no fruit was allowed to cross the border; it was an anti-pest measure rigidly enforced.

As I chatted to the officers, my cheeks burning from the long journey in the open air, a stocky white-haired man hurried over towards me. With an accent that was an indescribable mixture of Polish and Australian he asked if I was going to Adelaide. It turned out that he was a truck driver whose lorry had broken down. 'Will be goot navigeyetor,' he said, gold fillings glinting in the harsh light. Together we began the last stage of 130 miles or so, partners in a private rally which only a disaster could make us lose. At one point he yelled, 'Short cut here — save you seex mile.' He pointed to where a few tyre tracks were imprinted in the brick-red dust. We bumped and thumped our way through the parched scrub, startling a fox into sudden flight.

'You know I've only got about four inches clearance,' I shouted; 'this isn't a truck . . .' 'You OK. I push you,' he replied, and laughed hugely, throwing his head back and clapping his hands with delight. The road regained we put on speed, with my 'navi-geyetor' giving me warning of bends or bridges. We rolled into Adelaide after two in the morning and I dropped him at his home to loud protestations of thanks. Back at my bungalow I pulled into the drive and, shoulders aching, climbed out, taking a quick look at the trip-recorder as I did so. From Canberra, it had been a journey of 885 miles, much of it on dust roads; on the last leg from the border I had averaged 74 miles an hour. 'Next stop Monte Carlo,' I thought to myself as I unlatched the door. In the hall mirror I was confronted by a Red Indian, hair matted like a coconut's tuft. Despite the hour I could not sleep. As I lay in bed the ceiling seemed to rush towards me; my ears roared with the memory of the wind. Only when the first daylight filtered through the curtains did I drop off, exhausted but content.

I had much enjoyed the festival at Adelaide, but once it was over I found that university life was not to my liking. (I was only there on the understanding that it would be a six-month visit, no more; I had thought it might be interesting for once to have a taste of the cloistered calm of academe.) On first meeting my composition class of some fifteen students I suggested that as a project they should write an opera. We would solicit a libretto from the English faculty and each of them would provide one scene, fully composed and orchestrated and incorporating some or all of five small thematic germs which I gave them. (This I felt would give a unity of sorts to the music.) The copying of parts would be a good introduction to the facts of life. The time-span was by no means impractical, and at the end of my stay we could mount a concert performance to show that we had not been idle. The idea was greeted with enthusiasm; no visiting professor had dreamed up anything like a communal project before. I gave them a couple of detailed lectures on *Peter Grimes* to set the creative spark alight.

I had not counted on their almost infinite capacity to postpone work until the morrow. In six months, fifteen students produced not more than fifteen pages of manuscript. The one exception was an industrious girl who churned out music with machine-like efficiency, though not what I had asked for. As an extreme example of the student attitude I quote the saga of Jerry and *Hamlet*. During the festival I had been to a play by the notable Australian author, Patrick White. Jerry had written some incidental music for it, adequate but not an inspired contribution. At his first individual lesson I suggested that as an exercise he should write a score for *Hamlet*. I told him that I had worked a lot in theatre and radio and could well pass on the fruits of practical experience. He seemed to be quite fired by the idea, appreciating its relevance to real life. The following week he arrived with a piano trio written some eighteen months previously and extensively annotated by my predecessor. 'How's *Hamlet* coming on?' I asked him, thinking of the times that I had written entire film scores in a week. 'Oh, I jotted down a few things,' he replied vaguely, and handed me a single sheet of paper on which a few scattered dots appeared, barely recognisable as music notation. Each week the same evasive ritual was repeated; a work from the past would be resurrected, *Hamlet* would stay in the wings. After the Easter break he came in apologising for not having done anything. 'I was at the jazz camp,' he said, 'and they kept me busy.' I thought to myself that I was being too soft; too easily manipulated; perhaps these Aussies would prefer a firmer hand. 'As you've done virtually nothing since I've been here, Jerry, you can bloody well go away until you *have* got something to show me, and I don't mean something you wrote last year or the year before.' He looked stunned at the uncharacteristic outburst; he bit his lip, a tear spilled from his left eye. 'I wish you wouldn't adopt that attitude, Mr Hopkins; I only come because I'm so keen . . .'

He meant it, too, and went on to explain that he was reading three other subjects for his degree, music was a sideline, lessons with me a not-to-be-missed chance of communication with a distinguished intellect, had to put other subjects first, and so on.

'Do you think you could put my work first for just one week, Jerry, so that I can see what you can actually do.'

'Yes,' he said fervently, 'I will.' He paused a moment. 'But not this week.'

We agreed to meet in a fortnight's time, when he would return armed with an entire score of *Hamlet* composed for nine instruments of his choice. Shaking hands to seal the contract we parted. I never saw him again.

Bored with university life I made seventeen programmes for ABC television and gave a series of public lecture-recitals, suffering the familiar agonies about my playing. For the first time in my life I suffered a deep depression, a real Australian blues that only the great kindness of the pianist Lance Dossor and his wife prevented from becoming a serious breakdown.

One unusual episode gave me some gratification. During the festival there was a conference on film music which I was invited to attend. As an exercise, three Australian composers had been asked to write background music for a little five-minute film about the Alamein fountain in Sydney. The three different versions were shown in turn, whereupon the chairman asked members of the audience to make such criticism or comment as they wished. Several people had offered somewhat conflicting points of view when his eye lit on me. 'No doubt our distinguished visitor Mr Hopkins would like to say a few words . . .' Our distinguished visitor was hoping not to be noticed as he had thought all three scores rather dreary and quite irrelevant to the pictures. I said as much as politely as I could. The antagonism my remarks aroused seemed out of all proportion in any open forum, and for some minutes I had to weather quite a storm. Then a particularly indignant critic of mine stood up and pointed a positively quivering finger at me. 'If you think these scores are so poor I challenge you to do better . . .' The words had a suitably dramatic effect; the noise died down; all eyes were fixed on me. Feeling that the honour of the Old Country was at stake I said that if I was allowed to see the film again in silence I would then improvise some music on the piano. It was an uncanny recreation of an experience my father must have had when I was a very small child, for he used on occasion to play for the silent movies. Watching the screen closely I tried to remember the order of shots so that I could match the changes of mood. I then skated around the keyboard in a Debussyando manner, hoping that something reasonably suitable would emerge. After the ordeal was over I was approached by a heavily built man who shook my hand with the palm-crushing enthusiasm that musicians dread. 'That was great,' he said, beaming, 'just great. Would you consider writing music for a documentary film I'm making?'

The upshot of the conversation was a drive up to the Broken Hill mining complex and my first trip deep underground. I wrote a score for the film when I got back to England and recorded the music a few months after I had returned home. It was an unexpected bonus, one that I am sure would have enraged my challenger had he known what would be the outcome of his provocation.

We had felt that it would be well worth the expense for Alison to come out to Australia for the final month of my stay. Since she would rather have rowed there than flown, I booked her a passage on one of the P. and O. liners, a six-week voyage that she found totally enjoyable. Once in Adelaide she found it surprisingly cold and we would wander round the rather gloomy bungalow with blankets over our shoulders. The back door was a wire-mesh grille giving direct entry to winds that came off the Antarctic. The chilliest experience was a visit to Kangaroo Island, some ninety miles further south, where we stayed in the Ozone Hotel. It was being rebuilt during the winter recess and the entire south wall had been removed. A flapping plastic sheet was ineffectual protection from a wind that whistled in continually from the sea. She was reduced to wearing a thick polo-neck sweater even while she had a bath since the ventilation slats could not be closed.

I gave a public lecture there at a school where there was a small upright piano. I sat down to try it and thought that the pedal must be faulty since all the notes continued to jangle on after I had stopped playing. I opened the lid to investigate and found to my dismay that all the dampers had been pulled away from their rightful position. Some malicious soul had actually knotted them together, twisting the wires so that there was little chance of ever getting them straight. I spent forty minutes trying patiently to replace them but I wasn't able to do much good.

On our return journey we planned to have a week's holiday in Tunisia where a great friend, Bill Marchant, Sir Herbert Marchant, KCMG, was then the British Ambassador. He had had a remarkable career, starting as a schoolmaster at Harrow and progressing, via wartime Intelligence at Bletchley Park, to the élite circles of the Diplomatic Corps. From the relatively humble position of Press Attaché in Paris ('entering the Diplomatic by the backdoor,' as he put it), he was promoted to British Consul, a post he held in cities as varied as Zagreb, Düsseldorf and San Francisco, before being appointed British Ambassador to Cuba, just prior to the Bay of Pigs invasion. After he had coped admirably with the taxing situation under Castro, the Foreign Office reckoned that he had earned a rest. He was moved to Tunisia where, as Ambassador, he occupied a truly beautiful house some miles outside the city.

I had vaguely thought of taking the car for the thousand or so miles to Sydney, although the lack of luggage-space presented a considerable problem, however I need hardly say that the cheerful Sydney car-salesman refused to take the Healey back, so that I was forced to sell at quite a loss in Adelaide. The first leg of the return flight was therefore to Sydney, which to Alison's horror meant that we would mostly be flying over the 'dry' state of New South Wales. Even at thirty thousand feet no public drinking was allowed, a cruel blow to someone who ideally would like to be put on an intravenous gin drip for the duration of the flight. On the advice of sympathetic friends we bought a bottle of concentrated orange juice suitable for expectant mothers. (Alison was expecting only to have kittens, but it seemed comparable in a way.) The nourishing drink would clearly be ineffectual against her terror of flying, but the sole reason for its purchase was the extreme opacity of the bottle, whose emerald green hue prevented the contents from being seen at all. The drink so carefully prepared to give young mothers health and strength was poured down the sink; a potent mixture of Mother's Ruin was put in its place. Off we flew into the blue empyrean, with Alison quaffing from her bottle of 'orange-juice' with the fervour of a health fanatic.

At Sydney we changed planes and began the long dreary flight to Rome. By the time we had reached Malaysia and had had a couple of meals she was feeling ready to take over the controls if need be, but a four-hour wait in Rome in the early hours of the morning dampened both our spirits. After the giant Boeing, the Caravelle in which we were to fly to Tunis seemed claustrophobically small to her jaundiced eye, nor did she approve of the aircraft's design. To stick two engines on to the tail (where they could easily fall off) was an evident miscalculation that I had some difficulty in explaining.

Bill met us at Tunis airport in the Ambassadorial car. The sun beat down on the tarmac but a fresh breeze made the heat very tolerable. Our luggage was whisked through Customs without question and in a matter of moments we were driving in splendour towards the Residence. As the car came to a halt a bevy of servants gathered round, supervised by a mustachioed Arab wearing a flowing robe topped by a fez. Barking crisp but unintelligible orders to his two minions, he had the car unloaded in a trice. Bill's wife, Diana, had meanwhile come down the steps to greet us, leading us into the long cool room behind the verandah, and offering us a much needed drink. Refreshed, we made our way to the guest-room where we found an exquisitely dressed Tunisian girl, probably with some French blood in her I thought, since her complexion was too fair for an Arab. Her feet were bare, her clothes softly diaphanous. Hands clasped in an attitude of prayer she backed out of the room, murmuring inaudible phrases which I took to be assurances of devoted service. Tired travellers both, we slumped down on to the beds. Diana came in, sparkling with vitality, and suggested that we might like a swim in the pool. It was too tempting an idea to resist. Discarding our sticky and crumpled clothes, we rootled around in suitcases to find something to bathe in. Soon we were strolling through the luxuriantly flowered garden towards the swimming-pool at the far end. I could see the fez-topped major-domo directing the two underlings to scoop out a few leaves that were drifting on the water. 'Doesn't it get you down having servants on top of you all the time,' I asked Diana, speaking quietly for fear of giving offence. 'I mean, I realise the service is wonderful, but you don't get much privacy.' She shrugged. 'Oh, I don't know; you hardly notice it in time. It's a way of life . . .' We had reached the pool-side, and with a squeal of pleasure Alison dived in. I quickly joined her. We had been cooped up in aeroplanes for more than twenty-four hours and it was a sensual delight to feel the cool water sluicing around one's body. Suddenly there was a loud shout from the major-domo.

Expecting a guerilla attack at least I looked up in some alarm. To my astonishment he flung off his robe and leapt into the pool, as did the two servants with him. I knew the Marchants were democratic but for a fleeting moment I felt that egalitarianism could be taken too far. Then, as the major-domo's head emerged seal-like from the water beside me, I realised it was Tim, the Marchant's son, whom I had last seen when he was still a child. The 'underlings' were two friends while the pretty 'Tunisian' maid turned out to be the Marchant's niece. The assiduously attentive 'Arab' staff had taken us in completely in a splendid practical joke, carried out without a smile or a giggle to invite suspicion.

Holidays with the Marchants, whether in Zagreb or Tunis, were a total delight, not only for the hospitality, but for the sheer entertainment of Bill and Diana's company. He was certainly far removed from the conventional stuffed-shirt image of the diplomat, but his warmth and sense of fun served the British cause well. He was the perfect example of 'how to win friends and influence people'. If he reads these words he will mutter wryly that it sounds like an obituary; it isn't meant to, but an expression of gratitude is called for since all the giving seems to have been one-sided.

19
Screen Themes

Dec. 1956

Mon:	Write script. Record 'Talking about Music' BBC. 6.30-9.30
Tues:	Lecture-recital, East Grinstead
Wed:	Examine for ARCM diplomas. Lecture-recital Swindon 7.00
Thurs:	" " " Intimate Opera. Worthing 7.30
Fri:	Record programme BBC World Service
Sat:	Composers' Guild Luncheon
Sun:	To Liverpool to conduct carol concert, Philharmonic Hall

Not maybe as glamorous a week as one could find in the diary of the Daniel Barenboims of this world, but nevertheless a very typical page from my own. Throughout the nineteen-fifties and sixties I led an immensely varied life, composing, broadcasting, lecturing, adjudicating, conducting and writing. It seemed ironic that I had not foreseen a single one of these careers when I was a student. Without any conscious planning on my part, I had become a musical odd-job man, turning my hand to anything that offered itself. Since I was a free-lance, never having the security of a regular salary, I tended to take on more work than I actually needed. In the back of my mind there lurked an uneasy feeling that my luck couldn't last, that the flow of jobs might dry up. Even the 'Talking about Music' programmes for the BBC were only contracted on a three-monthly basis. I taught at the Royal College with the idea of keeping a foot in the door so that, if other sources of income dried up, I could increase my weekly stint from one day to three. I enjoyed teaching gifted students but found rather too often that individuals with no real talent had somehow been admitted. The work was poorly paid and I think I was justified in demanding a high standard. I gave a standing order to the man in the office who allocated pupils to teachers: 'Either they must be very talented or very pretty — otherwise I won't take them on.'

The only substantial sums I earned came from films, mostly undistinguished supporting features for which I could dash off a score in a week and collect four or five hundred pounds plus the subsequent performing rights. Some are still shown in the doldrum hours of television and duly noted in the Performing Rights Society returns. On one occasion I saw that I had been credited with a considerable sum for the television showing of a film called *The Beast of Marseilles*. I phoned the PRS and said that I had never written the music for any such epic; should I send the money back or keep it against future royalties? They promised to investigate; the following day they informed me that *The Beast of Marseilles* was the American title for a rather dreary escape film called *Seven Thunders* for which I had indeed written the score.

Although the financial rewards were well worth having, I cannot say that I derived much artistic satisfaction from composing film music. I enjoyed the challenge of fitting music to picture, working to the nearest third of a second, so that the shock chord coinciding with the heroine's scream occurred at exactly two minutes seventeen and two-thirds seconds, not more, not less. Even more I enjoyed recording the music, with the orchestra seated in front of the screen. First would come a purely musical rehearsal of the section, checking for wrong notes in the parts and clearing up little misunderstandings. ('No Jimmy, it's a tam-tam not a tom-tom!') The orchestral housework done I would call out, 'Roll the picture', and the screen would flicker into life, usually without a sound-track. The players would twist round in their chairs to see what the action was, supplying a ribald and witty commentary, while I mentally conducted the piece. It was always my aim to record a perfect 'take' the first time though it was surprisingly hard to do. Sometimes we would get a precise fit at every point to be told that an extraneous noise had spoiled the track. The recording engineers took great pride in their work and would always demand re-takes if they were in any way dissatisfied with the sound. I approved of their attitude though I quickly became cynical about the treatment of the music thereafter.

The worst instance of directorial interference with music was in the film version of *The Pickwick Papers* (1952). I was naturally delighted to be involved in such as project but soon found that the director, Noel Langley, was a less than ideal collaborator. I always believed that music should be used economically in films, that it should make a point and then disappear. Since much of Dickens' dialogue was retained, there were many places where music would merely be a distraction, and I argued as much with some vehemence. 'You write it, I'll cut it,' I was told with small consideration for artistic niceties.

For the opening titles he had asked for happy music that would suggest a huge Christmas party, with tunes as simple as nursery rhymes and as catchy. I obliged as best as I could, using a large orchestra to (as I thought) exhilarating effect. He seemed to be well pleased when we recorded it, and, considering that I had had to write about forty minutes of music in eleven days, I felt the job had been well done. I was unable to attend the première but some months later caught up with the film at a cinema in Cardiff. It was almost as distressing an experience as the one I had had in the Fulham Forum. Without a word of consultation Langley had jettisoned the whole of my title-music. In its place he had put a waltz from a much later point in the film which I had scored for about seven instruments. Designed to be heard from a distance by the slumbering Mr Pickwick, I had given it a deliberately sketchy treatment, implying harmonies rather than giving them in full. To compensate for the delicacy of the scoring (which was quite unsuitable for the opening titles) the volume had been coarsely over-amplified, giving the undesirable impression of a tiny orchestra working grotesquely hard. Throughout the film the music had been treated with an insensitivity I found hard to believe. Passages that I had planned to be in the foreground were suppressed beneath a carpet of sound-effects; passages that I had intended to be subtle comment were tweaked up so loudly that they became an intrusion; savage editing had caused the fruits of hours of labour to end up on the cutting-room floor. Small wonder that I much preferred writing for radio, for there I remained in control of the actual musical substance, even if it remained subservient to speech.

Even the film of *Billy Budd* in which I collaborated with Peter Ustinov had its unhappy moments. The American distributors were concerned about the ending; it was even suggested that the story should be changed so that the unfortunate Billy might be reprieved! After weeks of discussions that must have caused Peter a lot of worry, the film was cut by some fifteen minutes. Inevitably this meant that a number of music cues no longer fitted. An emergency recording session was arranged with the Philharmonia Orchestra; the orchestral parts were heavily edited with cuts, transpositions and written instructions. (*Play this bar three times then jump to A + 4; continue to B and then cut to last 4 bars.*) Such work is truly a sort of musical carpentry that any composer must find distasteful. On the evening of the session most of the orchestra managed to arrive at Elstree on time, weary though they must have felt after six hours' rehearsal for one of their normal concerts. Unfortunately the van containing their instruments was caught in a particularly stagnant traffic-jam. In increasing frustration we waited, powerless to do anything. At last, nearly an hour late the van appeared through the rain-swept darkness to be greeted with sardonic cheers from the thoroughly disgruntled players. While the van was being unloaded it was pointed out to me that one pays the man rather than his instrument; the players had been in the studio since 6.30, the hour at which for them the session had begun. If the recording went beyond the allotted three-hour span we would run into ruinous overtime; it counted for nothing that not a note had been played until 7.45. Working with fierce concentration I managed to record all but one section with ten minutes to spare. There remained the most complex of all the excerpts, involving synchronisation at about eight crucial points. (*Cut to drummer in close-up: 1 min 13 secs. Cut to bugler sounding alarm: 1 min 18⅓ secs. Wide shot of ship in action: 1 min. 24 secs. etc. etc.*) Quickly explaining to the orchestra the major surgery which re-editing had inflicted on the music, I gave my usual call, 'Roll the picture!' I think that the orchestra appreciated the difficulty of the task. We had no time to rehearse, no time for re-takes. The disembodied voice of the engineer called for silence. 'Recording now ... rolling ...' Descending figures, 5-4-3-2- flicked on to the screen. The tension was such that my baton felt as though it was charged with electricity as I gave the first down-beat. In the last available three minutes we managed to record a sequence lasting some two and a half — right first time. As the Iron Duke supposedly said, 'It was a damned close run thing.'

Recording the music for *Decameron Nights* I had a rather different sort of drama to cope with. For the opening titles I had specified several extra brass and percussion players, thinking to give the music the additional impact that brings gladness to the producer's heart. It was quite a splendid sound, and I made a point of conducting it through several times so that my employers would feel that they were getting their money's worth. Happy smiles indicated satisfaction. 'Let's move on to 5.M.2,' I said to the orchestra, technical talk for reel five, music cue two. After a good deal of rustling around there was general agreement that there was no such number; what was slightly worrying was that I didn't even have the score, although I could distinctly remember writing it. It was a duel on horseback, the only other number in which I had used the extra brass. I called Jack Simmons, the orchestral 'fixer', and in an urgent whisper asked him to phone Rosie Bramson, the music copyist, to see if the missing music was still with her. (Placid and imperturbable, she had an office off Charing Cross Road where four or five slaves toiled endlessly, copying every sort of music from symphonies to jazz arrangements.) Meanwhile we got on with recording another section, using the feeble excuse that the brass-players might want a breather as a pretext for the sudden change of plan. Soon Jack was beside me, his face grave. 'Any news?' I asked him anxiously between 'takes'. 'She hasn't got it and never had it,' he muttered, fully aware that I didn't want the bosses to know that something was wrong. 'Ring my home and ask my wife to look in the big pile of manuscript in the bathroom cupboard to see if it's there. If she finds it, tell her to rush it to Rosie's in a taxi. Can the extras stay on for this afternoon's session?' 'All except the tuba.' 'Well, get another tuba for the afternoon and tell Rosie to rush it — that's if Alison finds it . . .' He hurried away while, with my brains awhirl, I started to rehearse another section. Composers do not forget battle-scenes of any kind since they involve a lot of notes. I knew I'd written the duel. If it failed to turn up I'd have to score it again from my pencilled rough copy, call an extra recording session and pay for the whole orchestra myself. We ploughed on until the coffee-break, my thoughts more with Jack than on the screen. To my immense relief he looked a lot more cheerful as he came back into the studio. 'She's found it,' he whispered to me; 'she's taking it straight to Rosie's.'

At three o'clock in the afternoon a motor-cyclist roared up to the recording studio at Denham with a parcel containing the score and parts of 5.M.2. I learned afterwards that Rosie had put five copyists on to the job at the same time; nobody had stopped for lunch. Somehow we managed to keep the crisis to ourselves; neither producer nor director realised what was going on and the recording was completed on schedule. How I had been so careless as to shuffle the score into a pile of unused manuscript-paper I shall never understand; I imagine it was sheer exhaustion. Such music was invariably composed against the clock and I had probably written a hundred and fifty pages in less than two weeks.

Being by nature a sprinter rather than a long-distance runner the actual speed of composition never seemed to be a problem. Looking at the rough-cut of a film or reading through a radio script I found that noises in my head invariably made their presence felt straight away. The task was in itself an immediate stimulus. The procedure with my own 'real' compositions was somewhat different. I have described it as sending a message down to the kitchen. For example, I was commissioned by the Arts Council to write a little stage-work for the Opera Players; it was to be an opera to perform to children. The company had given innumerable performances of *Hansel and Gretel* all over the country and had a desperate need for something new. The distinguished writer Richard Church was suggested as librettist but he became engrossed in a novel and backed down. 'I'm sure you could do the words yourself,' said Elizabeth Parry, the company's director.

Walking across the lawn at home one sunny afternoon I suddenly stopped, hearing an inner voice say 'Doctor Musikus'. In a strange way it seemed to descend directly from the Marlowe play, *Dr Faustus*, with which my career had so curiously begun. There was a hint of magic in the name. I wrote to Elizabeth. 'I can tell you nothing about the opera except its title which is *Dr Musikus*.'

A few days later Alison and I went to Austria for a holiday, she badly bruised by a kicking horse, I still ignorant of what was going on in the kitchen of the subconscious. We stayed in a lakeside hotel at Pörtschach, close to the house where Brahms had composed his Second Symphony. One day I was sunning myself on our balcony reading a book on motor-racing. The sun was so bright that the print seemed to dance before my eyes; it became such an effort to read that I gave up and just sat, watching the small yachts tacking from side to side of the glittering water. Suddenly, without conscious thought, I saw the whole course of the opera in my imagination. I jotted down the action in a series of brief telegraphic phrases, using the inside cover of the book as my memo pad.

Symphony 29
Noises game
TV interviewer
Christening (Mother-Father-Baby gag)
Escape — soldiers
Wolves

And so the list continued, a thumbnail sketch that proved to be remarkably accurate in detail. The significance of 'Mother-Father-Baby gag' was a sharply defined visual image of the father and mother standing in a church for the baby's christening. For some reason the father was holding the baby upside-down like a rabbit, although at that stage I hadn't the faintest idea why. Once the kitchen had sent up this curious menu for the day I gave the matter no further thought. Back at home two weeks later, I put the book on motor-racing on the piano as a guide, stacked some manuscript paper beside it and started to write the opera, words and music simultaneously. Within six days the whole piece was written, forty-five minutes' worth, prepared one might say by the kitchen staff without interference from me. Since then it has been performed many times and has been translated into Swedish and Serbo-Croat for performance abroad.

Such facility is of course highly suspect and provides a useful stick for critics to beat me with. I cannot force myself to write more slowly nor would I suddenly become a more significant or profound composer if I were to do so. I, of all people, am the most aware of my limitations; I write to order, taking some pride in fulfilling the requirements of the customer in a professional way. Beyond that I have no pretensions. I know that my music has given pleasure to performers and that the kitchen has sent up some good tunes at a time when melody is an unfashionable virtue. For at least fifteen years I earned my living almost entirely by composition; there are many with higher aspirations who could not make the same claim.

20
'Come back, Ho'kinsan!'

Hong Kong Hotel: Kowloon   28 Mar. '73
... Tonight I had a lovely experience for a few moments. All evening I had been judging classes in choral church music, hymns in English, hymns in Chinese, plainsong in Latin, and then, to end with, two choirs singing 'God be in my head' and an 'own choice' anthem. The first choir was terrible, the second, a girls' school and boys' school combined, was nearly very good. They'd just started to go off stage when I called to them, 'Stay there', and I went up and started to rehearse with them. You should have seen their excitement and happiness; it was just fantastic, like an electric current of feeling. They were packed tight on raised tiers, each only a foot wide so that it was like looking at a tidal wave of faces; the response was tremendous. They were so excited that they made silly mistakes at first, but soon they settled in and sang as (I was sure) they had never done in their lives. Afterwards as they left the hall cheering and laughing the older boys, 17-18, started spontaneously to sing a marching song, and in seconds they had all joined in and went down the stone stairs with the sound booming and reverberating round the building ...

I had given up adjudicating in England years previously but Hong Kong was something special, a trip worth making for any pretext. My first visit had been in 1970, via Istanbul, Tehran, Shiraz, Persepolis, Isphaḥan, fortunately before there were any visible signs of social ferment in any of those places. Another of my strange coincidental encounters happened in Istanbul. Having spent two days sightseeing, I decided on the second night to go to a cinema; several of them were showing Western films, albeit with

Turkish subtitles. I asked the hotel porter which was the nearest; he told me the Astra, a mere five minutes' walk away. Fists lightly clenched against the potential assault of footpads, I strode briskly through the not too well-lit streets, feeling rather more adventurous than the situation probably warranted. Arriving at the cinema unharmed, I was astonished to find the foyer so crowded that it looked as though I mightn't be able to get in. Fortunately, being British, I was perfectly willing to queue, and, after not too long a wait, was rewarded with the last ticket before they put up the House Full barriers. (At the time there was virtually no television in Turkey; films were enormously popular still, regardless of language.)

The Astra was no palace, lacking even a raked floor. Thankful that the lights were still on, I looked frantically for an empty seat. The whole concrete box, resonant as a squash court, seemed to be packed full with an audience whose noisy excitement took me back to schooldays. Several times I tried to sit down only to be met with angry gesticulations indicating that the place was already taken. At last, right in the middle of the very back row, I found a vacant seat. Thankfully I sank down into it just as the lights dimmed. An interminable series of advertising slides ensued, followed by several trailers, including (to my surprise) one for the film I was expecting to see, James Stewart in, I think, *Corrigan's Bluff*. Suddenly, without the formalities of titles or censor's certificate, what I soon realised was the main film began. It was about a young pianist studying in Rome whose lover, a medical student, became a professional footballer of such prowess that he soon had a glorious scarlet Ferrari. After sundry marital upsets she returned one day to her dear old teacher at the Conservatoire. 'Let's see what you remember,' he breathed at her fondly. She played precisely two bars of a Mozart slow movement before he stopped her, breaking into Italian in his emotion. '*Bene*,' he said, '*molto bene*.' It was a short lesson. There was a continuous murmur of conversation around me since the spoken dialogue was meaningless to most of the audience. Catching the odd whisper in English to my left, I made a hesitant enquiry. 'Excuse me, can you tell me what film we're actually seeing — I thought it was going to be *Corrigan's Bluff* . . .' 'No, that's tomorrow night,' came the reply from my unseen neighbour, going on to give the evening's epic a name which has now escaped me. Within an hour the lights came up for an interval, signal for the hungry mob to make an unruly dash for the sweet counter. 'I hope I didn't disturb you,' I said politely to the young man beside me; 'it must have seemed very stupid not to know what film I'd come to see. According to the newspaper —' 'I know,' he replied; 'it's very confusing; they always advertise a day ahead. I say, aren't you Antony Hopkins?'

Now if I have any claim to fame it is as a voice rather than as a face; not for me the nightmare of instant recognition that is the lot of the film star, or nowadays, the telly-person. I do not expect to be recognised, least of all in the back row of a scruffy cinema in Istanbul. So far as I could tell, everyone else in the cinema was Turkish; to have sat next to someone with even a common language was stretching coincidence far enough. My surprise increased as our subsequent conversation revealed that he had been a boy at Berkhamsted School when I had given a lecture-recital there. He was possibly the only boy present who might have remembered me since he was an enthusiastic pianist. To add to the improbability of the encounter, he was currently living in America and had returned to Istanbul for a single week to intro-duce his German fiancée to his Turkish parents. After the film had ended (*why did they have to crash that beautiful Ferrari?*) I returned to his apartment and spent a pleasant hour or two with him and his attractive bride-to-be.

Once arrived in Hong Kong I fell totally under its spell even though the March skies were perpetually overcast. By day one never seems to be far from the vast expanse of the harbour, across whose crowded waters the Star Ferries chug to and fro in an almost continuous shuttle service. At night the view from the Peak must be without parallel in the world, so brilliant is the dis-play of multi-coloured lights, glowing magically against the dark backdrop of the surrounding hills. Times Square, Broadway and Blackpool combined could not eclipse this electric kaleidoscope whose vivid colouring merges into a haze at the water's edge. In recent years the skyscrapers have become too ostentatious, poking impudent fingers towards the hilltops in an effort to dwarf Nature; but on that first visit a decent proportion had still been preserved, the teeming city nestling in the hills' embrace.

The Competitive Festival involved some thirty thousand schoolchildren, most of them Chinese. Day after day I and my fellow adjudicators would sit in various halls scattered throughout

the twin cities of Hong Kong and Kowloon listening to a seemingly endless stream of young pianists, violinists, wind players, brass
players, singers, accordionists, guitarists, choirs and orchestras.
While many performers were mediocre or downright bad, the
good ones were so genuinely dedicated that it was impossible not
to be captivated by their enthusiasm. One teacher in particular,
Gloria Wong, brought such devoted fervour to her work that her
pupils were literally inspired. In one year they won nineteen out of
a possible twenty trophies, a record that led one of the judges to
remark that one could always tell when the pianists were playing
the Wong way because it was weally wight ... Comparable in
teaching ability to Gloria was a violinist called Henry Wong (no
relation) who taught all string instruments at a huge boys' school.
I will never forget a class for school orchestras in which I sat
listening to several groups in turn, culminating, as I thought,
with a splendid performance of Beethoven's 'Egmont' overture.
Mightily impressed, I wrote an enthusiastic critique, ending with
the phrase — 'Without exaggeration this is the finest school
orchestra I have ever heard.' As I finished my extravagant but
well-meant eulogy I became aware that another orchestra had
filed decorously into place and was waiting for a sign to begin. A
quick glance at the schedule revealed that they were intending to
play the slow movement of the Elgar 'Serenade for Strings'. 'Oh
God,' I thought to myself, 'this could be frightful.' The Oriental
faces topped by uniformly jet-black hair seemed too far removed
from Malvern or Worcester for any comprehension of Elgar's
idiom to be possible.

They started to play, bringing such tenderness to the opening
phrases that I laid my pencil down and sat back to listen to what I
sensed was something special. To say that something brought
tears to one's eyes has become a hackneyed cliché, yet it can also
be a simple statement of fact. There was something particularly
moving about this unlikely conjunction of East and West, with
Chinese children who lived in cramped and noisy apartments
evoking so sensitively an English countryside that they had never
seen. When they had finished I found that I had not written a
word. With an unsteady voice I asked them to stay where they
were, a request which caused a considerable stir in the audience. I
put a reassuring hand on the conductor's arm. 'Would it upset
you ... would you mind if I take them through it once? It was so

lovely; I'd just love to hear it again.' He gave a radiant smile and handed me his baton. I said a few encouraging words to the players, and then we began. It is a piece I have performed many times with highly accomplished professional chamber orchestras but it is that unrehearsed performance one afternoon in Hong Kong that dwells in the memory. The response was heart-warming; a nod to the violas to bring out a chromatic note would produce just the result I wanted; dark eyes followed my slightest gesture. Words were not needed; it was a communication far beyond the limitations of speech. So began my acquaintance with Henry Wong who, despite the rigidly unimaginative approach to teaching in Chinese schools, had liberated the souls of his pupils through the experience of music. Needless to say his string orchestra won the class even although the preceding group had seemed to be headed for a sure victory.

A less happy occasion came at the end of my stay. I had been asked to conduct a performance of Haydn's *Creation* in the City Hall with the Combined Christian Church Choirs and the so-called Hong Kong Philharmonic Orchestra — not in those days the enthusiastic and professionally competent body it has now become. The choir proved to be admirable but, from the first rehearsal, the orchestra filled me with foreboding. Not more than twenty players turned up to the session and, of those, only about seven seemed to have any standard of performance while a mere two or three had the least idea of Haydn's style. The following week an almost totally different group of players appeared, equal only in their general incompetence. On the day of the concert, a Sunday, the orchestral secretary rang me up, genuinely apolo-getic. 'Did I tell you we could only rehearse for half an hour?' he said. 'The orchestra is due to play for a fashion show at the Hilton at three.' In response to my anguished protests he agreed to try to telephone as many players as he could and ask them to come at one-thirty to give me an extra half hour. I duly arrived in the hall promptly at half-past. After twenty depressing minutes we had enough of a quorum to make a start. 'Half an orchestra is better than none,' I thought, wrongly as it turned out. The 'Repre-sentation of Chaos' with which the work begins can seldom have been played with such realism. Not more than thirty minutes after we had started to rehearse, players began to pack their instru-ments away and filter discreetly off the platform.

Huge smiles greeted me backstage that evening. 'Will be alrigh',' soothing voices assured me. 'You good conductor; we follow.' The soloists and choir were sympathetic, apologetic or apoplectic according to individual temperament. They all felt that I had had a singularly raw deal. I went on stage as though to my doom. Having acknowledged the warm applause from a nearly full hall, I turned to survey my ill-prepared forces. Dominating the stage were three squat but bulky trombone players, Filipinos all, whom I had never seen before. They were gazing at the music with puzzled expressions, obviously feeling that Haydn, whoever he might be, should have had a better arranger. Like all too many of the orchestra they normally played in night clubs. Presumably they could have coped admirably with the demands of 'Moon River' or 'Get me to the church on time', but Haydn baffled them. Every now and then, without prompting from me, they would offer a bar or two from 'The Heavens are Telling', looking up hopefully to see if I approved. Feeling more like a gardener than a conductor I would pluck out the offending sounds while wondering how I could indicate to the trombones which number we were actually playing. (There were some cuts but nobody had thought to tell them.) During the interval I searched them out and told them not to worry to come back. They seemed quite upset that I had failed to appreciate their contribution.

After my 1973 visit to Hong Kong I travelled on to Japan, where the British Council had arranged a lecture tour for me during which I was also to conduct some orchestras at universities. I arrived in Tokyo exhausted by the long hours of adjudicating. Previous experience had taught me how tiring Hong Kong could be so I had planned a five-day break to do some sightseeing. I took the 'bullet' express down to Kyoto (340 miles in less than three hours) and stayed in a rather gloomy hotel in whose lift was the firm injunction PLEASE DO NOT PROBE THE BUTTONS UN-NECESSARY.

Japanese urban architecture is hideous beyond belief, but the ancient temples of Kyoto and Nara were beautiful oases of tranquillity. I was taken round them by a young university student whose parents ran a small restaurant on the campus. I took him there for an evening meal, meaning to bring them good custom, but they refused to accept a single yen. Both in Hong Kong and Japan the kindness and hospitality were overwhelming.

I was soon caught up in a whirl of engagements, lecturing, teaching, conducting, recording talks and interviews.

Utsukushigaharaonsen Hotel
Matsumoto   24 Apr. '73

Yesterday I had tea at the Palace with the Crown Prince and Princess, just the three of us with only a discreet male secretary sitting in the background at a different level. The Palace must be the least ostentatious in the world, almost empty of furniture, and done in very quiet brown and grey. The room looked out on to a beautiful but quite wild-looking garden with a copse of silver birches and lovely green and gold pheasants adding a touch of exotic colour. I was supposed to stay less than an hour but they kept me for an hour and a half. We had two teas, one Japanese style with little salty biscuits made from seaweed, then a European one with teapots on a silver tray and a huge plate of gorgeous iced cakes. We talked about many things, music for children, education, the development of a child's personality, birds, insects, whales, Christmas in England, my St Francis opera . . .

This splendidly named hotel is up in the mountains, 6 hours by car from Tokyo, and I've come to see the famous Suzuki violin school. On the way up I saw the peak of Mt. Fuji like a ghost in the sky beyond another range of mountains . . . I am suddenly very very tired. The pace never lets up and it is quite a strain being a sort of fount of instant wisdom and charm and extreme politeness etc. My tummy is playing me up again and I'm feeling rotten . . .

In considerable discomfort I spent the best part of a day at the Suzuki school before slinking back to my hotel bedroom. After an hour of misery I phoned through to my British Council escort and asked whether he could arrange for a doctor to come and see me. I was running a fever I was sure, and felt that I couldn't face a long car journey the next day. 'No chance of him coming here,' said my escort later on the phone, 'but I've made an appointment for you to go down to a clinic at six.'

Feeling as though death was not far off I staggered out of the hotel and was driven down into the town. Outside the small surgery was a long line of shoes belonging to the waiting patients. Obedient to Japanese custom we added ours to the collection and shuffled inside, wearing the loose slippers provided. The waiting room was full but, to my embarrassment, I was swept in ahead of the locals. The doctor turned out to have scarcely a word of any language but his own. My British Council man, newly arrived from Malaya, knew hardly any Japanese while our amiable chauffeur only had the most rudimentary English. Like a drama student auditioning for RADA I tried to convey my symptoms in mime, finding vomiting easy to depict but diarrhoea something of a problem. Occasionally the good doctor would punctuate my performance with a word dragged from the furthermost recesses of his memory.

'Aa-aa-aa-h . . . anolexia?' 'No, not anorexia,' I would reply in growing desperation. 'Nee-moniah?' 'No, not pneumonia; bad STOMACH — down here — sore.' 'So?' 'No, not so, sore . . .'

In a moment of histrionic inspiration I stuck a rigid little finger under my tongue hoping that a thermometer might be forthcoming. A white-coated nurse stepped out of the shadows and offered me a cigarette. I refused it emphatically, shook my finger vigorously, checked to see if it registered below normal and stuck it back under my tongue again. Message received and understood. He produced a white plastic box the size of a pocket calculator to which was attached a coiled wire and a sort of prong which he thrust into my mouth. Silence reigned for a minute, broken by a gasp of satisfaction from the medico as the device in his hand flared into life giving a digital reading in illuminated figures. Unfortunately it gave my temperature in Centigrade, a meaningless number to someone educated in a pre-metric age. Apart from knowing that I was somewhere between death and delirium I was no wiser.

With a sudden air of determination the doctor strode into the next room, beckoning me to follow him. He picked up the phone, dialled a number, and, not taking his eye off me for a moment, began a considerable monologue in Japanese. He then handed me the telephone. To my relief a voice speaking 'leasonably fruent Engrish' came to me out of the unknown. It was another doctor, more linguistically versatile than mine, to whom I confided my symptoms without benefit of mime. The strange tripartite consultation continued for some time, comprehension gradually dawning on my man's face. An injection of some potent antibiotic was decreed. To the accompaniment of hysterical laughter from two young nurses I lowered my trousers and lay face down on the couch. Never having been giving the opportunity of seeing a Foreign Devil's bottom before, they savoured every moment, giggling helplessly as they squirted the magic potion first into the air and then into me. To my surprise it did the trick and I awoke the next morning much improved. My malaise may well have been caused by the sight of the menu at the Utsukushigaharaonsen; amongst other delicacies it offered Eentrees, Flesh fruit, Hamburg stake and Marined Oil Frog.

The hospitality and generosity I experienced in Japan were quite overwhelming, though perhaps even more gratifying was the musical respect. I find the word 'masterclass' a little too pretentious in my case since I am far from being a master performer; but I held what I prefer to call a piano clinic at the Conservatoire in Hiroshima and found the students wonderfully responsive. My interpreter, Tanimichi Sugita, head of the piano faculty there, said that of all the distinguished visitors they had had I was the one who was the most helpful in seeing the music from the Japanese viewpoint. As I left, the students formed two lines in the entrance hall and applauded me from the building. Through the rear window of the car that was taking me to the station I saw a dozen or so rushing into the street flagging down taxis to follow me. Waiting on the platform I was aware of running figures dashing from shop to shop in the little arcade along the station front. In a matter of moments they surrounded me, pressing beautifully wrapped gifts into my hands; some of the girls had tears running down their far from inscrutable Oriental faces. 'Please come back Ho'kinsan,' they pleaded. I was deeply touched and thought how little stir an exit from the College or the Academy would make.

Perhaps the most flattering incident occurred just as I was leaving the hotel at the end of my first visit to Tokyo. The British Council car had called for me to take me to the airport. Luggage in hand I was just crossing the foyer when a clerk behind the desk called my name in greater excitement. 'Mr Ho'kins, Mr Ho'kins, telephone call for you.' His eyes were alight with a look that combined awe and disbelief. 'From the Palace . . .' The last word was whispered; he handed me the phone as though it was about to burst into an incandescent glow, as close an encounter of the Royal kind as he was ever likely to experience. It was the Japanese equivalent to the Lord Chamberlain, phoning to wish me a safe journey and to say that were I to return another year would I please notify the Crown Prince and Princess as they would like to meet me again. The man from the British Council looked at me with some astonishment. 'I can't understand it,' he said. 'That just doesn't happen in Japan. I've never known anyone have a phone-call like that direct from the Palace. Whatever did you do to create such an impression?' 'Perhaps I treated them like human beings,' I replied.

In 1979 I went to Hong Kong, my fifth visit, to conduct the reconstituted Philharmonic Orchestra, no longer a motley group of night-club players, but an enthusiastic and competent body of young musicians who were a joy to work with. On the way back I stopped for a few days in Kuala Lumpur; I always try to do some sightseeing on journeys to and from distant parts. I had resolved to play some golf in Malaysia even though I was suffering from a groggy knee. (I had become addicted to the game in 1977 after a gap of over twenty years in which I had virtually never held a club in my hand. Having had chronic back trouble for most of my adult life I had felt that the game was not for me, but two exploratory rounds on a glorious course by the lake of Annecy turned me into a golf fanatic). The Royal Selangore Golf Club at Kuala Lumpur was unable to offer me a game as their largest Pro-Am tournament was taking place. Instead I went to Subang, a course which I played in solitary splendour in a heat of about 110 degrees. After fifteen holes I thought I might actually melt away; certainly my every shot watered the turf immediately surrounding me. I began to realise why I was alone; nobody plays at Subang except in the early morning and the late afternoon. 'There must be a cooler way,' I thought as I sat gasping on the clubhouse terrace, drinking four milkshakes in succession.

There was. COME TO GINTENG HIGHLAND RESORT said the brochures in my hotel lobby, and there were pictures of golfers on a wonderfully picturesque course. The next morning I took a minibus to the helicopter station and was quickly wafted up the 6500 feet to Ginteng. At the top of a mountain was a huge modern hotel of hideous design surrounded by cranes and bulldozers. Menacing clouds swirled around the adjacent hills; the air was damp and chilly. I asked where the golf-course was. 'You take cable car.' Helpful hands pointed towards the rather stark platform. Down three thousand feet I went, over ravines and jungle forest, wisps of cloud enveloping my glass cage as we creaked down the cable. Below me I caught an occasional glimpse of a dramatic-looking course with a strikingly modern clubhouse perched above it. It was several hundred yards distant from the cable car terminus. I walked down, my bad knee protesting at the steepness of the descent. There seemed to be no one about. I went into the building feeling rather foolish as I had no golfing equipment with me. All was silent. I called, clapped my hands. Nobody came. I could not believe that I could have come so far to no purpose. At last I heard footsteps; a smiling steward hurried along a polished corridor buttoning his jacket as he came. The sing-song voice called out, 'Sorry sir, not expecting anyone today.' I arranged to hire some clubs and a caddy, who turned out to be the head greenkeeper. (He could sink twenty-foot putts infallibly using only his right hand, a distressing facility that apparently earned him a tidy extra income from the betting fraternity). Using a club as a walking-stick I began my absurd round, staggering up hills and lurching into valleys but determined to finish the nine holes that were then available. The scenery was spectacular, the course a challenge even to a fit player. As I stood on the tee of the final hole the black clouds seemed to split with the weight of water; rain didn't fall, it gushed, a torrent that had me completely soaked in seconds. Keeping my head well down, since it was blindingly painful to look up, I addressed the ball carefully and struck it towards the barely visible green. For once it went straight. At a funeral pace I limped after it, shirt and trousers clinging wetly to my skin, shoes squelching through the rivulets of water that bubbled foaming across the fairway. Triumphantly I made my only par of the day, confirming my belief that one tends to play better when one cannot see where one is going. Five minutes later I had almost crawled back into the clubhouse. 'Not as hot as Subang,' I thought, 'but every bit as wet.'

My knee was so painful that I couldn't face the uphill walk to the cable car. When the storm had died out I persuaded a waiter to take me as a pillion passenger on his motorbike. The flight back to the city was dramatic with heavy rain beating on the windows and lightning flashing round us like anti-aircraft fire. The other passengers were praying audibly, white with terror, but it brought out my Flying Dutchman syndrome and I revelled in the battle with the elements. In three years since taking up golf again I have played eighty-four different courses, but my round at Ginteng holds an especial place in my memory. It is not every day that one travels by minibus, helicopter, cablecar and motorbike to play nine holes of lame golf ending in a tropical rainstorm.

21
Credit Given

Perhaps the most unexpected of my several careers has been that of author. After 'Talking about Music' had been running fairly regularly on the radio for six years I began to receive a number of requests from publishers for a book based on the series. (Conspicuously absent from the list was the BBC who to this day have never offered to publish a word of mine, apart from proposing that I might write programme notes for the occasional Promenade Concert.) Feeling that I was in no way qualified to write a book I turned down every overture. I at least realised that books and radio scripts were not at all the same: for one thing the proportion of words to music would need to differ substantially; for another, the choice of phrase would have to be far more selective with no human voice to give it the correct inflection. At last, after refusing offers from more than a dozen reputable firms, I agreed with some reluctance to attempt a book on symphonies. Not knowing quite how to go about it, I decided that Daisy Ashford should be my model; if she could write such an immortal classic as *The Young Visiters* in a notebook, I could surely do much the same. I went to the local branch of Smith's and bought three bound volumes of foolscap. It seemed plenty for my purpose. There is no better place to begin than at the beginning. With a sense of voyaging into the unknown I wrote TALKING ABOUT SYMPHONIES in fair capital letters on the first page, followed with a diminutive 'by' on the next line and ANTONY HOPKINS (capitals but smaller) on the next. It looked a bit bare so I added a little drawing of a windmill at the bottom of the page with a W and an H each side of it, the logo of my publisher-to-be. I turned the page. 'Better leave that one blank to list the chapters on,' I thought to myself. Another page turned. I was already on page three and gaining confidence all the time. I then wrote the book. It was never typed; like most of my books it was set up straight from manuscript. Used as I was to meeting a weekly deadline for my broadcasts I found the task less difficult than I had imagined. The arrival of the galley proofs brought a genuine frisson of pleasure coupled once again with the familiar sensation of disbelief. My mind works in a curious way, happily discarding things completed, whether notes or words. I have sat watching a television showing of a film for which I wrote the music without having the slightest idea what would come up next. Similarly I can dip into any book of mine and read on with quite a sense of discovery. The words seem surprisingly unfamiliar, as though written by another hand. Consequently I find proof-reading far from boring since I barely recognise the text as my own.

If there is one lesson life has taught me it is that the process of creating gives more satisfaction than the thing created. The achievement of an ambition seldom measures up to expectation; rehearsals are more rewarding than performances. I have been singularly fortunate in that I have done many things I had not even dared to contemplate in daydreams. But in the doing of them the critical self invariably spots the slightest deficiency. One can leave a concert hall having played ten thousand right notes, haunted by the memory of the dozen that were wrong; one can conduct a programme against all the odds of inadequate rehearsal and while acknowledging the applause, kick oneself for one small miscalculation; a single misprint, for which one may not even have been responsible can spoil the satisfaction of an entire book. Perhaps it is only in hobbies, when the professional self is quiescent, that one can achieve a satisfaction unsullied by regret. Winning a sports-car race at Snetterton in the wet, lapping Good-wood in a D-type, or even scoring a birdie on a difficult golf-hole, these are joys that bring no rebuke of conscience in their wake. Although I have undeniably tasted success I am continually aware of how much more I ought to have achieved. When I conduct youth orchestras today, I envy the players not only their ability but also their opportunities. Had my father lived I might have lacked the material advantages that came my way, but I am sure that he would have fostered my musical talent more effectively. Had higher standards of musical attainment been imposed from the start, how much better equipped I would have been for life as a professional musician. Had I only practised scales ... Futile reflections on the might-have-been may seem ungrateful to those who helped me on my way, but I cannot escape from the paradox that I failed in what I was trained to do and succeeded in fields I had not thought to enter. My father, writer and musician that he was, left me a gift for words and for music. Gifts should not be a cause for pride since one does not earn them by dedication or endeavour. The earnest but untalented student who works industriously day by day has more reason for self-congratulation than I, to whom things came too easily. If I deserve credit, it is for accepting opportunity when it arose, for being able to improvise, to trust in instinct.

Although most of the text of 'A Time for Growing' was provided by Nesta Pain (with whom I had had a number of happy collaborations on radio), I wrote the opening words myself. They represent a creed of sorts and are perhaps worth quoting:

Look upon me —
What am I?
A man, a body,
Arms, hands, legs, head, neck,
Rib-cage and spinal column;
'The knee-bone connected to the thigh-bone'
Everything in reasonable working order.
Others can run faster,
Think deeper,
Talk louder,
But I manage;
I am a man.
I look at you through this strange window
That I cannot bring myself to touch —
This magic eye
Through which I alone can see;
But you cannot look back,
You cannot see behind the mask,
Not see the hopes, doubts, fears,
Longing, desire or dread ...
I am the centre of my world,

> *Yet to the world I am nothing.*
> *How many millions are there like me,*
> *Each one a prisoner,*
> *Making the supplicatory gestures*
> *Of love and friendship*
> *As they try to escape from the truly solitary confinement*
> *To which they are eternally condemned.*
> *Let me out.*
> *Let me break loose from this containing shell.*
> *If only I could see for what inscrutable purpose I was born,*
> *The How, the Why of my creation . . .*

As I look back I suppose that I can see a purpose for which I may have been born. I sometimes wonder if it was not to live out the life my father was denied. When I first conducted music for a film I could not help thinking how wonderful it would have been for him to have had a full orchestra to play with instead of a jangling upright piano in a small cinema. When I opened the parcel containing six complimentary copies of my first book I thought of him, a professional writer who never had a book published. I feel as though I have been manipulated in some mysterious way, as though the route I planned to take has been diverted to an unforeseen destination. It is strange to feel so indebted to a man of whom I have not a single memory save for a fleeting vision of hands playing a piano directly in line with my childish eye. If I have succeeded in my life it is because I was endowed with some talent — small indeed in comparison to the almost supernatural gifts bestowed on some, but enough to carry me along the road. Credit for the gift must go to the giver rather than to the recipient; I can only hope that I have been a credit to him.

APPENDIX

For some years, from 1943-56, I kept a catalogue of my compositions. Although most of them were transient, the sheer quantity impresses me even now, offering proof that I was more of a composer than people realise. The flow of commissions for incidental music dried up completely some fifteen years ago. It was fortunate for me that the demand for words continued.

1943   Toccata for piano solo   (Publ. J & W Chester)
        Songs of Cyprus for *a cappella* choir
        String Quartet   (Cobbett Prize at R.C.M.)
        Earl o' Murray: setting for women's voices and piano

1944   Doctor Faustus: incidental music for Liverpool Old Vic
        Sonata No. 1 in D minor for piano solo
            (Publ. J & W Chester)
        Slow, Slow Fresh Fount: song for voice and piano
        The Golden Ass: incidental music for radio play
        Cupid and Psyche: "   "
        Suite for recorder and piano
        Angelus ad Virginem: prelude for piano solo
        A Child is Born: incidental music for radio Nativity play
        The Gentleman in the Parlour: incidental music for radio
        Julius Caesar: incidental music for BBC
        King John: "   "   "

1945   A Roman Holiday: incidental music for BBC
        The March Hare Resigns: "   "   "
        A little concerto for piano and massed recorders
        Three terzetti for two sopranos and viola d'amore
        Nine epigrams for violin and piano

A Humble Song to the Birds: cantata for high voice and
 piano   (Publ. J & W Chester)
Five preludes for piano solo   (Publ. J & W Chester)
Sonata No. 2 in F sharp minor
A Melancholy Song: for voice and piano
 (Publ. J & W Chester)
French folk-song arrangements:
 Le Roi Renaud   (Publ. J & W Chester)
 La Bergère aux Champs
An American Goes Home: incidental music for radio
 play
Oedipus: incidental music for Old Vic
The Crown of Gold: cantata for three solo voices, string
 quartet, cor anglais and piano
Telepathy: incidental music for radio feature
Five French folk-song arrangements
 (Publ. J & W Chester)

1945   Witchcraft: incidental music for radio feature
Atlantis: "   "   "
The Time of Your Life: incidental music for Lyric
 Theatre production of William Saroyan play
The Just Vengeance: choral music for Lichfield Cathedral
Sonata for viola and piano in four movements
Salute to All Fools: incidental music for radio play
Werewolves: "   "   "   feature
Nocturne: four Tudor sonnets for baritone and piano
Fairies: incidental music for radio feature
Three German folk-songs arranged for voice and piano
Address to Melancholy: ode for six voices
The Compleat Angler: ⎰ incidental music for radio
Dove Days: ⎱ version of Isaac Walton
The Assassin: incidental music for verse play
Antony and Cleopatra: incidental music for H.M.
 Tennent

1946   Moby Dick: incidental music for radio adaptation
Enemy of Cant: "   "   feature
The Heartless Giant: music for radio play
Animal Farm: "   "   adaptation
Fantasy for viola and piano
Four dances for recorder and spinet — originally music for
 Back to Methusalah, Arts Theatre — (Publ. Schott)

The Frogs: incidental music for radio play
Lady Rohesia: one-act opera, Sadler's Wells
The Sweet Nightingale: arrangement of Cornish
    folk-song
Duncan Gray: "   " Scottish
    folk-song
Piano Sonata No. 3 in C sharp minor
    (Publ. J & W Chester)
Thou Wilt Not Go and Leave Me Here
    (Arrangement of old English tune, later published by
    Basil Ramsey in version for female voices and piano)
Hark the Ecching Air: ⎫ realisation of Purcell Songs
Fairest Isle: ⎭
Dabbing in the Dew: arrangement
    (Publ. Basil Ramsey)
Co-ordination: ⎫ incidental music for two radio
          ⎬ fantasies
Other Kingdom: ⎭ by E.M. Forster
Lovers in the Grave: song for high voice and piano

1947   Vice-Versa: music for feature film
        Dangerous Drugs: incidental music for radio feature
        Mirages: ballet in three scenes
        Richard II: ⎫
        Henry IV Part I: ⎪
        Henry IV Part II: ⎬ fanfares for BBC Shakespeare
        Henry V: ⎪ Festival
        Henry VI: ⎪
        Richard III: ⎭
        Carillon: anthem for double choir
            (Publ: J & W Chester)

1948   The Cenci: incidental music for radio production
        Partita in G minor for solo violin(Publ. J & W Chester)
        The Skin of our Teeth: incidental music for Old Vic
            Australian Tour
        Music for Civil Service documentary film
        The Thracian Horses: incidental music for radio play
        Troylus and Cresside: song for radio version of Chaucer
        A Wedding Cantata for John Amis and Olive Zorian for
            tenor solo and small orchestra
        Air for dancing: written for *Movement* magazine
        Recueillement: for voice and piano
            (Publ. J & W Chester)

Music for Civil Service documentarv film

The Birds: incidental music for Berkhamsted School production, subsequently used for BBC

I'm the Girl from the Opera: satirical revue number for Rose Hill

Damon and Amaryllis Dancing in a Ring: song for tenor and piano

Prelude Fugue and Rondo for two violins

Here Come the Huggetts: feature film

It's Hard to be Good: "   "

Doctor Faustus: revised score for Old Vic

1949   Vote for Huggett: feature film

Full score of ballet Mirages, re-titled Etude

The Huggetts Abroad: feature film

Slide Softly Sleep: song for tenor and piano

The Song of Roland: incidental music for radio version

Scena: dramatic cantata for soprano and strings
        (Subsequently expanded and scored for full orchestra
        as an entry for the Radio Italia Prize.)

Five studies for voices and piano
        (Publ. J & W Chester)

Three pieces for flute and piano   (Publ. Schott)

Portrait of Istanbul: incidental music for radio feature

The White Deer: "   "   "   play

Commonwealth Christmas: "   "   world-wide
                                    Christmas programme

1950   Rothay Revisited: incidental music for radio feature

A Festival Overture: (two trumpets and strings) for the Aldeburgh Festival

The Travelling Fair: music for choir and orchestra for Kathleen Raine's radio poem

The Four-Poster: incidental music for Jan de Hartog's play

Twelfth Night: "   "   " Old Vic

The Face of Violence:"   "   " radio play (Italia Prize)

The New Canterbury Pilgrims: incidental music for radio feature

Cutty Sark: setting of Hart Crane's poem for bass-baritone, chorus, string orchestra, piano and percussion

The British Abroad: incidental music for overseas service

Auld Lang Syne: arrangement for BBC, New Year's Eve

1951 Henry V: music for Old Vic
  The Love of Four Colonels: incidental music for Ustinov
   play
  Fantasy for clarinet and piano (Publ. Schott)
  The Man From Tuscany: opera for two adults, boys, and
   piano duet, commissioned for Canterbury Choir
   School (with Christopher Hassall)
  Materials Handling: music for C.O.I. documentary film
  Spiders: incidental music for Nesta Pain radio feature
   (Entered for Italia Prize)
  The Moment of Truth: anthem for Ustinov play
  Ants: incidental music for radio feature
  Helena: "   " " " adaptation (Waugh)
  Time Gentlemen Please: music for feature film

1952 Beetles: incidental music for radio feature
  The Solitary Wasp:" " " "   "
  Coriolanus: music for Stratford
  The Young Elizabeth: music for Jeanette Dowling's play
  Macbeth: music for Stratford
  Suite for recorder and piano (Publ. Schott)
  Two French folk-songs arranged for voice and piano
  The Maid Freed From the Gallows:" " " "
  Pickwick Papers: music for feature film
  Gai lon la: French folk-song arranged for voice and piano
  Decameron Nights: music for feature film

1953 Child's Play: music for feature film
  Scorpions: incidental music for radio feature
  Johnny on the Run: music for feature film
  Antony and Cleopatra: music for Stratford
  White Ants: incidental music for radio feature
  This Music Crept by me Over the Waters: radio verse-
   play
  The Angel who Pawned her Harp: music for feature film
  Signature tune for radio (nautical magazine programme)
  The Neglected Tar: arrangement of 19th century song for
   above
  Three's Company: opera for three voices and piano
   (Publ. J & W Chester)
  Waltz for solo flute: for radio programme on Marshal
   Ney

1954   The Oboe Player: song for voice, oboe and piano
Comics: incidental music for radio feature
Café des Sports: ballet for Sadler's Wells Theatre
    Company
Romeo and Juliet: music for Stratford
Troilus and Cressida: "   "   "
Honeybees: incidental music for radio feature
Psalm 42 in George Wither's rhyming version: for choir
    and organ, for musicians' special service
    (Publ. J & W Chester)
Blue Peter: music for feature film
War in the Air: music for television film
Christmas Story: operatic sketch for Arts Theatre

1955   Two songs for baritone and piano
All's Well That Ends Well: music for Stratford
Macbeth: "   "   "
The Praying Mantis: incidental music for radio feature
Cast a Dark Shadow: music for feature film
The Fountain: cantata for chorus and strings for Imperial
    College Reunion

1956   The Oresteia: music for BBC production of the
    Aeschylus trilogy, for soloists, chorus and full
    orchestra
Grasshoppers: incidental music for radio feature
Music for three Menander Plays for BBC
Othello: music for Stratford
Ten o'clock Call: a satirical opera bouffe
Cicadas: incidental music for radio feature

The list ends here; from memory and without accurate dates I
    would add:

Radio programmes: Flies and Greenflies
                      Termites
                      Flies So-Called
                      The Dock Brief (Italia Prize)

Television programmes: The Adventures of Alice ('60)
                            Babar the Elephant ('66)

Other works: A Time for Growing: opera pageant ('67)

Rich Man, Poor Man, Beggarman, Saint: opera for young people

Dr Musikus: opera for four singers, piano and percussion   (Publ. Chester)

John and the Magic Music Man: for narrator and orchestra ('74)   (Recorded with Philharmonia on Unicorn)

Riding to Canonbie: Twenty-six songs for female voices and piano ('75)

Workspell for solo piano ('75)

Early one Morning ('80) — Cantata for solo mezzo-soprano female chorus and full orchestra (Weinberger)

Books:

Talking About Symphonies	Heinemann	(1961)
Talking About Concertos	"	(1964)
Talking About Sonatas	"	(1971)
Music All Around me	Leslie Frewin	(1967)
Lucy and Peterkin	" "	(1968)
Music Face to Face (with André Previn)	Hamish Hamilton	(1971)
Downbeat Music Guide	Oxford University Press (1977)	
Understanding Music	J & M Dent (1979) (Yorkshire Post Award)	
The Nine Symphonies of Beethoven	Heinemann (1981)	
Songs for Swinging Golfers	Michael Joseph (1981)	
Sounds of Music	J & M Dent (1982)	

Plus over a thousand scripts for broadcasts

INDEX